T5-ASQ-391

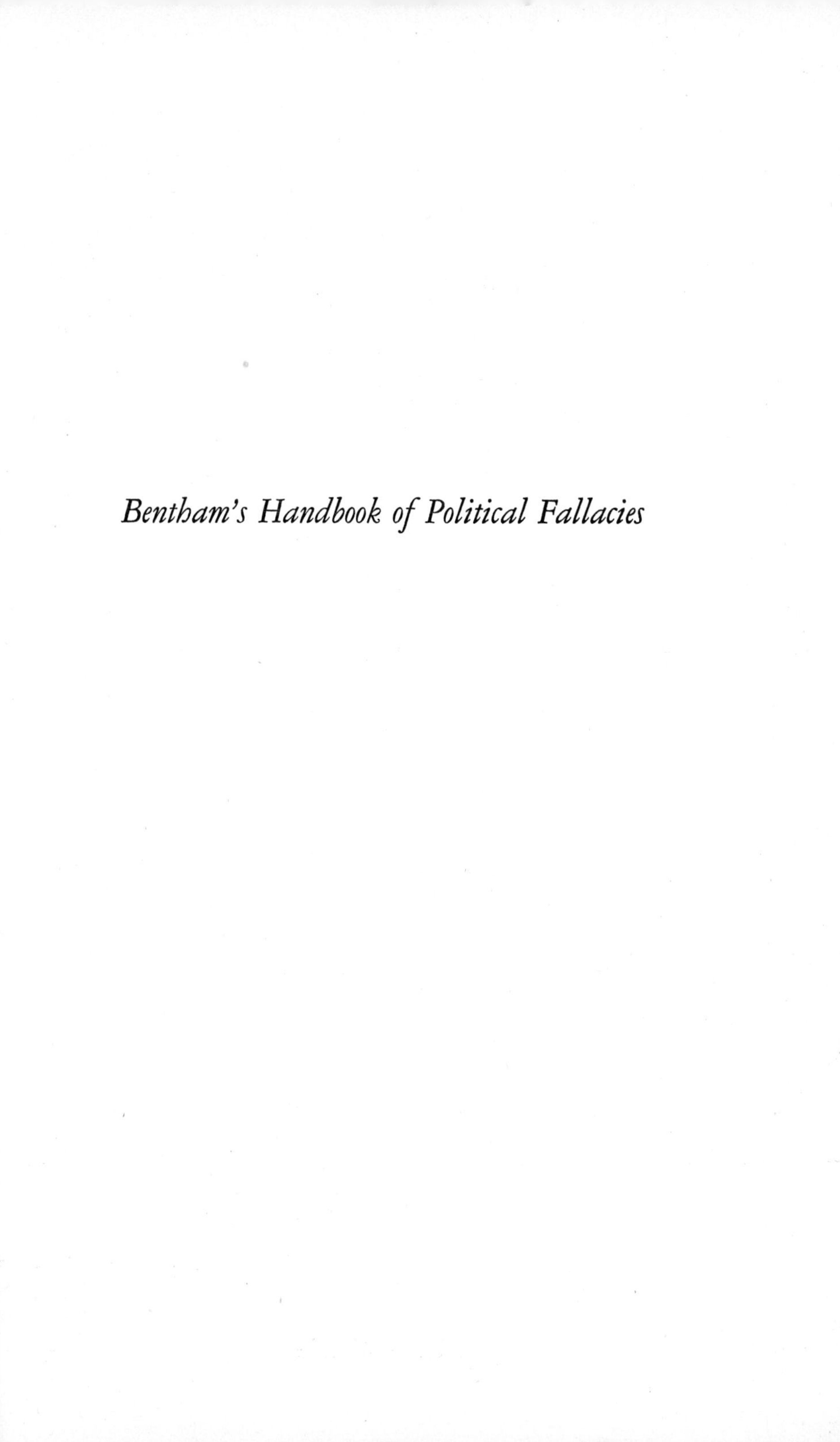

Bentham's Handbook of Political Fallacies

Jeremy Bentham

BENTHAM'S

Handbook of Political Fallacies

Revised, Edited and with a Preface by

HAROLD A. LARRABEE

1952

THE JOHNS HOPKINS PRESS

Baltimore

Baltimore: The Johns Hopkins Press
London: Geoffrey Cumberlege
Oxford University Press
Printed in the United States of America
by the J. H. Furst Company, Baltimore

EDITOR'S PREFACE

POLITICS AND LOGIC are sometimes reputed to be on less than speaking terms. But this book ventures to wed the two in a manual of political logic, a handbook of the art of verbal warfare in politics for the use of honest men. It was written out of a deep concern for human well-being, and from the ripe experience of a genius who had spent a long and laborious lifetime in efforts to bring about much-needed reforms by means of legislation. Jeremy Bentham (1748–1832) was the founder of Utilitarianism, or "the greatest happiness system" in ethics. With his whole heart he hated the manifold abuses that were unremedied by law throughout the world, and almost singlehandedly he set about the task of correcting them by a prodigious use of his pen.

In the long run, Bentham was almost incredibly successful. It is often claimed, and with justice, that nearly all of the improvements in the social and political life of England between 1825 and 1870 are traceable to him or to his followers, who are also credited with destroying more nonsense than any other school of thinkers in recorded history. But in the short run, Bentham encountered many bitter disappointments. In his early days, he tells us, "I was a great reformist, but never suspected that the 'people in power' were against reform. I supposed they only wanted to know what was good in order to embrace it."[1] He soon found out differently, and in his sixty years of struggle against the foes of better government as he conceived it, he learned and noted all their tricks. In the hard school of experience he discovered how very many ways there were by which a clearly

[1] Jeremy Bentham, *Works*, Bowring's edition, Vol. X, 66.

beneficial measure could be check-mated in a political assembly. He came to be especially on the alert for the sort of specious arguments called fallacies, the unsound, illogical contentions which might nevertheless be easily accepted as sound by the unwary.

His unfinished notes were freely edited and translated into French by the Swiss Étienne Dumont in 1816, with the title *Traité des sophismes politiques*. Bentham himself had been planning an English edition ever since 1808, but *The Book of Fallacies* was finally prepared by a disciple, Peregrine Bingham the younger (1788–1864), under Bentham's supervision.[2] For reasons which will be explained, the present version, edited and revised from the 1824 edition, but only in matters of style, is a double or a triple translation from Bentham's English to Dumont's Genevan French to Bentham's-and-Bingham's crabbed English to a language more acceptable to the modern reader. The meaning believed to have been intended by the author, however, has been scrupulously preserved throughout, and only a few outdated passages have been omitted. The aim has been to preserve the flavor and wit of the original without its linguistic extravagances.

Bentham's Purpose

It took the father of utilitarianism nearly half a lifetime to learn all the harsh, disillusioning lessons of the politics of reform. After repeated rebuffs, he came to understand the great variety of tactics employed by the defenders of entrenched abuses when confronted with an obviously good piece of legislation proposed by the reformers. Their first move was usually to invoke some sort of higher authority in order to rule out all discussion (Fallacies of Authority). As a second resource, they would try to accomplish the same end by exciting groundless alarms (Fallacies of Danger).

[2] *The Book of Fallacies; from unfinished papers of Jeremy Bentham.* By a Friend. London: J. and H. L. Hunt, 1824.

These stratagems failing, they would endeavor to postpone debate indefinitely (Fallacies of Delay). If all those devices availed them nothing, they could always resort to sheer confusion of the issue (Fallacies of Confusion).

But what annoyed Bentham the most was the fact that, all the while, these corrupt obstructionists of progress would pose before the world as reasonable and well-intentioned men. This seemed to him to be chicanery of the most detestable sort, and he resolved to expose it thoroughly. He made careful notes of all these maneuvers, naming and cataloguing some thirty principal species of political fallacies, which were later grouped by Dumont and Bingham under the four main headings of Authority, Danger, Delay, and Confusion. Before Bentham and his editors were through, they had furnished the political leader who finds himself facing opposition in the court of public opinion with a complete description of the weapons available to himself and his opponents.

Bentham became a mighty hunter of political fallacies because he believed profoundly in two things. The first was the power of reason in human affairs, once the veils of deception were torn from men's eyes. The second article of his faith was his belief in the greatest happiness *of the greatest number* — his conviction that men should "in case of collision and contest, happiness of each party being equal, prefer the happiness of the greater to that of the lesser number." [3] This meant that the smaller good — of the party, class, or family, must give way before the larger — of society or mankind.

It is hard to recover, in the middle of the turbulent twentieth century, Bentham's sublime confidence in the ability and inclination of most citizens and their representatives to listen to divergent points of view logically pre-

[3] Jeremy Bentham, *Works*, Bowring's edition, Vol. V, 211.

sented, and then to come to an honest and reasonable conclusion on the merits of the point in dispute. For our century has witnessed " the revolt against reason " in all its myriad manifestations. To Bentham, reason was patently the instrument which " alone could be productive of any useful effect " in the cause of political reform. And thanks in part to Bentham's pioneering effort, the modern reader has profited by the further probings of Freud and Marx and Pareto. Yet in their works, reason itself has seemed at times to be explained away as something irrational, as " really " consisting of disguised subconscious desires or class-warfare impulses or blind defense-reactions. Modern man is prey to a thousand assorted fears, not the least of which is the fear of being thought naïve enough to trust anything as old-fashioned as our ability to reason consistently.

It is not easy, therefore, to recreate the atmosphere in which *The Book of Fallacies* was originally composed. For the early nineteenth century in England was an age in which political leaders were intellectual enough, and innocent enough, to take bad thinking seriously. When it was done in public, by a responsible speaker in formal debate, it came to be reckoned as little short of a crime. In the words of a recent critic, that period was the heyday of parliamentary " fighting cocks like Pitt, who ran men out of public life for uttering fallacies in his presence . . . the great days of word-bandying, when men paid thirty guineas a seat to hear the metaphors whistle past Warren Hastings." [4]

Political swordplay of that sort is not likely to flourish again in Parliament as it did in the days of Pitt, but the value of Bentham's survey of political fallacies does not depend upon any such renaissance of rhetoric. The key moves on the chessboard of politics remain much the same

[4] Alva Johnston, " Alias Nero Wolfe, I," *The New Yorker*, Vol. XXV, No. 21, 26.

throughout the years, even though the players, and the content of their proposals, are constantly changing. There are signs, too, that the revolt against reason has spent its force. There are even indications that something approaching a " return to reason " may already be in progress. Our sophisticates are learning that extreme scepticism of the instruments of knowing leads eventually into the desert of complete sterility. If men are to act together, and they must, then reliance must be placed somewhere, both individually and socially. The modern substitutes for reason, most of which are actually very ancient, have not demonstrated their alleged superiority as foundations for satisfactory living.[5]

This does not mean that nothing has been learned from the modern rebellion against the extreme claims that were made in behalf of reason a century and more ago. It will be a chastened and a humbled reason that may in time be restored to public favor, and not a proud monarch reascending his throne. Reason in Bentham's day was something to be used primarily for the purpose of unmasking the bad thinking of others. He would have his fellow-men ever on the alert against being deceived by the clever sophistries of others, and his warnings are still worthy of the closest attention. But citizens today have been made conscious, as Bentham never was, of the more insidious dangers of deceiving themselves. And so, while many of them continue to share his burning indignation at the fallacies uttered by designing men, they smile at the naïve way in which his " love of mankind and an admiration of himself went hand in hand."

Bentham, in other words, was much too sure that he was always on the side of the angels, and that his opponents were plagued by evil motives rather than by apathy and ignorance. But at any rate his position on the relationship between logic

[5] Cf. Arthur E. Murphy, *The Uses of Reason* (New York, 1943), and Harold A. Larrabee, *Reliable Knowledge* (Boston, 1945).

and morals, unlike that of many of our contemporary social scientists, was perfectly clear. He was convinced by experience that there was a high correlation between political wickedness and bad logic: the slipshod thinker was probably up to no good morally, and the rascal in politics was almost sure to unmask himself by resorting to logical trickery. It was that conviction which lent force and vigor to his crusading exposure of political fallacies, and also deprived it of the objectivity of modern propaganda analysis.

There is, of course, much to be said for the purely descriptive approach to fallacies as neutral tools for the influencing of human behavior, and therefore open to exploitation for any ends, good or bad. More and more, however, it is coming to be recognized that this amoral attitude, although excellent for the purely scientific purposes of observation and analysis, can be devastating in its consequences when it is carried over into the realm of practical politics. In that arena it is likely to produce a Gerard Hamilton, denounced by Bentham (in Section 7 of the Introduction) for his readiness to make the worse appear the better reason for whichever party offered him the most attractive inducements.

The arts of political sophistry which Bentham exposes, in other words, are not something to be treated any longer as neutral objects for purely scientific scrutiny. They are too full of explosive possibilities. They deserve at least the same somewhat timorous respect that we give to the parallel skills of administering poisons and setting-off high explosives. The men of this generation have seen with their own eyes what political fallacies can accomplish in the hands of a Dr. Goebbels or a Politburo. By means of plausible but fallacious arguments, movements for needed reforms can be transformed into raging revolutions. But political sophistry may also be employed to make even the most imperative changes in the status quo difficult or impossible, thereby driving moderate reformers to the desperation of revolutionism. It was this latter use of fallacies which absorbed the attention of Jeremy Bentham. His whole life was a tireless war of the pen against the abuses, sired by feudalism and the industrial revolution, which he found to be defended by bad logic. His task was to show, in *The Book of Fallacies,* how bad the logic was. It would never have occurred to him to question the fact that logic, politics, and morals are inextricably interwoven in the social life of man.

The Author

Jeremy Bentham was fortunate enough to find his vocation early in life, and to have had both the inner and outer resources which enabled him to follow it with persistence and vigor. Born the precocious son of a worldly and ambitious lawyer-father, who fully intended to see him become Lord Chancellor, Jeremy was given the lavish education of a gentleman at the most fashionable college in Oxford, Queen's, where from thirteen to fifteen he imbibed some natural science along with the prescribed classics, and a minimum of that "mendacity and insincerity" which he later declared were "the sure and only sure effects of an English university education."

It was while combining a desultory preparation for the bar with wide reading and chemical experimenting on his own initiative in 1768, that he came across a striking passage near the end of Joseph Priestley's essay on government, and inwardly shouted "Eureka!" It read: "The good and happiness of the members, that is, of the majority of the members, of any state, is the great standard by which everything relating to that state must be finally determined." The effect of this upon the unwilling student of the vested absurdities of an antiquated legal system was electrifying. Bentham had found his key idea. He might have found substantially the same notion in Beccaria, Helvétius, Hume, or Hutcheson. But the important thing was that Bentham had found not only an idea but a mission: he was called to do for social science what Newton had done for natural science. At the age of twenty-one, he resolved to make himself the Newton of the unborn science of legislation, of "the Law as it ought to be."

In the commonplace book which he compiled during the next few years of self-education for his destined life-work are entries which already foreshadow his interest in hunting down sophistries and his disgust for the complacent supporters of "the Law as it is." In the years 1773–76 he took notes on "Vulgar errors, political"; and recorded such acid opinions as "Barristers are so called (a man of spleen might say) from barring against reforms the extremes of the law" and "It is as impossible for a lawyer to wish men out of litigation, as for a physician to wish them in health." In 1776 he began the immense undertaking of the systematic and detailed reformation of the law for all mankind, which was to keep his pen busy filling folio volumes from six in the morning until ten at night for over fifty years.

A surer recipe for avoiding immediate fame than Bentham's career up to this time is hard to imagine. But in the same year, 1776, at the conclusion of an unsuccessful suit for the hand of Caroline Fox, he published an anonymous *Fragment on Government,* a slashing attack upon Blackstone, to whose lectures he had listened in 1763 with an ear already attuned for detecting fallacies. The *Fragment* was one of the first calls to men of the law to break away from the extravagances of authority and ancestor worship. It was promptly attributed by various reviewers to Lord Mansfield, Lord Ashburton, or Lord Camden. Bentham's father, astonished and gratified by its success, could not keep the secret any longer. Chance brought the *Fragment* and its obscure author, now properly identified, to the attention of Lord Shelburne, later the Marquess of Lansdowne, a Tory radical who shared Bentham's antipathy to Blackstone. An invitation to Shelburne's estate Bowood opened a new social world to the young man, that of the law lords who had been mistakenly regarded as the authors of his *Fragment*.

He found these pillars of the legal system singularly uninterested in his far-reaching proposals for its reformation. They regarded the constitution of England as already " glorious " by comparison with Continental despotisms. The latter, indeed, seemed to offer greater immediate possibilities for change than complacent England. In 1785 Bentham set out for Russia to visit his brother Samuel, who was a naval engineer at the court of Empress Catherine the Great, journeying by way of Italy, Constantinople, and the Danube valley.

On his return to England in 1788, there was a brief flirtation with the idea of his entering Parliament by way of one of Lansdowne's pocket boroughs, but this soon proved to have been based upon a misunderstanding. Except for his incessant advocacy of schemes of his own like the famous Panopticon,[6] Bentham gave up the idea of direct participation in politics. " Beaten in the world of action, our philosopher fell back on his study chair from which he was to modify the laws of mankind." [7]

[6] The Panopticon, described by Bentham to Brissot as " a mill for grinding rogues honest, and idle men industrious " was suggested by his brother Sir Samuel as a design for a large workmen's house in Russia. It was to be a prison made up of tiers of cells so arranged that all of them could be seen from a central platform. Bentham devoted much of his time and fortune for over twenty years to the scheme, and finally received 23,000 pounds in compensation for expenses incurred up to the time of its abandonment. Joliet Penitentiary in the state of Illinois was constructed in 1920 substantially in the form of Bentham's Panopticon.

[7] Robert H. Murray, *Studies in the English Social and Political Thinkers of the Nineteenth Century*, Vol. I, 42.

Dumont and Other Disciples

As far as world-wide fame through publication was to be concerned, Bentham's career reached a turning point at a dinner in Lansdowne House in 1788. There he encountered a Swiss writer and former Protestant clergyman named Pierre Étienne-Louis Dumont (1759–1829), who had gone into voluntary exile from his native city of Geneva at the height of the long struggle over the extension of the suffrage in 1782. Dumont had spent eighteen months in St. Petersburg as the pastor of the French Reformed Church, and had then been invited to come to England by Lord Lansdowne to undertake the general supervision of his library and the education of his younger son. Greatly impressed by some of Bentham's manuscripts which were shown to him by their mutual friend Sir Samuel Romilly, Dumont offered to edit and popularize them in French. He was strongly attracted by the simplicity and concreteness of Bentham's detailed proposals for reform, perhaps because, as a reviewer in the *Foreign Quarterly Review* suggests, " he was wearied with the commonplaces of philanthropic declamation which passed for philosophy " at the time.[8] Dumont showed himself to be an able and enlightened, if somewhat deliberate editor, as well as an enthusiastic disciple. The finer points of Bentham's theory of fictions often escaped him, but as an editor of the political works for popular consumption, Dumont knew when to wield the blue-pencil, and when to call for additional illustrative material. Bentham complained that " the lazy rogue comes to me with everything he writes, and teases me to fill up every gap he has observed." Dumont, however, never failed to manifest a profound respect for the ideas, if not for the exact words of his master. According to Sismondi, he would often remark of " what he most admired in other

[8] *Foreign Quarterly Review,* Vol. V. (1829–30), 322.

philosophers, 'It is convincing, it is the truth itself, it is almost Benthamic.'" [9]

Beginning in 1802, at a time when Bentham's writings had been "praised only by a very few patient readers" in his own country, and continuing until 1823, Dumont published five volumes which he had edited (and in some instances remodelled) from the original manuscripts "half English, half English-French." [10] The bold ideas came from Bentham, but the lucidity and grace with which they were presented in French were contributed by Dumont. Through the Bossange brothers, publishers in Paris, upwards of 50,000 copies of these *Traités* were sold at a time when, as Bentham himself said, some of the English versions were "half devoured by the rats." It was thanks to these disinterested labors of Dumont that Bentham's reputation spread so widely and rapidly throughout the Latin world, bringing him such titles as that of citizen of France in 1792, and later through Spanish translations the resounding accolade of *El legislador del mundo.*

Yet it was only, as Elie Halévy remarks, "after many years and by a curious detour that Bentham was able to exercise any influence on his countrymen." Dumont returned to France in 1789, and through Romilly became the collaborator of the dazzling Count of Mirabeau, of whom it was said that "No man ever so thoroughly used other

[9] J. C. L. de Sismondi, "Notice nécrologique sur Dumont," *La Revue encyclopédique,* Vol. IV (1829), 258.

[10] They were (with the most nearly corresponding titles of Bentham's works in English): *Traités de Législation civile et penale,* 3 vols., Paris, 1802 (Theory of Legislation); *Théorie des peines et des recompenses,* 2 vols., London, 1811 (The Rationale of Punishment and The Rationale of Reward); *Tactique des Assemblées législatives, suivie d'un traité des sophismes politiques,* 2 vols., Geneva, 1816 (An Essay on Political Tactics and The Book of Fallacies); *Traité des preuves judiciaires,* 2 vols., Paris, 1823 (Rationale of Judicial Evidence); and *De l'organisation judiciaire et de la codification,* Paris, 1828.

men's work, and yet made it seem his own." Dumont wrote many of Mirabeau's famous addresses to the Assembly, but the Count supplied their oratorical force. After Mirabeau's death in 1791, Dumont lived in England and in Geneva. "The French Revolution," in Halévy's opinion, "injured Bentham's philosophical reputation" by aggravating Dumont's natural inertia, so that although the latter had kept Bentham's manuscripts since 1788, the first of his promised editions in French did not appear until 1802.[11]

The Book of Fallacies

It was not until 1816 that Dumont edited the *Traité des sophismes politiques* as the second volume of *Tactique des Assemblées législatives.* Of all the works of Bentham which he had a hand in shaping, the *Tactique* was the one to which his own contribution, despite the doubts of John Neal, was probably the greatest, since it was "the most unfinished of Mr. Bentham's manuscripts." Dumont grouped Bentham's thirty varieties of political fallacies under the three main headings of Authority, Delay, and Confusion (Danger was added later); and eliminated most of the examples dealing with British institutions and interests as unsuited to European readers.

When it came to an edition of *The Book of Fallacies* in its original English, Bentham, then over seventy, had been occupied with the project at intervals from 1808 to 1821, and was already involved in other and grander enterprises. He was always prone to be "running from a good scheme to a better," and looked to his disciples to undertake the piecing together of his earlier manuscripts. Sooner or later, nearly all of them were to have the privilege of "writing" one of his books. At this time, about 1819, his intellectual intimates (through his writings rather than through face-to-face

[11] Elie Halévy, *The Growth of Philosophic Radicalism*, 75, 178, 181, 296–98.

contacts) included Francis Place, John Cam Hobhouse (later Baron Broughton), Peregrine Bingham the younger, and James and John Stuart Mill.

At first, as Place remarks, "Even Hobhouse was pressed into service" to edit the *Fallacies*; but the future Lord Broughton was shortly to be under arrest for a pamphlet attacking Lord Erskine, and seems to have dropped out. "I never was to *translate* Mr. Bentham," he explained later in a letter to Place, "I was to arrange his Mss. and put his words into the vernacular, which, by the way, you may perhaps call translating . . . ."[12] The upshot of the affair was that the assignment went to Peregrine Bingham the younger. "Bingham, with a great deal of assistance from Place and (John Stuart) Mill, put together *The Book of Fallacies*."[13] Place described his own efforts as intended to "make the reading (of Bentham) more easy to the commonalty"; while John Stuart Mill, who worked mainly on the five volumes of the *Rationale of Evidence*, was even more explicit about the nature of the task of making the master's English presentable. "Bentham's later style, as the world knows," Mill wrote in his *Autobiography*, "was heavy and cumbersome, from the excess of a good quality, the love of precision, which made him introduce clause within clause into the heart of every sentence, that the reader might receive into his mind all the modifications and qualifications simultaneously with the main proposition; and the habit grew on him until his sentences became, to those not accustomed to them, most laborious reading." Mill found, therefore, that he must "unroll such of Bentham's involved and parenthetical sentences

[12] Letter from Hobhouse to Place, April 13, 1819, quoted in Graham Wallas, *The Life of Francis Place* (London, 1898), 8. (Italics his).

[13] Letter from Place to Hobhouse, August 7, 1819, quoted in Wallas, *The Life of Francis Place*, 83.

as seemed to overpass by their complexity the measure of what readers were likely to take the pains to understand." [14]

The main responsibility for editing *The Book of Fallacies* in English thus fell to a versatile legal and literary man-of-all-work in the Benthamite entourage. Peregrine Bingham the younger was the eldest son of an Anglican divine, and had been educated at Winchester and Magdalen College, Oxford, before being called to the bar at the Middle Temple in 1818. He became a legal reporter, invented a system of shorthand "of no practical value," and later was appointed a police magistrate. At the same time he retained a strong attachment to literary pursuits, writing no less than five of the articles in the first issue of the *Westminster Review*.[15]

But it must not be imagined that Bingham's editing of *The Book of Fallacies* in 1824 was just another piece of hack work done at Bentham's request. It was, rather, the beginning of a concerted effort on the part of the philosophic radicals to bring about the reformation of politics, a crusade which soon absorbed much of the energy which had been going into the broader activity of publishing the *Westminster Review* as a challenge to the *Edinburgh* and the *Quarterly* reviews of the conservatives. In 1826 Bingham became the editor of a new and ambitious periodical entitled *Parliamentary History and Review*. "The design of this work," said the first issue, "is to afford an annual record of the proceedings of the British Parliament, together with an examination of the principal topics discussed in that assembly, and of the manner in which its functions are performed." This was to be done by collecting all the debates on a certain subject under the general heading to which they belonged, with critical remarks upon the arguments brought forward. The editor promised an account "exempt from

[14] John Stuart Mill, *Autobiography*, 65.

[15] Mill, *Autobiography*, 54-55; and George L. Nesbitt, *Benthamite Reviewing*, 27.

vehemence or invective and impartially directed to what ought to be the only end of legislation – not the predominance of a particular party, sect, or portion of the community – but, the greatest happiness of the greatest number."

What was most remarkable about the new publication, however, was not its intention to supplement Hansard by critical analyses of the debates, but the fact that Bingham began his first volume on the session of 1825 by a " Prefatory Treatise on Political Fallacies," which condensed to twenty-eight pages the substance of *The Book of Fallacies.* The utilitarian disciple was losing no time in demonstrating the practical usefulness of his master's instrument. He describes the " Prefatory Treatise " as conveying " the spirit and principles in which the debates have been examined. It may not be unuseful to those who wish to form an estimate of the amount of talent and knowledge actually assembled in the two Houses of Parliament, and by degrees may have the effect of ridding the debates of a set of arguments almost always irrelevant, and but too generally delusive." Bingham believed that he was supplying his readers " with an instrument which will, we trust, enable them at once to discover and expose those fallacies, the prevalence of which has but too much contributed to retard political improvement . . . ." For a contemporary parallel, one would have to imagine an annual digest of the *Congressional Record* preceded by a condensed textbook of logic in politics.

The Doctrine of Sinister Interest

What the philosophic radicals believed they were combatting in the England of the days before the Reform Bill of 1832 is clearly indicated by Bingham's statement of the principal reasons for the wide prevalence of bad logic in Parliament: " Weakness of intellect; imperfections of language; and the sinister interest of erring individuals." The latter defect, a key concept in Bentham's analysis of political fallacies, he defined in these words: " By a sinister interest, we mean an interest attaching to an individual or class, incompatible with the interests of the community . . . . we call an interest confined to himself *sinister*, when it operates in a direction contrary to those which attach to him as a member of the community."

The " great object aimed at in the formation or reformation of every government " should be " to prevent the sinister interest of an individual or class of individuals from operating detrimentally on the interests of the rest of the community." How is this to be done? Not by abolishing or even by diminishing the force of self-interest. " The objection ought to be, not that self-interest exists and predominates, but that our political institutions have not been so framed as to make it conduce to the benefit of the community as well as to that of the individual, or at all events, that it has not been prevented from operating in a direction opposed to the interests of the community." Bingham reaffirms the Benthamite doctrine of the artificial identification of interests through government, declaring that it is incontestable that self-interest can be " so directed or controlled by political institutions constructed to such an end."

That the members of Parliament are " exposed to the action of sinister interest " is proved by the fact that they conduct, " subject to no immediate check, the expenditure of an immense fund raised by taxation: subject to no immediate check, because they are neither elected nor removable by the people whom they are said *virtually* to represent, but in considerable numbers avowedly purchase their seats, while a majority of them are indisputably placed in the House by about 180 powerful families, who either in possession or expectancy have a direct interest in a prodigal expenditure of the public money, and as far as possible in appropriating it to their own purposes."

But it is only in a country which has a combination of

corrupt influences upon government and a relatively free press that we find political fallacies flourishing. " In countries where freedom of the press and public discussion do not exist, the interests of the many are openly and unhesitatingly sacrificed by force to the interests of the few: the people have it not in their power to require reasons, and no reason is given but the supreme will of the ruler. In England, on the contrary, these ends can only be obtained by fraud. In consequence of long-established habits of public discussion, the people are too mindful of their own interests, and too strong to allow them to be openly violated: reasons must be given, and reasons sufficient to satisfy or deceive a majority of the persons to whom they are addressed. Now it is impossible by fair reasoning, with reference to the avowed ends of government, to justify the sacrifice of the interests of the many to the interests of the few, and as we have shown that the members of the British Parliament are placed in a position which must induce them more or less to attempt the sacrifice, it follows that for effecting this purpose they must have recourse to every kind of fallacy, and address themselves, when occasion requires it, to the passions, the prejudices, and the ignorance of mankind." [16]

Bentham's doctrine of sinister interest has often been regarded as an anticipation of Karl Marx's concept of inevitable class-warfare. But even a cursory examination of the two theories reveals a vast gulf between them: the one leading to reformist gradualism, and the other to violent revolution. For the basis of Bentham's notion of sinister interest is purely individualistic. He does not regard even the most greedy holder of power as incapable of occasional manifestations of disinterestedness, nor does he doubt that many of the sinister interests cancel each other out. Hence Bentham directly contradicts Marx by showing that class-

[16] *Parliamentary History and Review,* Vol. I (1826), 1–4.

warfare is avoidable through a relentless exposure of sinister interests. The cure is reform, not revolution.

Current Significance

It has been justly claimed that " there never was a more thoroughly and essentially practical mind " than Bentham's; and that, indeed, " in order to stimulate him to exertion, it was necessary that something to be *done* be at least the ultimate object." [17] Of his many practical projects, there was none " to which Bentham looked with more satisfaction than this rooting out, from the field of political thought, of the tares which the enemies of truth had sown in it." [18] At the conclusion of *The Book of Fallacies* there is a clear hint of what Bentham wanted to be done with it. It was to be used as an instrument for the logical dissection of legislative debates, and hence as a weapon for parliamentary reform. By furnishing the public with a handy edition of the new instrument, Bentham and Bingham seemed to have hoped quite literally to force a drastic reduction in the volume of illogical nonsense uttered on the floors of the two houses by making it possible to recognize and label the various spurious arguments as fallacies.

Their project proved to be a good many generations ahead of its time, and it might be questioned whether the volume of political fallacies uttered in our legislatures has increased or diminished in the last century and a quarter. Many of the concrete abuses against which Bentham crusaded have disappeared; but some of them are still in existence, and many of them will continue to thrive as long as there is a discrepancy between government as it is, and government as it ought to be. Bentham grew up in the midst of a Tory aristocracy which he came to recognize as " systematized corruption." Even as a child of eleven he perceived " the

[17] Bentham, *Works*, Bowring's edition, Vol. I, ix. (Italics his.)

[18] John Hill Burton, *Benthamiana*, 368.

Daemon of Chicane in all his hideousness," and vowed eternal enmity against it.[19] The American and French revolutions showed the way to better things, but had served mainly to terrify the British upholders of "things as they were." Yet a façade of reasonableness had to be presented to the world, with the result that "civil life was one great and continuous practical lesson in the art of saying one thing and meaning another." [20]

It was upon this tissue of hypocritical fictions and fallacies that Bentham the realist and hater of shams declared war. Educated himself as a lawyer, in his early *Fragment on Government* he found the law full of "fiction, tautology, technicality, circuity, irregularity, inconsistency. But above all, the pestilential breath of Fiction poisons the sense of every instrument it comes near." [21] Bentham's aggressive sincerity was affronted to find fiction "the great staple of the law." For a fiction of law seemed to him to be nothing less than "a wilful falsehood, having for its object the stealing of legislative power, by and for hands which durst not, or could not, openly claim it; and, but for the delusion thus produced, could not exercise it."

At times this rage against illusions blinded Bentham to the legitimacy of some fictional devices in human relationships, and carried him to extremes of condemnation which were wholly excessive. But to a man of his moral sensitivity the provocation was great. The intolerable social evils of Bentham's world seemed to him to be caused mainly by arbitrary power supported by word-magic, a "vast mass of mischief" from which there could be no escape except by the clarification of thought and its vehicle, language. By calling attention to the fundamental importance of the problems of language in the fields of law and politics, Bentham not only

[19] *Works*, Bowring's edition, Vol. X, 35.
[20] *Ibid.*, Vol. I, vi.
[21] *Ibid.*, Vol. I, 235.

anticipated the modern semanticists and positivists, but placed himself solidly, as Ogden suggests, in that great line of British empiricists which began with the names of Bacon, Hobbes, Locke, Berkeley, and Hume.[22]

In a century that was to be preoccupied with surface appearances of Victorian respectability, Bentham insisted upon probing deeply into the secrets of selfish interests and laying them bare for all to see. He did not, of course, carry his analysis of human motivation, as Freud did later, into the region of the unconscious, nor did he explain many of the political fallacies as rationalizations. The psychology of political accusation and counter-accusation is more complicated than Bentham suspected. As an English Marxist expresses it: " A wrongful imputation of conscious trickery and deception provokes the ego to adopt means of self-justification which, since there is no conscious intent to deceive, impels it to maintain and develop the attacked point of view." [23]

Bentham is sometimes acclaimed as " the first Fabian " in his passion for reform, but he was by no means a " leveller " or communist. In 1820 he took the trouble to point out in his *Radicalism Not Dangerous* that the philosophic radicals were seeking neither the abolition of all government nor the overthrow by violence of any existing regime. Against the anarchists and demagogues with their promises of utopia, the Utilitarians advocated the gradual, orderly extension of the suffrage as a means of artificially harmonizing men's incurably selfish interests. This platform, as Halévy points out, was assimilated by traditional English Liberalism of the Manchester variety,[24] and has passed in its turn into the gradualism of the Labour Party.

What Bentham kept repeating was, that the cure for all

[22] C. K. Ogden, *Bentham's Theory of Fictions*, ix.

[23] R. Osborn, *Freud and Marx* (London, 1937), 284.

[24] Halévy, *The Growth of Philosophic Radicalism*, 264.

the "persevering propagation of immorality and misery" through deliberately muddy thinking was clear thinking. But "the still small voice of one weighing the meaning of words was not heeded" in Bentham's day.[25] Will it be heeded today? A century and a quarter after Bentham attacked them so vigorously, the British landed aristocracy and its supporting castes of clergy and bar are no longer the all-powerful closed corporations whose egoism and complacency aroused his resentment. The number of feudal anachronisms, such as the requirement of religious oaths for admission to the universities, which can be punctured by a single sharp criticism has been, thanks largely to Bentham and his followers, materially reduced.

But the value of *The Book of Fallacies*, if its lessons are taken to heart and transposed into contemporary situations, remains and will continue to do so, because it rests upon the lasting framework of human nature: upon man's propensity to defend his selfishness with bad logic, and upon reason as ultimately the cure. As long as there continue to be vested interests which are "sinister" in their devotion to something less than the well-being of all mankind, and which defend themselves with spurious arguments, Bentham's manual of political fallacies will supply the honest citizen with an invaluable counter-weapon of rational exposure.

HAROLD A. LARRABEE

Union College
Schenectady, New York
August 1, 1952

[25] Bentham, *Works*, Bowring's edition, Vol. I, 43.

ACKNOWLEDGMENTS

MY BEST THANKS are due to Professor Herbert W. Schneider of Columbia University, who first called to my attention, many years ago, the virtues of *The Book of Fallacies* in the teaching of logic and politics to college undergraduates. The task of editing has been appreciably lightened by the hospitality of the Widener Library of Harvard University, and by the assistance of Professor Helmer L. Webb, Librarian of the Union College Library, in securing wanted books. I am also indebted to my colleagues Harrison C. Coffin, Frank Bailey professor of Greek, and D. Richard Weeks, associate professor of English, for their aid in tracking down some of Bentham's more obscure references in their respective fields.

H. A. L.

CONTENTS

Introduction

PART THE FIRST

Fallacies of Authority

PART THE SECOND

Fallacies of Danger

PART THE THIRD

Fallacies of Delay

PART THE FOURTH

Fallacies of Confusion

PART THE FIFTH

Causes of Fallacies

Appendix:

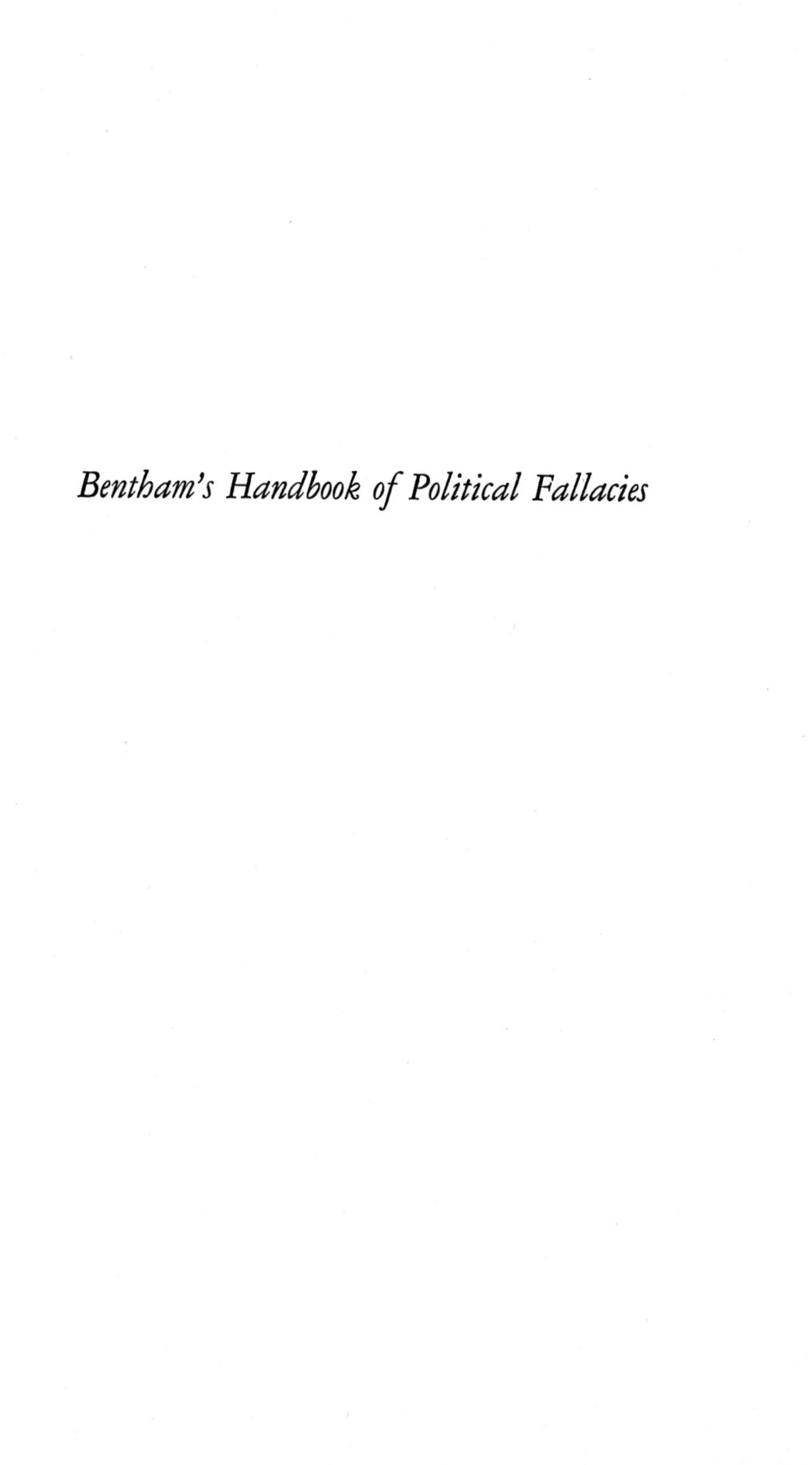

Bentham's Handbook of Political Fallacies

INTRODUCTION

Sec. 1. A Fallacy, What

BY THE NAME OF *fallacy* it is common to designate any argument employed or topic suggested for the purpose, or with the probability of producing the effect of deception, or of causing some erroneous opinion to be entertained by any person to whose mind such an argument may have been presented.

Sec. 2. Fallacies, by whom Treated Heretofore

The earliest author extant in whose works any mention is made of the subject of fallacies is Aristotle. In his treatise on logic, not only is the topic originated, but a list is given of the varieties of arguments to which the name fallacy may properly be applied. Aristotle's term for them has become the English word *sophism,* being derived from the ironical application of the root meaning of the Greek word *sophos,* or wise man, to that tribe of wranglers, the Sophists, whose pretension to the praise of wisdom had no better ground than an abuse of words. Upon the principle of the exhaustive method employed at so early a period by that astonishing genius, and so little turned to account since his day, Aristotle distributed the whole mass of fallacies into two parts: fallacies in the diction, of which he listed six, and fallacies not in the diction, of which there were seven, or a total of thirteen varieties in all.

But just as from Aristotle down to Locke with regard to the origin of our ideas of all sorts, so from Aristotle down to the present day with regard to the ways in which ideas are employable as instruments of deception, all is a blank. To do something about filling up that blank is the object of the present work.

In speaking of Aristotle's collection of fallacies as a stock to which from his time to the present no addition has been made, all that is meant is that no new arguments, besides those exposed by Aristotle, have been brought to view under that name. Yet between his days and the present, treatises on the art of oratory or popular argumentation have not been wanting, nor will any of them be found in which a person who might want to deceive his hearers might not find plentiful instruction.

What these books of instruction profess to teach is this: how, by means of words aptly employed, to gain your point; and how to produce upon your hearers the impression most favorable to your purpose, no matter what that purpose may be. Whether the impression in question was correct or deceptious, and whether the probable consequences to the individual or the community were likely to be salutary, indifferent, or pernicious – these were questions which seem never to have crossed the authors' minds. Apparently they would have regarded such issues as foreign to the subject, just as in a treatise on the art of war, a discussion of the justice of any particular war would be irrelevant. Dionysius of Halicarnassus, Cicero, Quintilian, Isaac Voss,[1] and, though last and least in bulk, yet not the least interesting, our own Gerard Hamilton,[2] are of this stamp.

[1] Isaac Voss (or Isaak Vossius) 1618–89, was one of several precocious sons of the Dutch scholar Gerard John Vos. After a brilliant career in Sweden, where he taught Queen Christina Greek, he went to England in 1670, and was given a place as residentiary canon at Windsor. Reputed to have the finest private library in the world, he was so much of a sceptic that Charles II remarked of him that "he would believe anything if only it were not in the Bible." – Ed.

[2] William Gerard Hamilton, who lived from 1729 to 1796, was known somewhat unjustly as "Single-speech Hamilton" for his maiden effort in the House of Commons debate on the address, November 13, 1755. After his death, two of his speeches in the Irish House of Commons, together with some miscellaneous papers, were published

After so many ages of teaching with equal complacency and indifference the art of true instruction and the art of deception, the art of producing good effects and bad effects, the art of the honest man and the knave, the means of promoting the purposes of the benefactor and the enemy of the human race — after so many ages during which no instruction has been given with a view to persuasion and action except in the same strain of imperturbable impartiality, it seemed to be not too early in the nineteenth century to take up the subject on the ground of morality, and to invite common honesty for the first time to mount the bench and take her seat as judge.

As for the fallacies enumerated by Aristotle, with the possible exception of those of Begging the Question and Mistaking an Obstacle for a Cause, so little danger of deception will be found in them on close examination, that had the philosopher left them unexposed to do their worst, the omission need not have hung very heavily upon his conscience. For about all the inconvenience they seem capable of producing is a slight sensation of embarrassment in not being able to describe exactly where the absurdity of the argument lies.

Sec. 3. Relation of Fallacies to Vulgar Errors

Vulgar error is the name given to an opinion which, being thought to be false, is considered in itself only, and not with a view to any consequences which it may produce. It is termed vulgar with respect to the multitude of persons by whom it is supposed to be entertained. *Fallacy* is applied to discourse in any shape considered as having a tendency, with or without design, to cause any erroneous opinion to be embraced, or, through the medium of some erroneous opinion

under the title *Parliamentary Logic,* which is discussed by Bentham in Section 7 below. — Ed.

already entertained, a pernicious course of action to be engaged in or persevered in. Thus to believe that the persons who lived in early or old times were, because they lived in those times, wiser or better than those who live in later or modern times, is a vulgar error; but to employ that error in the endeavor to cause pernicious practices and institutions to be retained is a fallacy.

Most of those who employed the term fallacy originally, considered deception not merely as a more or less probable consequence of such arguments, but as the end aimed at by at least some of their utterers. The thirteen arguments enumerated by Aristotle to which his Latin commentators gave the name of *fallaciae* (from *fallere,* to deceive), were undoubtedly regarded by him as instruments of deception, since on every occasion on which they are mentioned by him, the intent to deceive is either directly asserted or assumed.

Sec. 4. Political Fallacies the Subject of this Work

The present work confines itself to the examination and exposure of only one class of fallacies: those relating to the adoption or rejection of some measure of government, whether of legislation or of administration. The latter pair are so intimately connected that for our purposes they need not be distinguished from one another.

Under the name of a *Treatise on Political Fallacies* this work will possess the character and effect of a manual on the art of government, having for its practical object and tendency the introduction of such features of good government as remain to be introduced, and their perpetuation by means of that instrument, reason, which alone will be productive of any useful effect.

Now there are two ways in which the instrument of reason can be employed in this endeavor. The first and more direct is by showing positively, with respect to each measure proposed, in what ways and with what consequences it is likely to accomplish the end which it professes to have in view. The second and less direct is by pointing out the irrelevancy, and thus anticipating and destroying the persuasive force of such deceptious arguments as are likely to be used in dissuading men from supporting it.

Of these two different but harmonizing modes of applying this same instrument of reason to its several purposes, the more direct is that of which a sample has been before the public since 1802 in the collection of unfinished papers of legislation published at Paris in French by M. Dumont,[3] but for whose labors it would scarcely, in the author's life-time at least, have seen the light. To exhibit the less direct, but in its application the more extensive use, is the business of the present work.

To give existence to good arguments was the object of the former work; to provide for the exposure of bad ones is the object of the present one – to provide for the exposure of their real nature, and hence for the destruction of their pernicious force. Sophistry is a hydra of which, if all the necks could be exposed, the force would be destroyed. In this work they have been diligently looked out for, and in the course of it the principal and most active of them have been brought in view.

Sec. 5. Classification of Fallacies

So numerous are the instruments of persuasion which the present work will expose in the character of fallacies that to enable the mind to obtain any tolerably satisfactory command of the subject a scheme of classification is altogether indispensable. To frame such a classification with perfect logical accuracy would be an undertaking requiring more

[3] *Traités de la législation civile et pénale,* 3 vols. Translated as *Bentham's Theory of Legislation* by Charles Milner Atkinson, London, 1914. – Ed.

time than either author or editor has been able to spare. An imperfect classification, however, being preferable to no classification at all, the author [Bentham] adopted several principles of division into classes. One was the situation of the utterers of fallacies, especially in a legislative body such as a parliament: the fallacies of the *Ins*; the fallacies of the *Outs*; and *Either-side* fallacies. Another principle relates to the quarter to which the fallacy applies itself in the persons on whom it is designed to operate: fallacies of *the affections*; fallacies of *the judgment*; and fallacies of *the imagination.*

To the several clusters of fallacies marked out by this principle, a Latin affix expressive of the faculty or affection aimed at, was attached, not for ostentation, but for prominence, impressiveness, and hence for clearness. Thus we have arguments 1. *Ad verecundiam* (to modesty); *Ad superstitionem* (to superstition); 3. *Ad amicitiam* (to friendship); 4. *Ad metum* (to fear); 5. *Ad odium* (to hatred); 6. *Ad invidentiam* (to envy); 7. *Ad quietem* (to rest); 8. *Ad socordiam* (to weakmindedness); 9. *Ad superbiam* (to pride); 10. *Ad judicium* (to judgment); and 11. *Ad imaginationem* (to fancy). In the same manner, John Locke has employed Latin names to distinguish four kinds of argument: *Ad verecundiam, Ad ignorantiam, Ad hominem,* and *Ad judicium.*

M. Dumont, who some few years ago published a translation, or rather a *redaction,* of a considerable portion of the present work, divided the fallacies into three classes according to the particular object to which each class appeared to be immediately applicable. Some of them he supposed destined to repress discussion altogether; others to postpone it; and still others to perplex, when discussion could no longer be avoided. The first class he called the fallacies of *authority,* the second, fallacies of *delay,* and the third, fallacies of *confusion,* adding to the name of each the Latin affix which indicated the faculty or affection to which it was chiefly addressed.

The present editor [Bingham] has preferred Dumont's arrangement to that pursued by the author, and with some little variation he has adopted it in this volume. In addition to the immediate object of each class of fallacies, he has considered the subject-matter of each, with a view to placing all the fallacies that are similar in subject-matter in the same class. The classes he has arranged in the order in which the enemies of improvement may be expected to resort to them according to the emergency of the moment:

First, the fallacies of *authority*, including laudatory personalities, the subject-matter of which is authority in various shapes, and the immediate object to repress, on the ground of the weight of such authority, all exercise of the reasoning faculty.

Secondly, the fallacies of *danger*, including vituperative personalities, the subject-matter of which is the suggestion of danger in various shapes, and the object to repress altogether, on the ground of such danger, the discussion of a proposed measure.

Thirdly, the fallacies of *delay*, the subject-matter of which is the assigning of reasons for delay in various shapes, and the object, to postpone such discussion, with a view to eluding it altogether.

Fourthly, the fallacies of *confusion*, the subject-matter of which consists chiefly of vague and indefinite generalities, while the object is to produce, when discussion can no longer be avoided, such confusion in the minds of the hearers as to incapacitate them for forming a correct judgment on the question at issue.

In this classification, imperfections will be found, the removal of which (should it be practicable and worth the trouble) must be left to some more expert hand. The classes are not in every instance sufficiently distinct from each other; yet, imperfect as the classification is, it is to be hoped that the reflecting reader will not find it altogether without use.

Sec. 6. Nomenclature of Political Fallacies

Between the business of classification and that of nomenclature, the connection is most intimate. To the work of classification no expression can be given except by means of nomenclature, whereby a name is applied to a class marked out, and, as far as the work of the mind is creation, created. Of the class marked out, a description may be given of any length and degree of complication, amounting sometimes to entire sentences. But a name properly so-called consists of no more than one word or phrase. Without prodigious circumlocution and inconvenience, a class of objects, however well marked out by description, cannot be designated unless we substitute a word or a very small cluster of words for those constituting its description.

A class having been marked out by description, but lacking a name, it will be necessary to find and apply one. If already named, care should be taken to see whether or not a still better name cannot be devised.

Blessed be he forevermore, in whatever robe arrayed, to whose creative genius we are indebted for the first conception of those too short-lived vehicles which convey to us as in a nutshell the essential character of those awful volumes which ăt the touch of the sceptre become the rules of our conduct and the arbiters of our destiny: "The Alien Act," "The Turnpike Act," "The Middlesex Waterworks Bill," and so on.

How much better they serve than those authoritative masses of words called *titles,* by which so large a proportion of sound and so small a proportion of instruction are at so large an expense of attention granted to us, such as — "An Act to explain and amend an act entitled An Act to explain and amend . . ." Coinages of commodious titles are thus issued day by day throughout the session from an invisible though not unlicensed mint. But no sooner has the last newspaper of the last day of the session made its way to the most distant of its readers, than all this learning, all this circulating medium, is as completely buried in oblivion as a French assignat. So many yearly strings of words, not one of which is to be found in the works of Dryden, with whom the art of coining words fit to be used became numbered among the lost arts, and the art of giving birth to new ideas among the prohibited ones!

Let the workshop of invention be shut up forever, rather than that the eardrum of taste should be grated by a new sound! Rigorous decree! More rigorous, if obedience or enforcement kept pace with design, than even the continent-blockading and commerce-crushing decrees proclaimed by Bonaparte.

So necessary is it that, when a thing is talked of, there should be a name to call it by; so conducive, not to say necessary, to the prevalence of reason and common sense and moral honesty, that instruments of deception should be talked of, well talked of, and talked out of fashion — in a word, talked down; that, without any other license than the old one granted by Horace and seldom used,[4] the author has struck out under the spur of necessity a separate barbarism for each of these fallacies, such as the tools at his command have enabled him to produce. The objections of a class of readers, however, who under the name of *men of taste* attach more importance to the manner than the matter of a com-

[4] The reference is to Horace, *Ars Poetica,* lines 47–73, where permission to invent new words is granted on condition that it be used with moderation. The death of old words and the birth of new ones follows the order of nature. "As the forests change their foliage when the years turn to their closing, and the leaves of spring fall, so the old generation of words passes away, and new ones burst into life, like generations of men." Bentham himself took full advantage of this license granted by Horace, and not always with moderation. As Tom Moore sang: "There's Bentham, whose English is all his own making." Neal, *Short Title,* 146. — Ed.

position, have induced the editor to suppress for the present some of these characteristic names, and to substitute for them a number of less expressive titles.

Sec. 7. Contrast Between the Present Work and Hamilton's "Parliamentary Logic"

The general conception of this work had been formed, and some little progress in its composition had been made, when advertisements brought to the author's notice the posthumous work of the late William Gerard Hamilton entitled *Parliamentary Logic.*[5] The author had neither the hope nor the fear of finding the need of such a work as the present one superseded in any considerable degree by that of the right honorable orator. But his surprise was not inconsiderable upon finding in the two works hardly the slightest degree of coincidence. In respect to practical views and objects, it would not indeed be true to say that between the two works there exists no relation; for there exists a pretty close one, namely – the relation of contrariety.

Gerard Hamilton's book is a sort of school, in which the means of advocating a good cause and a bad cause are brought to view with equal frankness, and inculcated with equal solicitude for success. In other words, what Machiavelli has sometimes been supposed to have aimed at, Gerard Hamilton not only aims at, but aims at it without disguise.

Sketched out by himself and finished by his editor and panegyrist, the political character of Gerard Hamilton may be outlined in a few words: he was determined to join a party; he was as ready to side with one party as another; and whichever party he joined, he was as ready to say one thing as another in support of it. Independently of party, and personal profit to be derived from party, right and wrong, good and evil, were in his eyes matters of indifference. But having

[5] Published in 1808. – Ed.

consecrated himself to that party, whatever it was, from which the most was to be got — that party being the party of the *Ins*, standing constantly pledged for the protection of abuse in every shape, and opposing its extirpation; hence it was to the opposing of whatever was good in honest eyes that his powers, such as they were, were bent and pushed with peculiar energy.

One thing only he recognized as being evil in itself, to be opposed at any price, even on the unlikely assumption that it might be brought forward by his own party. That was *parliamentary reform*. In his eyes, Parliament was a sort of gaming-house; the members on the two sides of each house the players; and the property of the people, insofar as any pretense could be found for extracting it from them, the stakes to be played for. Insincerity in all its shapes, disingenuousness, lying, hypocrisy, fallacy — all are instruments employed by the players on both sides for obtaining advantages in the game. Whatever question is raised, the one consideration that is never taken into account by anyone is: what course will be for the advantage of the universal interest? Instead, the only question really taken into consideration is that of personal advantage in its several shapes. According to the answer given to that question in his own mind, a man takes sides: the side of those in office, if there is room for him; the side of those who expect to succeed to office, if that contingency presents the more encouraging prospect of the two.

To such persons, parliamentary reform is bound to be an object of extreme abhorrence. How could it be otherwise? By parliamentary reform the prey, the perpetually renascent prey, the fruit and object of the game, would be snatched out of their hands. It would mean official pay no greater than is sufficient for securing adequate service: no sinecures, no pensions, for hiring flatterers and pampering parasites; and no plundering in any shape or for any purpose. Amid the cries of "No theory! No theory!" the example of America would be a lesson, and the practice of America would be transferred to Britain.

The notion of the general predominance of self-regarding over social interest has been represented as a weakness incident to the situation of those whose converse has been more with books than with men. Be it so. Then look to those teachers, those supposed men of practical wisdom, whose converse has been at least as much with men as with books. Look in particular to this right honorable gentleman who in the house of commons had doubled the twenty years of lucubration necessary for law, who had served the equivalent of six apprenticeships and five complete clerkships; what says he? Is self-regarding interest predominant over social interest? Is self-regard merely predominant? No; self-regard is sole occupant. The universal interest, no matter how much talked of, is never so much as really thought of; and right and wrong are objects of complete and avowed indifference.

In Gerard Hamilton's book for the first time the veil of decorum has been cast aside and profligacy revealed stark naked. In the reign of Charles the Second, Sir Charles Sedley and others were indicted for exposing themselves on a balcony in a state of perfect nudity.[6] In Gerard Hamilton may be seen the Sir Charles Sedley of political morality. Sedley might have stood in his balcony until he was frozen, and nobody would have been the better, nobody much the worse; but Hamilton's self-exposure is most instructive.

If a man were to say that parliamentary reform is a good thing because Gerard Hamilton is against it, he would fall

[6] Sir Charles Sedley (1639–1701), wit and dramatist, M.P. for New Romney in Kent, was fined £500 for his part in the indecent frolic at the Cock Tavern in Bow Street, and according to Samuel Pepys (*Diary*, July 1, 1663) given "a most high reproofe" by the whole bench. Other participants were Lord Buckhurst (later Earl of Dorset) and Sir Thomas Ogle. – Ed.

into the use of one of the fallacies against the influence of which it is one of the objects of this work to raise a barrier. But this, however, may be said, and without fallacy, that it is the influence exercised by such men, and the use to which it is put, which constitutes no small part of the political disease which has produced the demand for parliamentary reform as a remedy. It is in the hope of substituting men for puppets, and the will of the people for the will of noble lords, puppets themselves to ministers or secret advisers, that parliamentary reform has recently become once more an object of general desire.

It might be pled in Hamilton's defense that instructions on how to administer poisons may have the effect of enabling a person who reads them with an opposite end in view, to secure himself the more effectually against attack by poisons. But in Hamilton's case, the manner in which he writes leaves little room for doubt as to whether he means his suggestions to be embraced or rejected. The object he has in view is plainly, on the occasion of a debate in parliament or any legislative assembly, to gain his point, no matter what it may be. The means he indicates as conducive to that end are sometimes fair, and sometimes foul ones. Be they fair or foul, they are delivered throughout in the same tone of seriousness and composure.

Come unto me all ye who have a point to gain, and I will show you how. It matters not whether it be bad or good; as long as it is not parliamentary reform, to me it is a matter of indifference. Here then, whatever be the influence of authority, either in general or of Gerard Hamilton in particular, it is exerted in the propagation of insincerity in that form of service in which it wins its richest reward.

To secure their children from falling into the vice of drunkenness, we are told that it was the policy of Spartan fathers to exhibit their slaves before them in a state of inebriation, so that the children might experience the contempt which is felt for a man whose intellect has been thrown into disorder by drink. An English father who has any regard for the morals of his son, especially in the vital matter of sincerity, will perhaps nowhere else find so instructive an example as that supplied by Gerard Hamilton in his book. In that mirror may be seen to what a state of corruption the moral part of a man's frame is capable of being reduced; to what a state of degradation, in the present state of parliamentary morality, a man is capable of sinking even when sober, and without any help from wine; and with what deliberate zeal he may exert his powers in the endeavor to propagate the infection in other minds.[7]

[7] That Bentham was not alone in his castigation of Hamilton may be seen from the review of *Parliamentary Logic* by Lord Jeffrey in the *Edinburgh Review,* Vol. XV (1809–10), 151–61, which concludes: "Throughout the whole work, indeed, it does not seem to have once occurred to the author, that it could ever be the object of debate, or at least of parliamentary debate, to promote the cause of justice or truth; all that he professes to teach is, how to get the better of an antagonist; and judging, wisely, that they who are in the right stand little in need of his instructions, nine-tenths of them are professedly devised for the assistance of those who know they are in the wrong. We have nowhere seen a more barefaced manual of sophistry; and should think its tendency pernicious, if we had any idea that it could at all affect the practice of its readers." – Ed.

PART THE FIRST

FALLACIES OF AUTHORITY

The subject of which is Authority in various shapes, and the object, to repress all exercise of the reasoning faculty.

CHAPTER I

The Nature of Authority

WITH REFERENCE to any proposed measures having for their object the greatest happiness of the greatest number, the course pursued by the adversaries of such measures has commonly been, in the first instance, to try to repress altogether the exercise of the reasoning faculty by invoking authority in various shapes as conclusive regarding the measure proposed.

But before any clear view can be given of the deception liable to be produced by the abuse of authority, it will be necessary to understand its nature, and to distinguish between its proper and its improper use. In the ensuing analysis, one distinction ought to be borne in mind: that between what may be termed a question of *opinion* and a question of *fact*. It will frequently happen that, while the authority of a person in respect to a question of fact is entitled to more or less regard, it is not so entitled in respect to a question of opinion.

Sec. 1. Analysis of Authority

What on any given occasion is the legitimate weight or influence to be attached to authority, regard being had to the circumstances surrounding the person who is claimed to be the authority? The answer depends upon: (1) the degree of relative and adequate intelligence of the person in question; (2) the degree of relative probity of the same person; (3) the nearness or remoteness between the subject of his opinion and the question in hand; and (4) the fidelity of the medium through which such supposed opinion has been transmitted, including both correctness and completeness.

Such are the sources upon which the legitimately persuasive force of authority seems to depend, and in which any deficiency of persuasive force, if it exists, is to be sought. Such deficiency may be in the intensity and steadiness of attention to the circumstances upon which the opinion needs to be grounded, or in respect of information in regard to the specific question in hand, or in distance in time or place from the scene of the proposed measures. The latter defects: distance in point of time or space, operate as causes of a deficiency in relevant and adequate information, and thus of a deficiency in intelligence.

As to relative probity of the alleged authority, any deficiency under this head will be occasioned by the exposure of the person in question to sinister interest, which is discussed in Part V. The most common and conspicuous deficiency in probity is that of insincerity: the opposition or discrepancy between the opinion expressed and that which is really entertained. Sinister interest operates either to keep the relevant means and materials out of the mind, or keeps the attention from fixing upon them with that degree of intensity which is proportioned to their legitimately persuasive force.

As to the mass of information accumulated by any person in relation to a given subject, its correctness and completeness (and hence the probability of the correctness of the opinion grounded upon it) will depend upon the joint ratio of the sufficiency of the *means* of collecting such information, and the strength of the *motives* by which he was urged to employ such means.

On both of these accounts taken together, at the top of the scale of trustworthiness stands that mass of authority which is constituted by scientific or professional opinion. This is opinion entertained in relation to a subject by a person who, through special means and motives attached to a particular situation in life, may with reason be considered as possessed of exceptional facilities for insuring the correctness of his opinions.

As to the special motives in question, they will in every case be found to consist of good or evil, profit or loss presenting themselves as eventually likely to befall the person in question: profit in case of the correctness of his opinion, loss in the event of its incorrectness. These motives operate in determining the degree of his attention in looking out for information, and the use made of the information in the way of reflection during the forming of his opinions. Thus in every occupation which may yield a profit, the hope of gaining a livelihood, or the fear of not gaining it, are the motives which impel a man to apply himself to the collection of information that may contribute to the correctness of his opinions, and hence to increased advantages in profit-making.

The following is a scale of the probable degrees of legitimately persuasive force of supposed expressions of authority:

1. Authority derived from *professional status,* being taken as the highest term in the scale for reasons already given.

2. Authority derived from *power,* since the greater quantity of power a man has, of any sort, the nearer the authority of his opinion comes to professional authority in respect of ease of obtaining the means conducive to correctness of opinion.

3. Authority derived from *opulence,* since opulence, being an instrument of power, seems to stand next after power in the scale of instruments of facility as above.

4. Authority derived from *reputation,* meaning general reputation, and not special and relative reputation, which

might rank this species of authority with professional status, as above.

Only the first of these four classes of authority embraces both motives and means. By having the motives which tend to correctness of information, the professional man has the means likewise; since it is to the force of his motives that he is indebted for whatever means he has acquired. It is from his having the motives that it follows that he has the means. But in the other three cases, whatever the means which a man's situation places within his reach, it does not follow that he has the motives to make use of the means.

On the contrary, in proportion as in the scale of power the man in question rises above the ordinary level, in that same proportion, in respect of motives for exertion, he is apt to sink below the same level. This is because the greater the quantity of the general mass of his objects of desire a man is already in possession of, the greater the portion of his desires that are in a state of saturation, and consequently the less the amount of that portion which, remaining unsatisfied, is free to operate on his mind as a motive.

Under Oriental despotism, the person at whose command the means of information exist in larger proportion than they do in the instance of any other person whatever, is the despot. But, necessary motives being wanting, no use is made by him of those means, and the general result is a state of almost infantile imbecility and ignorance. Such in kind, varying only in degree, is the case with every hand in which power is lodged when it is unencumbered with obligation, or, in other words, with a sense of eventual danger.

In England the king, the peer, the opulent borough-holding or county-holding country gentleman should, on the above principle, present an instance of the inverse ratio according to which, as the means decrease, the motives rise. But as long as he takes part at all in public affairs, the sense of that weak kind of eventual responsibility to which, notwithstanding the prevailing habits of idolatry, the monarch, as such, stands at all times exposed, suffices to keep his intellectual facilities at a point more or less above utter ignorance. But in either of the other two situations mentioned, short of provable idiocy, there is no degree of imbecility that can make it dangerous or inconvenient for the possessor of power to leave it altogether unexercised, or, without the smallest regard for the public welfare, to exercise his power in whatever manner may be most agreeable or convenient to himself.

All this while, it is only on the supposition of perfect relative probity, that is — of complete sincerity, that the title of a man's authority to respect bears any proportion either to motives or means of information as above. On the contrary, if immediately, or through the medium of the will, a man's understanding be exposed to the dominion of sinister interest, then the more complete, as well as correct, the mass of relevant information he possesses, the less will his real or pretended opinion be entitled to be regarded as authoritative.

For example, concerning the question: what is the system of remuneration best adapted to the purpose of obtaining the highest degree of official aptitude throughout the whole field of government service? the authority of any person who, here or elsewhere, now or formerly, was in possession or expectation of any such situation as that of minister of state, is not equal to zero, but is less than zero, in that it affords a reason for looking upon the opposite opinion as the right and true one. Similarly concerning the question: what, in so far as concerns intelligibility, economy, or expeditiousness of procedure, the state of the law *ought* to be? the authority of any person who, here or elsewhere, recently or formerly, was in possession or expectation of any situation, professional or official, the profitableness of which, in the shape of money, power, ease, and occasionally vengeance, depended upon the unintelligibility, the expensiveness, the dilatoriness, and the vexatiousness of the system of judicial procedure, is likewise not merely equal to zero, but in the mathematical sense negative, or less than zero.

So far it has been taken for granted that the direction in which the authority is offered is the same as that in which the sinister interest acts. Should the contrary be true – the sinister interest lying one way, the direction of the authority the other way – then the title of the opinion to credit as authority, far from being destroyed or weakened, is much increased. This is because the motives and the means which lead to correctness, being within the reach of men of this description, and the forces which tend to promote aberration having spent themselves in vain, the chance of ultimate correctness is thereby enhanced. This is in accord with one of the few rational rules that have so far gained acceptance among the established rules of evidence: In a man's own favor his own testimony is the weakest; in his disfavor the strongest evidence.

Whenever a man is furnished to a superior degree with the means and motives for obtaining relevant information concerning a question, the stronger the force of the sinister interest upon him, the stronger is his title to our attention. For there is a high probability that he will produce and use such information. If, then, instead he produces no such information, or uses arguments of an irrelevant sort, the use of such bad arguments affords circumstantial evidence of no mean degree of probative force, of the inability of the side thus advocated to furnish any good ones.

Of the third circumstance which should be considered in estimating the credit due to authority, closeness of the relation between the subject of the supposed opinion and the immediate topic in hand, it is evident that there cannot be any common and generally applicable measure. It is the sort of quantity concerning which a judgment can only be pronounced in each individual case.

As to the fourth requisite – the fidelity of the medium

through which the opinion constitutive of the authority in question has been transmitted — of its inclusion in the list the propriety is, on the bare mention, as manifest as it is in the power of reason to make it.

The need for the legitimately persuasive force of authority, that is — the probability of comparatively superior information on the one hand, is in inverse ratio to the information of the person on whom it is designed to operate, on the other. The less the degree in which each man is qualified to form a judgment on any subject on the ground of specific and relevant information, or direct evidence, the more cogent the necessity he is under of trusting, with a degree of confidence more or less implicit, to indirect or circumstantial evidence. But in proportion to the number of persons who possess, each within himself, the means of forming an opinion on any given subject on the ground of direct evidence, the greater the number of persons to whom it ought to be a matter of shame to frame and pronounce their respective decisions on no better ground than that of such inconclusive and necessarily fallacious evidence.

Of the truth of this observation, men belonging to several classes, whose situation in the community has given them both efficient power and a separate and sinister interest opposite to that of the community in general, have seldom failed to be sufficiently aware. This is one cause, although only one, of the anxiety betrayed and the pains taken by lawyers to keep the rule of legal action in a state of as complete unintelligibility as possible on the part of the people whose conduct is professed to be directed by it, and whose fate is in fact disposed of by it. Another example is to be seen in the pains taken by the clergy of old times in the Romish church, to keep in the same state of unintelligibility the acknowledged rule of action in matters of sacred and supernatural law. And in the instance of the English clergy of times later than those of the Romish church, one sees a similar partial explanation of the exertions made by so large a proportion of the governing classes of that hierarchy to keep back and if possible to render abortive that system of invention which has for its object the giving to the exercise of the art of reading the highest degree of universality possible.

But to return to the definition of legitimate authority, no fallacy can be alleged when the sole object of citing an authority is to point out a place where relevant arguments may be found and brought forth in a more complete or perspicuous state than would otherwise be possible. In the case thus supposed there is no question of irrelevance. The arguments are relevant ones, such as, if the person by whom they are presented were altogether unknown, would not lose any of their weight. The opinion is not presented as itself constitutive of authority, as carrying any weight of itself and independently of the considerations which the arguer has brought to view. Neither is there any fallacy in referring to the opinion of this or that professional person, in a case to such a degree professional or scientific that it is beyond the competence of the members of the audience to form a correct judgment on the basis of relevant and specific arguments. In matters touching medical science, chemistry, astronomy, the mechanical arts, and the various branches of the art of war, and so forth, no other course could be pursued.

Sec. 2. Appeal to Authority, in What Cases Fallacious[1]

Reference to authority is open to the charge of fallacy when, in the course of a debate on a subject lying within the comprehension of the debaters, so that arguments bearing the closest relation to it would be perfectly within the sphere of their comprehension, authority (or an irrelevant argument) is employed in the place of such relevant arguments as might have been brought forward.

The most fallacious use of authority is in instances where the debaters are capable of forming a correct judgment on the basis of relevant arguments, but in which the *opinion*, real or supposed, of some person whose profession or other particular situation involves an interest opposite to that of the general public, is brought forth in the character of an argument in the place of such relevant arguments as ought to be furnished. (In an appendix to this chapter will be given examples of persons whose declared opinions, on a question of legislation, are in a peculiar degree liable to be tinged with falsity by the action of sinister interest).

He who refers to authority as decisive of the propriety of any law or established practice assumes the truth of one or the other of two positions: either (1) that the principle of utility — the greatest happiness of the greatest number, is not at the time the proper standard for judging the merits

[1] An unquestionable maxim (it is said) is this: "Reason and not authority should determine the judgment." Said, and by whom? Even by a bishop, and by what bishop? Even Bishop Warburton, and this not in one work, but in two. The above words are from his *Div. Legat.* 2, 302; and in his *Alliance,* etc. is a passage to the same effect. Here then we have authority against authority. Ed. note: The works referred to are *Divine Legation of Moses demonstrated on the Principles of a Religious Deist* (2 vols., 1737–41) and *Alliance between Church and State* (1736) by William Warburton (1698–1779), bishop of Gloucester, who was noted for his "passion for paradox."

of the question; or (2) that the practice of other and former times, or the opinion of other persons, ought to be regarded in all cases as conclusive evidence, superseding the necessity and propriety of any recourse to reason or present experience.

In the first instance, being really an enemy to the community, that he should be esteemed as such by all to whom the happiness of the community is an object of regard, is no more than right and reasonable. In the second case, what he does is virtually to acknowledge himself not to possess any powers of reasoning which he himself can venture to think it safe to trust. Incapable of forming for himself any judgment by which he thinks it safe to be governed, he betakes himself for safety to some other men, or set of men, of whom he knows little or nothing, except that they lived so many years ago, and consequently in a period possessing for its guidance so much the less experience than his own.

When a man gives this account of himself – when he represents his own mind as laboring under this kind and degree of imbecility, what can be more reasonable than that he should be taken at his word? Why should he not be considered as a person laboring under a general and incurable imbecility, one from whom nothing relevant can reasonably be expected?

He who employs authority in the place of reasoning makes no secret of the opinion he entertains of his hearers and his readers. He assumes that those he addresses are incapable, each of them, of forming a judgment of their own. If they submit to this insult, may it not be presumed that they acknowledge the justice of it?

Now of imbecility, at any rate of self-conscious and self-avowed imbecility, proportionable humility ought naturally to be the result. On the contrary, of this species of idolatry, of this worshipping of dead men's bones, all the passions the most opposite to humility: pride, anger, obstinacy, and overbearingness, are the frequent, not to say the constant accompaniments. With the utmost strength of mind that can be displayed in the field of reasoning, no reasonable man ever manifests so much heat, assumes so much, or exhibits himself disposed to hear so little, as these men, whose title to regard and notice is thus surrendered by themselves.

Whence this inconsistency? Whence this violence? From this alone, that having some abuse to defend, some abuse in which they have an interest and a profit, and finding it on the ground of present public interest indefensible, they fly for refuge to the only sort of argument in which so much as the pretension of being sincere in error can find countenance.

By authority, support, the strength of which is proportioned to the number of persons joining in it, is given to systems of opinion at once absurd and pernicious, to the religion of Buddha, of Brahma, or of Mahomet. Hence it may be inferred that the probative force of authority is not increased by the number of those who may have professed a given opinion, unless indeed it could be proved that each individual of the multitudes who so professed, possessed in the highest degree the means and motives for insuring its correctness. Even in such a case it would not warrant the substitution of the authority for such direct evidence and arguments as any case in debate might be able to supply, supposing the debaters capable of comprehending such direct evidence and arguments.

The following considerations will render it sufficiently apparent that in ordinary cases, no such circumstantial evidence should possess any such legitimately probative force as to warrant its addition, much less its substitution in place of that sort of information which belongs to direct evidence:

1. If distance in point of time were not sufficient to destroy the probative force of such authority, the Catholic religion would be restored to the exclusive dominion it pos-

sessed and exercised for so many centuries; the Toleration laws would be repealed, and persecution to the point of extirpation would be substituted for whatever liberty in conduct and discourse is enjoyed at present. And in this way, after the abolished religion had thus been triumphantly restored, an inexorable door would be shut against every imaginable change in it, and thence against every imaginable reform or improvement in it, through all future ages.

2. If distance in point of place were not understood to have the same effect, some other religion than the Christian, the religion of Mahomet for example, or the way of thinking in matters of religion prevalent in China, would have to be substituted by law for the Christian religion.

In authority, defense, such as it is, has been found for every imperfection, for every abuse, for every most pernicious and most execrable abomination that the most corrupt system of government has ever husbanded in its bosom. And here may be seen the mischief necessarily attached to the course of him whose footsteps are regulated by the finger of this blind guide. What is more, what inferences may be deduced respecting the probity or improbity, the sincerity or insincerity of him who, standing in a public situation, blushes not to look to this blind guide to the exclusion of and in preference to reason – the only guide that does not begin by shutting his own eyes, for the purpose of closing the eyes of his followers.

As the world grows older, if at the same time it grows wiser (which it will do unless the time comes when experience, the mother of wisdom, becomes barren), the influence of authority will in each situation, and particularly in Parliament, become less and less. Take any part of the field of moral science: private morality, constitutional law, private law – go back a few centuries, and you will find argument consisting of reference to authority, not exclusively, but in as large a proportion as possible. As experience has increased, authority has gradually been set aside, and reasoning, drawn from facts and guided by reference to the end in view has taken its place.

Of the enormous mass of Roman law heaped up in the school of Justinian, a mass, the perusal of which would employ several lives occupied by nothing else, materials of the following description constitute by far the greater part: A. throws out at random some loose thought; B. catching it up, tells you what A. thinks — at least, what A. said; C. tells you what has been said by A. and B.; and thus like an avalanche the mass rolls on. Happily it is only in matters of law and religion that endeavors are made, by the favor shown and currency given to this fallacy, to limit and debilitate the exercise of the right of private inquiry in as great a degree as possible, although in these days the exercise of this essential right can no longer be suppressed in a complete and direct way by legal punishment.

In mechanics, in astronomy, in mathematics, in the new-born science of chemistry, no one today has either effrontery or folly enough to avow, or so much as insinuate, that the most rational and desirable course in those branches of useful knowledge would be to substitute decision on the ground of authority for decision on the ground of direct and specific evidence. In every branch of physical art and science, the folly of this substitution is a matter of demonstration, a matter of intuition, and as such is universally acknowledged. In the moral branch of science, religion not excluded, the folly of the same recipe for correctness of opinion would not be less universally recognized, if the wealth, ease, and dignity attached to and supported by the maintenance of the opposite opinion did not so steadily resist such recognition.

Causes of the employment and prevalence of this fallacy

It is obvious that this fallacy in all its branches is frequently resorted to by those who are interested in the support of abuses, or of institutions pernicious to the great body of the people, with the intention of suppressing all exercise of reason. A foolish or untenable proposition resting on its own supports, or on the mere credit of the utterer, could not fail speedily to encounter detection and exposure. The same proposition, extracted from a page of Blackstone, or from the mouth of any other person to whom the idle and unthinking are in the habit of unconditionally surrendering their understandings, will disarm all opposition.

Blind obsequiousness, ignorance, idleness, irresponsibility are the causes which enable the fallacy to maintain such an ascendancy in the governing assemblies of the British empire.

(1) In this situation one man is ready to borrow the opinion of another, because through ignorance and imbecility he feels himself unable, or through want of solicitude unwilling, to form one for himself; and he is thus ignorant, if natural talent does not fail him, because he is so idle. Knowledge, especially in so wide and extensive a field, requires study; and study requires labor of mind bestowed with more or less energy, for a greater or lesser length of time.

(2) In a situation for which the strongest talents would not be more than adequate, there is frequently a failure of natural talent, because in so many instances admission to that situation requires so little talent that no degree of intellectual deficiency, short of palpable idiocy, can have the effect of excluding a man from it.

(3) The sense of responsibility is in a large proportion of the members altogether wanting, because so few of them are at any time in any degree dependent upon the people

whose fate is in their hands, and those few only for short periods of time. While so few are dependent on those on whom they ought to be dependent, so many are dependent on those who ought to be dependent on them: those servants of the crown on whose conduct they are commissioned by their constituents to act as judges. What share of knowledge, intelligence, and natural talent is in the house, is thus divided between those who are, and their rivals who hope to be, servants of the crown. The consequence is that, those excepted in whom knowledge, intelligence, and talent are worse than useless, the house is composed of men the furniture of whose minds is made up of discordant prejudices, of which on each occasion they follow that by which the interest or passion of the moment is most promoted.

Then, with regard to responsibility, so happily have matters been managed by the house that a seat in it is not less clear of obligation than a seat in the opera house: in both, a man takes his seat only when he cannot find more amusement elsewhere; for both, the qualifications are the same, a ticket begged or bought; in neither is a man charged with any obligation other than the negative one of not being a nuisance to the company; in both, the length as well as the number of attendances depends on the amusement a man finds, except, in the house, as regards the members dependent upon the crown. True it is, that a self-styled independent member is not necessarily ignorant and weak: if by accident a man possessed of knowledge and intelligence is placed in the house, his seat will not deprive him of his talents. All therefore that is meant is, only, that ignorance does not disqualify, not that knowledge does. Of the crown and its creatures it is the interest that this ignorance be as thick as possible. Why? Because the thicker the ignorance, the more completely is the furniture of men's minds made up of those interest-begotten prejudices, which render them blindly obsequious to all those who with power in their hands stand up to take the lead.

But the Emperor of Morocco is not more irresponsible, and therefore more likely to be ignorant and prone to be deceived by the fallacy of authority, than a member of the British Parliament. The Emperor's power is clear of obligation; so is the member's. The Emperor's power, it is true, is an integer, and the member's but a fraction; but no ignorance prevents a man from becoming or continuing Emperor of Morocco, nor from becoming or continuing a member of Parliament. The Emperor's title is derived from birth; so is that of many a member. To enjoy his despotism, no fraud, insincerity, hypocrisy or jargon is necessary to the Emperor; much of all of them to the member. By ascending and maintaining his throne, no principle is violated by the Emperor; by the member, if a borough-holder, many principles are violated on his taking and retaining his seat. In being a despot, the Emperor is not an impostor; the member is. The Emperor pretends not to be a trustee, agent, deputy, delegate, representative; lying is not among the accompaniments of his tyranny and insolence; the member does pretend all this, and, if a borough-holder, he lies. A trust-holder, yes; but he is a trust-breaker. An agent, yes; but for himself. A representative of the people, yes; but as Mr. Kemble represents Macbeth.[2] A deputy, yes; because it has not been in their power to depute or delegate anyone else. Deputy? Delegate? Neither title does he assume except for argument, and when he cannot help it. Deputation refers to a matter of fact, and reveals the fewness of the electors and their want of freedom. Representation is a more convenient word. The acts of the electors are kept out of sight by it. It is a mere fiction, the offspring of lawyer-craft. Any one person or thing

[2] John Philip Kemble (1757–1823) of the famous theatrical family, was manager of Covent Garden, and shone especially in the role of Macbeth. – Ed.

may be represented by any other. By canvas with colors, a man is represented; by a king, the whole people; by an ambassador, the king, and thus the people.

Remedy against the influence of this fallacy

For banishing ignorance, and for replacing it with a constantly competent measure of useful, appropriate, and general instruction, the proper, necessary, and only means lie not deep beneath the surface. The sources of instruction being at command, and the quantity of natural talent given, the quantity of information obtained will in every case be as the quantity of mental labor employed in the collection of it; and the quantity of such labor as the aggregate strength of the motives by which a man is incited to labor.

In the existing order of things, there is, comparatively speaking, no instruction obtained, because no labor is bestowed. And no labor is bestowed, because none of the motives by which men are excited to labor are applied in that direction. The situation of member of Parliament being by supposition an object of desire, if without labor being employed in obtaining instruction, there would be no chance of obtaining such a situation, or an inferior chance, while with labor so employed there would be a certainty, or a superior chance, then instruction would have its motives and efficient cause, and so would labor applied to the attainment of instruction.

The quality, that is, the relative applicability of the mass of information obtained is also an object not to be overlooked. The goodness of the quality will depend upon the liberty enjoyed in respect of the choice. By prohibitions, with penalties attached to the delivery of alleged information relative to a subject in question, or any part of it, the quality of the whole mass is impaired, and an implied certificate is given attesting to the truth and utility of whatever is thus endeavored to be suppressed.

APPENDIX

Examples of persons whose declared opinions upon a question of legislation are peculiarly liable to be tinged with falsity by the action of sinister interest.

1. Lawyers: oppositeness of their interest to the universal interest

THE OPINIONS OF LAWYERS on a question of legislation, particularly of such lawyers as are or have been practicing advocates, are peculiarly liable to be tinged with falsity by the operation of sinister interest. To the interest of the community at large, that of every advocate is in a state of such direct and constant opposition, especially in civil matters, that the above assertion requires an apology to redeem it from the appearance of trifling. It is to the people's interest that delay, vexation, and expense of procedure should be as small as possible; it is to the advocate's that they should be as great as possible: the expense in so far as his profit is proportioned to it; the factitious vexation and delay, in so far as they are inseparable from the profit-yielding part of the expense. As to uncertainty in the law, it is to the people's interest that each man's security against wrong should be as complete as possible: that all his rights should be known to him; that all acts, which in the case of his doing them will be treated as offenses, may be known to him as such, together with their eventual punishment, that he may avoid committing them, and that others may, in as few instances as possible, suffer either from the wrong or from the expensive and vexatious remedy. Hence it is to the people's interest that in all these matters the rule of action as it applies to each man should at all times be not only discoverable, but actually present to his mind.

Such knowledge, which it is to every man's interest to

possess to the greatest, it is to the lawyer's interest that he possess to the narrowest degree possible. It is to every man's interest to keep out of lawyers' hands as much as possible; it is to the lawyer's interest to get him in as often, and keep him in as long as possible. Hence it is to the lawyer's interest to prevent any written expression of the words necessary to keep non-lawyers out of his hands from coming into existence, and when and if in existence from being present to the lay mind, and when presented from staying there.[1] It is to the lawyer's interest, therefore, that people should continually suffer for the non-observance of laws, which, so far from having received efficient promulgation, have never yet found any authoritative expression in words. This is the very perfection of oppression. Yet, propose that access to knowledge of the laws be afforded by means of a code, and lawyers, one and all, will join in declaring it impossible. To any effect, as occasion arises, a judge will forge a rule of law; but propose to make a law to that same effect, in any determinate form of words, and that same judge will declare it impossible. . .

It is to the judge's interest that on every occasion his declared opinion be taken for the standard of right and wrong; that whatever he declares right or wrong be universally received as such, no matter how contrary such declaration may be to truth or utility, or to his own declaration at other times. Hence it is to his interest that, within the whole field of law, men's opinion of right and wrong should be as contradictory, unsettled, and hence as obsequious to

[1] A considerable proportion of what is termed the common law of England is in this oral and unwritten state. The cases in which it has been clothed with words, that is, in which it has been framed and pronounced, are to be found in the various collections of reported decisions. These decisions, not having the sanction of a law passed by the legislature, are confirmed or overruled at pleasure by the existing judges; so that, except in matters of the most common and daily occurrence, they afford no rule of action at all.

him as possible; that the same conduct which to others would occasion shame and punishment, should to him and his bring honor and reward; that on condition of telling a lie, it should be in his power to do what he pleases, the injustice and falsehood being regarded with complacency and reverence; and that as often as by falsehood, money or other advantage can be secured, it should be regarded as proper for him to employ reward or punishment, or both, for the procurement of such falsehood. Consistently with men's abstaining from violent acts, by which the person and property of him and his would be alarmingly endangered, it is to his interest that intellectual as well as moral depravity should be as intense and extensive as possible; that transgressions cognizable by him should be as numerous as possible; that injuries and other transgressions committed by him should be reverenced as acts of virtue; and that the suffering produced by such injuries should be placed, not to his account, but to the immutable nature of things, or to the wrongdoer who, but for encouragement from him, would not have become such.

His professional and personal interest being thus adverse to that of the public, from a lawyer's declaration that the tendency of a proposed law relative to procedure is pernicious, the contrary inference may not unreasonably be drawn. From those habits of misrepresenting their own opinion, that is, of insincerity, which are almost peculiar to this in comparison with other professions, one presumption is, that he does not entertain the opinion thus declared. Another one is, that if he does, he has been deceived into it by sinister interest and the authority of his fellow professional men, in like manner deceivers or deceived. In other words, it is the result of interest-begotten prejudice.

In the case of every other body of men, it is generally expected that their conduct and language will be for the most part directed by their own interest, that is, by their own view of it. In the case of the lawyer, the ground of this persuasion, so far from being weaker, is stronger than in any other instance. His evidence being thus *interested evidence*, according to his own rules his declaration of opinion on the subject here pointed out would not be so much as hearable. It is true that, were those rules consistently observed, judicature would be useless, and society would be dissolved. Accordingly they are not so observed, but observed or broken pretty much at pleasure. But they are none the less among those rules, the excellence and inviolability of which the lawyer is never tired of trumpeting. But on any point, such as those in question, nothing could be more unreasonable, nothing more inconsistent with what has been said above, than to refuse him a hearing. On every such point, his habits and experience afford him facilities not possessed by any one else for finding relevant and specific arguments, when the nature of the case affords any such arguments. But the surer he is of being able to find such arguments, if any are to be found, the stronger the reason for treating his naked declaration of opinion as unworthy of all regard. Accompanied by specific arguments, it is useless; destitute of them, it amounts to a virtual confession of their non-existence. So matters stand on the question of what *ought* to be law.

On the question what the law *is*, as long as the rule of action is kept in the state of common, alias unwritten, alias imaginary law, authority, though next to nothing, is everything. The question is: what on a given occasion A. (the judge) is likely to think? Wait till your fortune has been spent in the inquiry, and you will know. But, inasmuch as it is naturally a man's wish to be able to give a guess what the result will eventually be, before he has spent his fortune, with a view if possible to avoid spending his fortune and getting nothing in return for it, he applies through the medium of B. (an attorney) for an opinion to C. (a counsel) who, considering what D. (a former judge) has, on a subject supposed to be more or less analogous to the one in question, said or been supposed to say, deduces therefore his guess as to what, when the time comes, Judge A., he thinks, will say, and gives it to you. A shorter way would be to put the question at once to A., but for obvious reasons, that is not permitted.

On many cases, again, as well-grounded a guess might be had of an astrologer for five shillings, as of a counsel for twice or thrice as many guineas, but that the lawyer considers the astrologer as a smuggler, and puts him down.

But Packwood's opinion on the goodness of his own razors would be a safer guide for judging of their goodness, than a judge's opinion on the goodness of a proposed law. It is to Packwood's interest that his razors be as good as possible; it is to the judge's interest that the law be as bad, yet thought to be as good as possible. It would not be to the judge's interest that his commodity should be thus bad, if, as in the case of Packwood, the customer had other shops to go to; but in this case, even when there are two shops to go to, the shops being in confederacy, the commodity is equally bad in both, and the worse the commodity, the better it is said to be. And in the case of the judge's commodity, no experience seems to suffice to undeceive men, for the bad quality of it is referred to any cause except the true one.

2. Churchmen: oppositeness of their interest to the universal interest

In the lawyer's case it has been shown that concerning the question, what on such or such a point *ought* to be the law, to refer to a lawyer's opinion given without or against specific reasons is a fallacy; its tendency, in proportion to the regard paid to it, deceptious; the cause of this deceptious tendency, sinister interest, to the action of which all advocates and (being made from advocates) all judges stand exposed. To the churchman's case the same reasoning applies: it is not a question as to what in matters of religion *is* law, but as to what *ought* to be. On a question not connected with religion, reference to a churchman's opinion as such, as authority, can scarcely be considered as a fallacy, such opinion not being likely to be considered as constitutive of authority.

To understand how great would be the probability of deception, if on the question what in matters of religion ought to be law, the unsupported opinion of a churchman were to be regarded as authority, we must develop the nature and form of the sinister interest, by which any declaration of opinion from such a quarter is divested of all title to regard.

The sources of a churchman's sinister interest are as follows:

1. On entering the profession, as condition precedent to advantage from it in the shape of subsistence and all other shapes, he makes of necessity a solemn and recorded declaration of his belief in the truth of 39 articles framed in 1562, the date of which, the ignorance and violence of that time being considered, should suffice to satisfy a reflecting mind of the impossibility of their being all of them really believed by any person at present.

2. In this declaration is generally understood to be included an engagement or undertaking, in case of original belief and subsequent change, never to declare, but, if questioned, to deny any such change.

3. In the institution thus established, he beholds shame and punishment attached to sincerity, rewards in the largest quantity to absurdity and insincerity. Now the presumptions resulting from such an application of reward and punishment to engage men to declare assent to a given proposition are (1) that the proposition is not believed by the proposer; (2) hence, that it is not true; and (3) that it is not believed by the acceptor. It is impossible to produce real and immediate belief by rewards and punishments. But the follow-

ing effects may certainly be produced: (1) the abstaining from any declaration of disbelief; (2) declaration of belief; and (3) the turning aside from all considerations tending to produce belief, authority especially, by which a sort of vague and indistinct belief in the most absurd propositions has everywhere been produced.

In no other part of the field of knowledge are rewards and punishments considered nowadays as fit instruments for the production of assent or dissent. A schoolmaster would not be looked upon as sane, who, instead of putting Euclid's demonstrations into the hands of his pupil, should, without the demonstrations, put Euclid's propositions into his hand, and then give him a guinea for signing a paper declarative of his belief in them, or lock him up for a couple of days without food on his refusal to sign. And so it is in chemistry, mechanics, husbandry, astronomy, or any other branch of knowledge. It is true that in those parts of knowledge in which assent and dissent are left free, the importance of arriving at the truth may not be esteemed as great as here, where it is thus influenced. But the more important the truth, the more flagrant the absurdity and tyranny of employing, for the propagation of it, instruments the employment of which has a stronger tendency to propagate error than truth.

4. For teaching such religious truths as men are allowed to teach, together with such religious errors as they are thus forced to teach, the churchman sees rewards allotted in larger quantities than for the most useful services. In Ireland, of nine-tenths of those on pretense of instructing whom this vast mass of reward is extorted, it is known that, being by conscience precluded from hearing such instruction, it is impossible that they should derive any benefit from it. In Scotland, where government reward is not employed in giving support to it, Church-of-Englandism is reduced to next to nothing.

The opinions which, in this state of things, interest engages a churchman to support are: (1) that reward to the highest extent has no tendency to promote insincerity, even where practicable, to an unlimited extent, and without chance of detection; (2) that money given in case of compliance, refused in case of non-compliance, is not reward for compliance; (3) that punishment applied in case of non-compliance, withheld in case of compliance, is not punishment; (4) that insincerity is not vice but virtue, and as such ought to be promoted; and (5) that it is not merely consistent with, but requisite to good government to extort money from poor and rich to be applied as reward for doing nothing, or for doing but a small part of what is done by others for a small proportion of the same reward, and this on pretense of rendering service, which nine-tenths of the people in a country refuse to receive.

It is in the interest of the persons thus engaged upon a course of insincerity, that by the same means perseverance in the same course should be universal and perpetual; for suppose, in case of the reward being withheld, the number annually making the same declaration should be reduced one-half, this would be presumptive evidence of insincerity on the part of half of those who made it before. The more flagrant the absurdity, thc stronger is each man's interest in engaging as many as possible in joining with him in the profession of assent to it, for the greater the number of such co-declarants, the greater the number of those of whose professions the elements of authority are composed, and of those who stand precluded from casting on the rest the imputation of insincerity.

The following, then, are the abuses in the defense of which all churchmen are enlisted: (1) perpetuation of immorality in the shape of insincerity; (2) perpetuation of absurdity in subjects of the highest importance; (3) extortion inflicted on the many for the benefit of the few; (4)

reward bestowed on idleness and incapacity to the exclusion of labor and ability; (5) the matter of corruption applied to the purposes of corruption in a constant stream; and (6) in one of these kingdoms a vast majority of the people kept in degradation avowedly for none other than the above purposes. But whoever is engaged by interest in the support of any one government abuse, is engaged in the support of all, each giving to the others his support in exchange.

It being the characteristic of abuse to need and receive support from fallacy, it is the interest of every man who derives profit from abuse in any shape to give the utmost currency to fallacy in every shape: to those which render more particular service to the abuses of others as well as those which render such service to his own. It being to the interest of each person so situated to give the utmost support to abuse, and the utmost currency to fallacy in every shape, it is also to his interest to make most efficient that system of education by which men are most effectively divested both of the power and the will to detect and expose fallacies, and hence to suppress every system of education which has the contrary tendency. And lastly, the stronger the interest by which a man is urged to give currency to fallacy, and thus to propagate deception, the more likely it is that such will be his endeavor, and the less fit, therefore, will his opinion be to serve in the character of authority, as a standard and model for the opinions of others.

CHAPTER II

The Wisdom of our Ancestors, or Chinese Argument

Ad verecundiam.

Exposition

THIS ARGUMENT CONSISTS in stating a supposed repugnancy between the proposed measure and the opinions of men by whom the country of those who are discussing the measure was inhabited in former times: these opinions being collected either from the express words of some writer living at the time in question, or from laws or institutions that were then in existence.

Our wise ancestors — the wisdom of our ancestors — the wisdom of ages — venerable antiquity — wisdom of old times — such are the leading terms and phrases of propositions the object of which is to cause the alleged repugnance to be regarded as a sufficient cause for the rejection of the measure.

Exposure

This fallacy affords one of the most striking of the numerous instances in which, under the conciliatory influence of custom, that is of prejudice, opinions the most repugnant to one another are capable of maintaining their ground in the same intellect. This fallacy, prevalent as it is in matters of law, is directly contrary to a principle or maxim universally admitted in almost every other department of human intelligence, and which is the foundation of all useful knowledge and all rational conduct.

"Experience is the mother of wisdom," is among the maxims handed down to the present and all future ages, by the wisdom, such as it has been, of past ages. "No!" says this fallacy, "the true mother of wisdom is not experience, but inexperience."

An absurdity so glaring carries in itself its own refutation. All that we can do is to trace the causes which have contributed to give this fallacy such an ascendancy in matters of legislation. Among the several branches of the fallacies of authority, the cause of delusion is more impressive in this than in any other. From inaccuracy of expression arises incorrectness of expression, from which expression conception is produced again. Thus error, beginning as a momentary cause, comes to be a permanent effect.

In the very name commonly employed to signify the portion of time to which the fallacy refers, there is virtually involved a false and deceptious proposition, which, from its being used by every mouth, is at length, and without examination, received as true. What in common language is called *old* time, ought (with reference to any period at which the fallacy in question is employed) to be called *young* or early time.

As between individual and individual living at the same time and in the same situation, he who is old possesses, as such, more experience than he who is young. But, as between generation and generation, the reverse of this is true. If, as in ordinary language, a preceding generation be called old, this old or preceding generation could not have had as much experience as the succeeding generation. With respect to such materials or sources of wisdom as have been presented to their own senses, the two generations are on a par; but with respect to such of those materials and sources as are derived from the reports of others, the later of the two generations possesses an indisputable advantage. In giving the name of old or elder to the earlier generation of the two, the misrepresentation is not less gross, nor the folly of it less contestable, than if the name of old man or old woman were given to an infant in its cradle.

What then is the wisdom of the times called old? Is it the wisdom of gray hairs? No. It is the wisdom of the cradle.[1] The learned and honorable gentlemen of Tibet do homage to superior wisdom – superiority raised to the degree of divinity – in the person of an infant lying and squalling in his cradle. The learned and honorable gentlemen of Westminster set down as impostors the Lamas of Tibet, and laugh at the folly of the deluded people on whom such imposture passes for sincerity and wisdom. But the worship paid in Tibet to the infant body of the present day is, if not the exact counterpart, the type at least of the homage paid at Westminster to the infant minds of those who have lived in earlier ages.

Another cause of delusion which promotes the employment of this fallacy is the reigning prejudice in favor of the dead. This prejudice contributed, more than anything else, to the practice of idolatry: the dead were speedily elevated to the rank of divinities, the superstitious invoked them, and ascribed a miraculous efficacy to their relics.

This prejudice, when examined, will be seen to be no less indefensible than pernicious, and no less pernicious than indefensible. By propagating this mischievous notion, and acting accordingly, the man of selfishness and malice obtains the praise that is due to humanity and social virtue. With this jargon in his mouth, he is permitted to sacrifice the real interests of the living to the imaginary interests of the dead. Thus imposture, in this shape, finds in the folly or improbity

[1] No one will deny that preceding ages have produced men eminently distinguished by benevolence and genius. It is to them that we owe all the advances which have hitherto been made in the career of human improvement. But as their talents could only be developed in proportion to the state of knowledge at the period in which they lived, and could only have been called into action with a view to the then-existing circumstances, it is absurd to rely on their authority, at a period and under a state of things altogether different.

of mankind a never-failing fund of encouragement and reward.

De mortuis nihil nisi bonum — Speak only good of the dead — with all its absurdity, the adage is but too frequently received as a leading principle of morals. But of two attacks, which is the more barbarous, on a man who can feel it, or on one who cannot? On the man who can feel it, says the principle of utility. On the man who cannot, says the principle of caprice and prejudice — the principle of sentimentalism — the principle in which imagination is the sole mover — the principle in and by which feelings are disregarded as not worth notice.

The same man who bepraises you when you are dead, would have plagued you without mercy while you were living. Thus it was between Pitt and Fox. While both were living, the friends of each reckoned as so many adversaries the friends of the other. On the death of him who died first, his adversaries were converted into friends. At what price this friendship was paid for by the people is no secret. For the payment of Pitt's creditors was voted 40,000 pounds of the public money; for Fox's widow, the sum of 1,500 pounds a year.

The cause of this so extensively prevalent and pernicious propensity lies not very deep. A dead man has no rivals. To nobody is he an object of envy. No matter in whose way he may have stood while living, when dead he no longer stands in anyone's way. If he was a man of genius, those who denied him any merit during his life, even his very enemies, changing their tone all at once, assume an air of justice and kindness. This costs them nothing, and enables them, under the pretense of respect for the dead, to continue to gratify their malignity toward the living.

Another class of persons habitually exalts the past for the express purpose of depressing and discouraging the present generation. It is characteristic of these persons to idolize, under the name of wisdom of our ancestors, the wisdom of untaught, inexperienced generations, and to undervalue and cover with every expression of contempt that the language of pride can furnish, the supposed ignorance and folly of the great body of the people.

As long as they keep to vague generalities, as long as the two objects of comparison are each of them taken in the lump: wise ancestors in one lump, ignorant and foolish mob of modern times in the other, the weakness of the fallacy may escape detection. Let them but assign for the period of superior wisdom any determinate period whatever, not only will the groundlessness of the notion be apparent (class being compared with class in that period and the present one), but, unless the earlier period be comparatively speaking a very modern one, so wide will be the disparity, and to such an amount in favor of modern times, that, in comparison with the lowest class of the people in modern times (always supposing them proficient in the art of reading, and their proficiency employed in reading newspapers), the very highest and best informed class of these wise ancestors will turn out to be grossly ignorant.

Take for example any year in the reign of Henry the Eighth, from 1509 to 1547. At that time the House of Lords would probably have been in possession of by far the larger proportion of what little instruction the age afforded. In the House of Lords, among the laity, it might even then be a question whether without exception their lordships were all of them able so much as to read. But even supposing them all in the fullest possession of that useful art, political science being the science in question, what instruction on the subject could they meet with at that period?

On no single branch of legislation was any book extant from which, with regard to the circumstances of the times, any useful instruction could have been derived: distributive law, penal law, international law, political economy, so far from existing as sciences, had scarcely obtained a name. In all those departments, as concerned plans for the future, a mere blank. The whole literature of the age consisted of a meagre chronicle or two, containing short memoranda of the usual occurrences of war and peace, battles, sieges, executions, revels, deaths, births, processions, ceremonies, and other external events; but with scarce a speech or an incident that could enter into the composition of any such work as a history of the human mind, and with scarce an attempt at investigation into causes, characters, or the state of the people at large. Even when at last, little by little, a scrap or two of political instruction came to be obtainable, the proportion of error and mischievous doctrine mixed up with it was so great, that whether a blank unfilled might not have been less prejudicial than a blank filled, may reasonably be a matter of doubt.

If we come down to the reign of James the First, we shall find that Solomon of his time, eminently eloquent as well as learned, not only among crowned but among uncrowned heads, marking out for prohibition and punishment the practices of devils and witches, and, without the slightest objection on the part of the great characters of that day in their high situations, consigning men to death and torment for the misfortune of not being so well acquainted as he was with the composition of the Godhead.

Passing on to the days of Charles the Second, even after Bacon had laid the foundations of a sound philosophy, we find Lord Chief Justice Hale (to the present hour chief god of the man-of-law's idolatry) [2] unable to tell, so he says himself, what theft was; but knowing at the same time too well

[2] Sir Matthew Hale (1609–1676) held the office of Lord Chief Justice from 1671 to 1676. Two women were tried before him in 1664 for witchcraft, condemned and executed, although such cases were already becoming rare.— Ed.

what witchcraft was, and hanging men with the most perfect complacency for both crimes, amid the applause of all who were wise and learned in that blessed age.

Under the name of exorcism the Catholic liturgy contains a form of procedure for driving out devils; and even with the help of this instrument, the operation cannot be performed with the desired success but by an operator qualified by holy orders for the working of this as well as so many other wonders. But in our days and in our country the same object is attained, and beyond comparison more effectually, by so cheap an instrument as a common newspaper: before this talisman, not only devils but ghosts, vampires, witches and all their kindred tribes are driven out of the land, never to return again, for the touch of holy water is not as intolerable to them as the bare smell of printer's ink.

If it is absurd to rely on the wisdom of our ancestors, it is not less so to vaunt their probity. They were as much inferior to us on that point as in all others. The further we look back, the more abuses we shall discover in every department of government. Nothing but the enormity of those abuses has produced that degree of comparative amendment on which at present we value ourselves so highly. Until the human race was rescued from that absolute slavery under which nine-tenths of every nation groaned, not a single step could be taken in the career of improvement; and take what period we will in the lapse of preceding ages, there is not one which presents such a state of things as any rational man would wish to see entirely re-established.

Undoubtedly the history of past ages is not wanting in some splendid instances of probity and self-devotion. But in the admiration which these excite, we commonly overrate their amount, and become the dupes of an illusion created by the very nature of an extensive retrospect. Such a retrospect is often made by a single glance of the mind; in this glance the splendid actions of several ages (as if for the very purpose of conveying a false estimate of their number and contiguity) present themselves as it were in a lump, leaving the intervals between them altogether unnoticed. Thus groves of trees, which at a distance present the appearance of thick and impenetrable masses, turn out on nearer approach to consist of trunks widely separated from each other.

Would you then have us speak and act as if we had never had any ancestors? Would you, because recorded experience, and, along with it, wisdom, increases from year to year, annually change the whole body of our laws? By no means; such a mode of reasoning and acting would be more absurd even than that which has just been exposed. Provisional adherence to existing establishments is grounded on considerations much more rational than a reliance upon the wisdom of our ancestors. Though the *opinions* of our ancestors are as such of little value, their *practice* is not the less worth attending to – that is, in so far as their practice forms a part of our own experience. It is not so much, however, from what they did, as from what they underwent (good included as well as evil) that our instruction comes. Independently of consequences, what they did is no more than evidence of what they thought; nor yet, in legislation, is it evidence of what they thought best for the whole community. It is only evidence of what the rulers thought would be best for themselves in periods when every species of abuse prevailed unmitigated, without the existence of either public press or public opinion.

From the facts of their times, much information may be derived; from the opinions, little or none. As to the latter, it is rather from those which were foolish than from those which were well-grounded, that any instruction can be gleaned. From foolish opinions comes foolish conduct; from the most foolish conduct, the severest disaster; and from the severest disaster, the most useful warning. It is from the folly, not from the wisdom of our ancestors that we have so much to learn; and yet it is to their supposed wisdom, and not to their folly, that the fallacy under consideration sends us for instruction.

It seems, then, that our ancestors, considering the disadvantages under which they labored, could not have been capable of exercising as sound a judgment of their interests as we of ours. Since a knowledge of the facts on which a judgment is to be pronounced is an indispensable preliminary to arriving at a just conclusion, and since the relevant facts of the later period must all of them individually, and most of them specifically, have been unknown to the men of the earlier period, it is clear that any judgment derived from the authority of our ancestors, and applied to existing affairs, must be a judgment pronounced without evidence. It is that sort of judgment which the fallacy in question calls on us to abide by, to the exclusion of a judgment formed on the completest evidence that the nature of each case may admit.

Causes of the propensity to be influenced by this fallacy

Wisdom of our ancestors being the most impressive of all the arguments that can be employed in defense of established abuses and imperfections, persons interested in this or that particular abuse are most forward in employing it. But their exertions would be of little avail, were it not for the propensity which they find on the part of their antagonists to attribute to this argument nearly the same weight as those who rely upon it.

This propensity may be traced to two intimately connected causes: (1) both parties having been trained up alike in the school of the English lawyers, headed by Blackstone;

and (2) their consequent inability, for want of practice, to draw from the principle of utility the justificative reason of everything that is susceptible of justification.

In the hands of a defender of abuse, authority answers a double purpose – by affording an argument in favor of any particular abuse which may happen to call for protection, and by causing men to regard with a mingled emotion of hatred and terror the principle of general utility, in which alone the true standard and measure of right and wrong is to be found.

In no other department of the field of knowledge and wisdom (unless that which pertains to religion be an exception) do the leading men of the present time recommend to us this recipe for thinking and acting wisely. By no gentleman, honorable or right honorable, are we sent in these days to the wisdom of our ancestors for the best mode of marshalling armies, navigating ships, attacking or defending towns; for the best modes of cultivating and improving land, and preparing and preserving its products for the purposes of food, clothing, artificial light and heat; for the promptest and most commodious means of conveyance of ourselves and our goods from one portion of the earth's surface to another; for the best modes of curing, alleviating, or preventing disorders of our own bodies and those of the animals which we contrive to apply to our use.

Why this difference? Only because in any other part of the field of knowledge, legislation excepted (and religion, insofar as it has been the subject of legislation), leading men are not affected with that sinister interest which is so unhappily combined with power in the persons of those leaders who conduct governments as they are generally at present established.

Sir Humphry Davy has never had anything to gain, either

from the unnecessary length, the miscarriage, or the unnecessary part of the expenses attendant upon his chemical experiments. He therefore sends us either to his own experiments or to those of the most enlightened and fortunate of his contemporaries, and not to the notions of Stahl, Van Helmont, or Paracelsus.[3]

[3] Sir Humphry Davy (1778–1829) performed many classical experiments in electro-chemistry, and was the inventor of the miner's safety-lamp. George Ernst Stahl (1660–1734) is chiefly remembered for his phlogiston theory of heat. Jean Baptiste Van Helmont (1577–1644) was a disciple of Paracelsus, and "deserves to be regarded as the founder of pneumatic chemistry." Paracelsus (c. 1490–1541) was the name adopted by Theophrastus Bombast von Hohenheim, who combined a career as healer with the advocacy of the doctrine of signatures, or the supposed dependence of every part of man upon a corresponding part of Nature.—Ed.

CHAPTER III

Fallacies of Irrevocable Laws and of Vows

Ad superstitionem.

THE TWO FALLACIES BROUGHT to view in this chapter are intimately connected, and should be considered together. The object in view is the same in both; the difference lies only in the instrument employed. Both of them are in effect the fallacy of the wisdom of our ancestors, pushed to the highest degree of extravagance and absurdity. The object is to tie up the hands of future legislators by obligations supposed to be indissoluble.

In the fallacy derived from the alleged irrevocable nature of certain laws, the instrument employed is a contract—a contract entered into by the ruling powers of the state in question with the ruling powers of some other party, who may be either the sovereign of some other state, or the whole or some part of the people of the state in question. In the fallacy derived from vows, a supernatural power is called in and employed in the character of guarantee.

Sec. 1. Fallacy of Irrevocable Laws: Exposition

A law, no matter to what effect, is proposed to a legislative assembly, and, no matter in what way, it is by the whole or a majority of the assembly regarded as being of a beneficial tendency. This fallacy consists in calling upon the assembly to reject it notwithstanding, upon the single ground that a regulation was made by the predecessors of the present legislators precluding forever, or to the end of a period not yet expired, all succeeding legislators from enacting a law to any such effect as that now proposed.

Exposure

To consider the matter in the first place on the ground of general utility. At each point of time the existing sovereign possesses such means as the nature of the case affords, for making himself acquainted with the exigencies of his own time. With relation to the future, the sovereign has no such means of information. It is only by a sort of vague anticipation, a sort of rough and almost random guess drawn by analogy, that the sovereign of this year can pretend to say what will be the exigencies of the country ten years from now.

Here then, to the extent of the pretended immutable law, is the government transferred from those who possess the best possible means of information, to those who, by their very position, are necessarily incapacitated from knowing anything at all about the matter. Instead of being guided by their own judgment, the men of the 19th century shut their own eyes, and give themselves up to be led blindfold by the men of the 18th century. The men who have the means of knowing the whole body of facts on which the correctness of the judgment to be formed depends, must give up their own judgment to that of a set of men entirely destitute of the requisite knowledge of such facts. Men who have a century more of experience to ground their judgments on, surrender their intellect to men who have had a century less of experience, and who, unless that deficiency constitutes a claim, have no claim to preference.

Even if the prior generation were, in respect of intellectual qualification, ever so much superior to the present generation, if it understood so much better than the later generation itself the interest of that later generation – could it have been in an equal degree anxious to promote that interest, and consequently equally attentive to those facts with which it should have been (but could not have been) acquainted? In a word, will its love for that later generation be quite so great as that same generation's love for itself? The answer, after even a moment's deliberate reflection, can hardly be in the affirmative.

Yet it is their prodigious anxiety for the welfare of their posterity that accounts for the propensity of these sages to tie up the hands of this same posterity for evermore, to act as guardians of its perpetual and incurable weakness, and to take its conduct forever out of its own hands.

If it be right that the conduct of the 19th century should be determined not by its own judgment but by that of the 18th, it will be equally right that the conduct of the 20th century should be determined not by its own judgment but by that of the 19th. The same principle still pursued, what at length would be the consequence? In the process of time the practice of legislation would be at an end: the conduct and fate of all men would be determined by those who neither knew nor cared anything about the matter. The aggregate body of the living would then remain forever in subjection to an inexorable tyranny exercised, as it were, by the aggregate body of the dead.

Suppose that this irrevocable law, whether good or bad at the moment of its enactment, is found at some succeeding time to be productive of mischief — uncompensated mischief — to any amount. Now of this mischief, what possibility has the country of being rid? A despotism, though it were that of a Caligula or a Nero, would be less intolerable than any such immutable law. By benevolence (for even a tyrant has his moments of benovolence), by prudence, in a word, by caprice, the living tyrant might be induced to revoke his law, and release the country from its consequences. But the dead tyrant! Who shall make *him* feel? Who shall make *him* hear?

Let it not be forgotten that it is only to a bad purpose that this and every other instrument of deception will, in general, be employed. It is only when the law in question is mischievous and generally felt and understood to be such, that an argument of this stamp will be employed in the support of it. Suppose the law is a good one, then it will be supported not by absurdity and deception, but by reasons drawn from its own excellence.

But is it possible that the restraint of an irrevocable law should be imposed on so many millions of living beings by a few score, or a few hundreds of persons whose existence has ceased? Can a system of tyranny be established under which the living are all slaves, and a few among the dead, their tyrants? The production of any such effect in the way of constraint being physically impossible, if produced in any degree it must be by force of argument — by the force of fallacy, and not by that of legislative power.

The means employed to give effect to this device are two in number, the first of them exhibiting a contrivance not less flagitious than the position itself is absurd. In speaking of a law which is considered as repugnant to any law of the pretended immutable class, the method has been to call it void. But to what purpose? Only to excite the people to rebellion in the event of the legislator's passing any such void law. In speaking of a law as void, either this is meant or nothing.

Are the people to consider the law void? They are then to consider it as an act of injustice and tyranny under the name of law, as an act of power exercised by men who have no right to exercise it. They are to deal with it as they would with the command of a robber; they are to deal with those who, having passed it, take upon themselves to enforce the execution of it, as they would deal, whenever they found themselves strong enough, with the robber himself.[1]

[1] Lord Coke was for holding void every act contrary to Magna Carta. If his doctrine were tenable, every act imposing law-taxes would be void. Ed. note: Sir Edward Coke (1552–1634) was Chief Justice

The other contrivance for maintaining the immutability of a given law, is derived from the notion of a contract or engagement. The faithful observance of contracts being one of the most important of the ties that bind society together, an argument drawn from this source cannot fail to have the appearance of plausibility. But be the interested parties who they may, a contract is not itself an end; it is but a means toward some end; and in cases where the public is one of the parties concerned, it is only such a means insofar as the end consists of the happiness of the whole community taken in the aggregate. Then, and only then, is such a contract worthy to be observed.

Let us examine the various kinds of contract to which statesmen have endeavored to impart this character of perpetuity: (1) Treaties between state and foreign state, by which each respectively engages its government and people; (2) Grants of privileges from the sovereign to the whole community in the character of subjects; (3) Grants of privileges from the sovereign to a particular class of subjects; (4) New arrangements of power between different portions or branches of the sovereignty, or new declarations of the rights of the community; and (5) Incorporative unions between two sovereignties having or not having a common head.

As long as the happiness of the whole community, taken in the aggregate, is promoted in a greater degree by the exact observance of the contract than it would be by any alteration of it, then the contract should be exactly observed. On the contrary, if by any given change, the aggregate of happiness would be in a greater degree promoted than by the exact observance, such change should be made. True it is, that considering the alarm and danger which is the natural result of every breach of contract to which the sovereign is

of the King's Bench from 1613 to 1616, and was generally regarded as the leading legal light of his day.

a party, the aggregate of public happiness will ordinarily be diminished rather than promoted by a change in such contract, unless any disadvantage to any party that is brought about by the change is made up by adequate compensation.

To apply the foregoing principles to the cases above enumerated:

(1) Concerning contracts or treaties between state and foreign state, the dogma of immutability has seldom been productive of any considerable practical inconvenience. Complaints have arisen more often from the tendency to change such treaties than from too rigid an adherence to their terms. Some commercial treaties between state and state, however, which have been entered into in times of political ignorance or error, and which have proved pernicious to the general interests of commerce, are frequently upheld under a pretense of regard for the supposed inviolability of such contracts, when the real reasons are the same ignorance, error, antipathy or sinister interest which brought them into existence in the first place. It can seldom or never happen that a forced direction thus given to the employment of capital can ultimately prove advantageous to either of the contracting parties; and when the pernicious effect of the operation of the treaty on the interests of both parties has been clearly pointed out, there can be no longer any pretense for continuing it. Notice of any proposed departure from the treaty ought to be given to all the parties concerned; sufficient time should be afforded to individuals engaged in traffic under the faith of the treaty to withdraw their capital; and they should be compensated for unavoidable losses.

(2) When grants of privileges are made by the sovereign to the whole community, this principle should prevail: if, by the supposed change in such grants, privileges of equal value are given in place of those which are abrogated by it, then adequate compensation has been made. If greater privileges

are substituted by the terms of the change, there is all the more reason for supporting it.

(3) In regard to grants of privileges by the sovereign to a particular class of subjects, no such special privilege ought to have been granted in the first place if the aggregate happiness of the community was likely to be diminished thereby. Compensation should be made if such a privilege is withdrawn, since the happiness of the portion of the community affected by the change is a legitimate part of the aggregate happiness of the whole community.

(4) The same general principle holds for new arrangements or distributions of powers as between different branches of the sovereignty: if a change will not be productive of a real addition to the aggregate stock of happiness of the community, it ought not to be made. Supposing the reverse to be true, then, notwithstanding the existence of the prior contract, it is right and fitting that the change should be made. Compensation in such instances is merely a matter to be arranged among the members of the sovereignty who may manage to satisfy one another without charge or disadvantage to the people, for whom they are trustees.

The frame or constitution of the several American United States, so far from being declared immutable or imprescriptible, contains an express provision [2] that a convention shall be held at intervals for the avowed object of revising and improving the constitution as the exigencies of succeeding times may require. In Europe, the effect of declaring this or that article in a new distribution of powers or in the original frame of a constitution as immutable, has been to weaken the sanction of all laws. The article in question often turns out to be mischievous or impracticable. Instead

[2] Article V provides only that such conventions shall be called by Congress "on the application of the Legislatures of two-thirds of the several States." – Ed.

of being repealed, it is openly or covertly violated; and the violation affords a precedent or pretext for the non-observance of other arrangements which are clearly calculated to promote the aggregate happiness of the community.

(5) Of all of the cases listed, this is the only one which is attended with difficulty: incorporative unions between two sovereignties having or not having a common head. Distressing indeed would be the difficulty, were it not for one circumstance which happily is interwoven in the very nature of such a case. At the time of the intended union, the two states are related to one another, in a greater or less degree, as foreign and independent states. Of the two uniting states, one will generally be more, the other less powerful. If the inequality be considerable, the more powerful state naturally will not consent to the union unless it can retain in the government of the new-framed compound state a share that is greater by a difference bearing some proportion to the difference in prosperity existing between the two states.

On the part of the less powerful state, there will be an equally natural tendency to take precautions against possible oppression by the stronger. Wherever a multitude of human beings are brought together, there is but too much room for jealousy, suspicion, and mutual ill-will. Each group fears that the other, if it should obtain possession of the powers to be exercised by the common government, may apply them unjustly. They are afraid that the new compound government, under the influence of the group that is predominant in it, may in some manner render the burdens proportionably more severe upon one part of the new compounded state than upon the other, or force upon it new customs, new religious ceremonies, or new laws.

It appears to result in a dilemma: let the hands of the new government remain altogether loose, then one of the two compound nations may be injured and oppressed by the other. But, tie up the hands of the joint government in such a degree as is requisite to give to each nation security against injustice at the hands of the other, and sooner or later comes the time when the inconveniences resulting from the restrictions will become intolerable to one or the other or both.

But sooner or later the very duration of the union produces the natural remedy. For sooner or later the two nations will by habit have become melted into one, and their mutual apprehensions will have been dissipated by conjunct experience.

Yet all this while, in one or both of the conjoined states, the individuals will be all too numerous and powerful who, because of sinister interest and interest-begotten prejudice, will give every possible countenance and intensity to these mutual fears and jealousies. If in either of the united communities at the time of union there was a set of men more or less numerous and powerful to whom abuse and imperfection of any sort was a source of profit, they will of course lay hold of any restrictions expressed in the contract which will give protection and continuance to a state of things so agreeable and beneficial to themselves.

At the time of the union between England and Scotland (1603), the Tory party, of whom a large proportion were Jacobites, and all or most of them high-church men, had acquired an ascendancy in the House of Commons. Here, then, a favorable occasion presented itself to these partisans of episcopacy for giving perpetuity to the triumph they had obtained over the English presbyterians, by the Act of Uniformity proclaimed in the time of Charles the Second.

In treaties between unconnected nations, where an advantage in substance is given to one nation, it has been the custom, for the purpose of saving the honor of the other, to make the articles bear the appearance of reciprocity upon the face of them. For example, when making a treaty to facilitate the sale of French wines in England, the provision might be made that the wine grown in either country might be imported into the other duty free.

By the combined astuteness of priestcraft and lawyer-craft, advantage was taken of this custom to try to rivet forever those chains of ecclesiastical tyranny which, in the haste that attended the Restoration, had been fastened upon the people of England. To secure the 45 Scottish members from being outnumbered by the 513 English ones, provision had been made in favor of the Church of Scotland; therefore, on the principle of reciprocity, to secure the 513 English members from being outnumbered by the 45 Scottish ones, like provision was made in favor of the Church of England.

Blackstone avails himself of this transaction for giving perpetuity to whatever imperfections may be found in the ecclesiastical branch of the law and in the official establishment of England. On a general account he gives of the articles and act of union, he grounds three observations:

1. That the two kingdoms of England and Scotland are now so inseparably united that nothing can ever disunite them again, except the mutual consent of both, or the successful resistance of either upon apprehending an infringement of those points which, when they were separate and independent nations, it was mutually stipulated should be "fundamental and essential conditions of the union."

2. That whatever else may be deemed "fundamental and essential conditions," the preservation of the two churches of England and Scotland in the same state that they were in at the time of the union, and the maintenance of the acts of uniformity which establish our common prayer book, are expressly declared to be such.

3. That therefore any alteration in the constitution of either of those churches, or in the liturgy of the Church of England, unless with the consent of the respective churches collectively or representatively given, would be an infringe-

ment of the "fundamental and essential conditions," and would greatly endanger the union.

Thus we see that an improvement has been made upon the original device by the ingenuity of the orthodox and learned commentator. If as, for example by the alteration of any of the 39 articles, or by the abolition of any of the English ecclesiastical sinecures, or by any efficient measure for insuring the performance of duty in return for salary, the ecclesiastical branch of the English official establishment were brought so much the nearer to what it is in Scotland, the Scots, fired by the injury done to them, would cry out "A breach of faith!" and call for a dissolution of the union.

To obviate this danger, "a great one," he calls it, his ingenuity in concert with his piety has however furnished us with an expedient. "The consent of the church collectively or representatively given" is to be taken; by which is meant, if anything, that by the revival of the convocation, or some other means, the clergy of England are to be erected into a fourth estate. It should be obvious that in any attempt to force the discipline of the Church of Scotland upon the Church of England, the 45 Scottish members in the House of Commons, supposing them all unanimous, would have to outnumber, or somehow or other subdue, the 513 English ones; and that in the House of Lords the 16 Scottish members, supposing all the lay lords to be indifferent to the fate of the Church of England, would in like manner have to outnumber the 26 English bishops and archbishops. But the Tories, who were then in vigor, feared that they might not always be so, and seized their opportunity to fetter posterity by an act which should be deemed irrevocable.

According to the 20th article of the act of union, entitled "heritable offices, including heritable jurisdictions," those public trusts are on the footing of "rights of property" reserved to the owners, yet without any expression of that fanatic spirit which, in the field of religion, had in the same statute endeavored to invest the conceits of mortal man with the attribute of immortality. Yet nine-and-thirty years later came the act for abolishing these same heritable jurisdictions. Here was an act made in the very teeth of the act of union.

Mark now the sort of discernment, or of sincerity, that is to be learned from Blackstone. In a point-blank violation of the articles of union, in the abolition of those heritable jurisdictions which it was the declared object of the 20th article to preserve, Blackstone saw nothing " to endanger the union." But suppose any such opinion to prevail, as that it is not exactly true that by the mere act of being born every human being merits damnation (if by damnation be meant everlasting torment or punishment in any other shape), and a corresponding change were to be made in the set of propositions called the 39 articles, then the union would be " greatly endangered."

Between twenty and thirty years afterwards, at the suggestion of an honest member of the Court of Session, there came upon the carpet for the first time the idea of applying remedies to some of the most flagrant imperfections in the administration of Scottish justice. Thereupon came out a pamphlet by James Boswell, declaiming in schoolboy style upon the injury that would be done to the people of Scotland by rendering justice a little less inaccessible to them, and the breach that would be made in the faith plighted by that treaty which, to judge by what he says of it, he had never looked at. Again in 1806, when another attempt was made to apply a remedy to the abuses and imperfections of the system of judicature in Scotland, everything that could be done in that direction was immediately reprobated by the Scottish lawyers as an infringement of that most sacred of all sacred bonds, the union.

Upon the whole, the following is the conclusion that seems to be dictated by the foregoing considerations: every arrangement by which the hands of the sovereignty for the time being are attempted to be tied up and precluded from making a fresh arrangement is absurd and mischievous; and if the utility of a fresh arrangement is sufficiently established, the existence of a prohibitive clause ought not to be considered as opposing any bar to its establishment.

It is true that all laws and all political institutions are essentially dispositions for the future. The professed object of all of them is to afford a steady and permanent security to the interests of mankind. In this sense, all of them may be said to be framed with a view to perpetuity. But perpetual is not synonymous with irrevocable; and the principle on which all laws ought to be, and the greater part of them have been established is that of *defeasible perpetuity*: a perpetuity defeasible only by a change in the circumstances and reasons upon which the law is founded.

To comprise all in a single word, reason, and that alone, is the proper anchor for a law, and for everything which goes by that name. At the time of passing his law, let the legislator deliver in the character of reasons the considerations by which he was led to the passage of it. This done, as long as in the eyes of succeeding legislators the state of facts on which the reasons are grounded appear to continue without material change, and the reasons to appear satisfactory, so long the law should continue. But no sooner do the reasons cease to appear satisfactory, or the state of the facts to have undergone such change as to call for a change in the law, then an alteration in it, or abrogation of it, should take place accordingly.

A declaration or assertion that this or that law is immutable, so far from being a proper instrument to insure its permanence, is rather a presumption that it has some mischievous tendency. The better the law, the less is any such extraneous argument likely to be recurred to for the support of it. The worse the law, and hence the more completely destitute it is of all intrinsic support, the more likely it is that support should be sought for it from this extraneous source.

To draw up laws without reasons, and laws for which good reasons are not in the nature of the case to be found, requires no more than the union of will and power. But to the framing of laws good in themselves and accompanied by good and sufficient reasons, there would be required in the legislator a probity not to be diverted by sinister interests, and an intelligence adequate to an enlarged comprehension and close application of the principle of general utility – that of the greatest happiness of the greatest number.

The man who should produce such a body of good laws with an accompaniment of good reasons, could feel an honest pride at the prospect of thus holding in bondage a succession of willing generations. His triumph would be to leave them the power, but to deprive them of the will to escape. But to the champions of abuse, by whom among other devices the conceit of immutable laws is played off against reform in whatever shape it presents itself, every use of reason is as odious as the light of the sun to moles and burglars.

Sec. 2. Fallacy of Vows, or Promissory Oaths

The object of this fallacy is the same as the preceding one; but to the absurdity involved in the notion of tying up the hands of generations yet to come is added, in this case, that which consists in seeking to use supernatural power. The arm pressed into service is that of the invisible and supreme ruler of the universe.

The oath being taken, the formularies involved in it being pronounced, is or is not the Almighty bound to do what is expected of Him? Of the two contradictory propositions, which one do you believe? If He is *not* bound, then the security, the sanction, the obligation amounts to nothing.

If He *is* bound, then observe what follows: the Almighty is bound, and by whom? Of all the worms that crawl about the earth in the shape of men there is not one who may not thus impose conditions on the supreme ruler of the universe.

And to what is He bound? To any number of contradictory and incompatible observances, which legislators, tyrants, madmen, may, in the shape of an oath, be pleased to assign Him. Eventual, it must be admitted, and no more, is the power thus exercised over, the task thus imposed upon the Almighty. For so long as the vow is kept, there is nothing for Him to do. True; but no sooner is the vow broken, than His task commences: a task which consists in inflicting upon him by whom the vow is broken a punishment which, when it is inflicted, is of no use by way of example, since nobody ever sees it.

This punishment, it may be said, will be, when inflicted, exactly what, in the judgment of the almighty and infallible judge, will be best adapted to the nature of the offense. Yes, but what offense? Not the act which the oath was intended to prevent, for that act may be indifferent, or even meritorious, and if criminal ought to be punished independently of the oath. The only offense peculiar to this case is the profanation of a ceremony, and the profanation is the same, whether the act by which it arises be pernicious or beneficial.

It is in vain to urge, in this or that particular instance, as proof of the reasonableness of the oath, the reasonableness of the prohibition or command which it is thus employed to perpetuate. The objection is to the principle itself: to any idea of employing an instrument so unfit to be employed in human affairs. No sort of security is given, or can be given, that it will be applied to the most beneficial purpose rather than to the most pernicious.

On the contrary, it is more likely to be applied to a pernicious than to a beneficial purpose. Because the more manifestly and undeniably beneficial the observance of the prohibition in question would be in the eyes of future generations, the more likely it is to be observed independently of the oath. On the other hand, the more likely the prohibition is not to be observed otherwise, the greater is the demand for a security of this extraordinary complexion to enforce its observance.

We now come to an instance in which, by the operation of the fallacy here in question, the ceremony of an oath has been endeavored to be applied to the perpetuation of misrule. Among the statutes passed in the first parliament of William and Mary in 1688 is one entitled "An Act for the Establishing the Coronation Oath." The form in which this ceremony is performed is as follows: by the archbishop or bishop certain questions are put to the monarch; and it is of the answers given to these questions that the oath is composed. Of these questions, the third is as follows: "Will you, to the utmost of your power, maintain the laws of God, the true profession of the Gospel, and the Protestant reformed religion established by law? And will you preserve unto the bishops and clergy of this realm, and to the churches committed to their charge, all such rights and privileges as by law do or shall appertain unto them, or any of them?"

Answer: "All this I promise to do."

After this, in the year 1706, comes the Act of Union, in the concluding article of which it is said, "That after the demise of her majesty . . . the sovereign next succeeding her majesty in the royal government of the kingdom of Great Britain, and so forever hereafter, every king or queen succeeding and coming to the royal government of the kingdom of Great Britain, at his or her coronation," etc., "take and subscribe an oath to maintain and preserve inviolate the said settlement of the church, and the doctrine, worship, discipline and government thereof, as by law established, within the kingdoms of England and Ireland, the dominion of Wales, and town of Berwick-upon-Tweed, and the territories thereunto belonging."

Now a notion was once started, and on occasion may but too probably be broached again, that by the above clause in the coronation oath, the king stands precluded from joining in the putting of the majority of the Irish people upon an equal footing with the minority, as well as from affording to both together any relief against the abuses of the ecclesiastical establishment of that country.

In relation to such a notion, the following propositions have already, it is hoped, been put sufficiently beyond all doubt: (1) That it ought not to be in the power of the sovereignty to tie up its own hands, or the hands of its successors; (2) That, on the part of the sovereignty, no such power can have existence, either here or anywhere else; (3) That therefore all attempts to exercise such power are in their own nature, to use the technical language of lawyers, null and void; and (4) That no such anarchical wish or expectation was entertained by the original framers of the oath.

It is plainly in what is called his executive, and not in his legislative capacity that the obligation in question was meant to rest upon the monarch. So loose are the words of the act that, if they were deemed to apply to the monarch in his legislative capacity, he might find in them a pretense for refusing assent to almost anything he did not like. By the first clause of the oath he is made "solemnly to promise and swear to govern the people . . . according to the statutes in parliament agreed on, and the laws and customs of the same." But in governing according to any new law whatever, he could not govern by the old law abrogated by it. If Henry the Eighth at his coronation had sworn to "maintain" that Catholic religion which for so many previous centuries had been "established by law" and by fire and sword to keep out the Protestant religion, and had been considered bound by such an oath, he could never have taken one step towards the Reformation, and the religion of the state must have continued to be Catholic.

Would you put a force upon the conscience of your sovereign? By any construction of words, which in your judgment might be the proper one, would you preclude him from the free exercise of his own conscience? Most assuredly not.

All I plead for is, that on so easy a condition as that of pronouncing the word conscience, it may not be in his power either to make himself absolute, or in any shape to give continuance to misrule.

Chains to the man in power? Yes; but such as he wears upon the stage: to the spectators as imposing, to himself as light as possible. Modelled by the wearer to suit his own purposes, they serve to rattle but not to restrain.

Suppose a king of Great Britain and Ireland to have expressed his fixed determination, in the event of any proposed law being tendered to him for his assent, to refuse such assent, not on the persuasion that the law would not be "for the utility of the subjects," but because his coronation oath precludes such action. Then the course proper to be taken by Parliament, the course pointed out by principle and precedent, would be a vote of abdication, a vote declaring that the king had abdicated his royal authority, and that, as in the case of death or incurable mental derangement, now is the time for the person next in succession to take his place.

Appendix: Note on the Longevity of Laws

The variety of the notions entertained at different periods and at different stages respecting the duration of laws presents a curious and not uninstructive picture of human weakness.

1. At one time we see, under the name of king, a single

person whose will makes law, or at any rate a person without whose will no law is made. When this law-giver dies, his laws die with him. Such was the state of things in Saxon times, and continued to be the state of things for several reigns after the Norman conquest, to Richard the First (1189-1199) inclusive.

2. Next comes a period in which the duration of the law, during the life-time of the monarch to whom it owed its birth, was unsettled and left to chance. (John through Edward II, 1327).

3. In the third place comes a period in which the notions respecting the duration of the law concur with the dictates of reason and utility, not so much from reflection as because no occasion of a nature to suggest and urge any attempt so absurd as that of tyrannizing over futurity had as yet happened to present itself.

4. Lastly, upon the spur of an occasion of the sort in question, comes the attempt to give eternity to human laws.

Provisional and eventual perpetuity is an attribute which, in that stage of society at which laws have ceased to expire with the individual legislator, is understood to be inherent in all laws in which no expression is found to the contrary. But, if a particular length of time be marked out, during which it is declared that that law shall not be liable to suffer abrogation or alteration, the determination to tie up the hands of succeeding legislators is expressed in unequivocal terms. Such, in respect of their constitutional code, was the pretension set up by the first assembly of legislators brought together by the French Revolution.

A position not less absurd in principle, but by the limitation in point of time not pregnant with anything like equal mischief, was before that time acted upon, and still continues to be acted upon, in English legislation. In various statutes, a clause may be found by which the statute is declared capable of being altered or repealed in the course of the same session. In this clause is contained, in the way of necessary implication, that a statute in which no such clause is inserted is not capable of being repealed or altered during the session, no, not by the very hands by which it was made.

CHAPTER IV

No-Precedent Argument

Ad verecundiam.

Exposition

" THE PROPOSITION IS of a novel and unprecedented complexion: the present is surely the first time that any such thing was ever heard of in this house."

Whatever may happen to be the subject introduced, the above is a specimen of the infinite variety of forms in which the opposing predicate may be clothed. There could be no objection to such a comment, if its object were only to fix attention upon a new or difficult subject, with the advice: " Deliberate well before you act, since you have no precedent to direct your course."

Exposure

But as a ground for the rejection of the proposed measure, this is obviously a fallacy. Whether or not the alleged novelty actually exists, is an inquiry which it can never be worth-while to make. That it is impossible that it should in any case afford the smallest ground for the rejection of the measure, that it is completely irrelevant to the question whether the measure should be adopted – these are propositions difficult to deny. If no specific good is indicated as likely to be produced by the proposed measure, this deficiency in itself is enough to warrant its rejection. If any such specific good *is* indicated, then that good must be minute indeed if an observation of this kind can lead to its rejection.

If the lack of a precedent presents a conclusive objection against the particular measure in question, so it would against any other measure that ever was proposed. This includes every measure that has ever been adopted, and so every institution which exists at the present time. If the argument proves that this ought not to be done, it proves that nothing else ought ever to have been done.

It may be urged that if the measure had been a fit one, it would have been brought upon the carpet before. But there are several obstacles besides the inexpediency of a measure which, for any length of time, may prevent its being brought forward. If, for example, a measure is beyond dispute promotive of the interest of the many, yet contains something adverse to the interests, prejudices, or humors of the ruling few, then the wonder is, not that it should not have been brought forward before, but that it should be brought forward even now. Or if it required a special degree of ingenuity in its formulation, that of itself would be enough to account for the tardiness of its appearance.

In legislation, the birth of ingenuity is obstructed and retarded by difficulties which are greater than those which prevail in other matters. Besides, the more general sinister interest affecting the body of lawyers is one to which any given measure is likely to be adverse in proportion to the ingenuity displayed in framing it. Measures which may be classified as indirect legislation, and in particular those which have the quality of executing themselves, possess the most efficiency when once established, but require greater ingenuity in their contrivance. Now in proportion as laws execute themselves, or are attended with voluntary obedience, in that proportion they are efficient; but it is only in proportion as they fail of being efficient that, to a man of law, they are beneficial and productive, for it is only as they stand in need of enforcement, that business makes its way into the hands of the lawyer.

CHAPTER V

Self-Assumed Authority

Ad ignorantiam; ad verecundiam.

THIS FALLACY PRESENTS itself in two shapes: (1) an avowal made with a sort of mock modesty and caution by a person in an exalted station, to the effect that he is incapable of forming a judgment on the question in debate, such incapacity being sometimes real and sometimes pretended; and (2) an open assertion by a person so situated with respect to the purity of his motives and the integrity of his life, that entire reliance may consequently be reposed on all he says and does.

Sec. 1. Unpreparedness to Assert

The first variety is commonly played off as follows: an evil or defect in our institutions is pointed out clearly and a remedy is proposed to which no objection can be made. Up rises a man high in office, and, instead of stating any specific objection, says: " I am not prepared to do so and so," " I am not prepared to say," and so on. The meaning he evidently intends to convey is: " If I, who am so dignified and supposed to be so capable of forming a judgment, openly avow myself incompetent to do so, what presumption, what folly must there be in the conclusion formed by anyone else! " In truth, this is nothing but an indirect way of browbeating. It is arrogance hiding under a thin veil of modesty.

If you are not prepared to pass any judgment, then you are not prepared to condemn, and you ought not, therefore, to oppose. If you are sincere, the utmost that you are warranted in doing, is to ask for a little time for further consideration. Supposing the unpreparedness real, the reasonable and practical inference is: say nothing, take no part whatever in the business.

A proposition for the reforming of this or that abuse in the administration of justice is the most common occasion for the employment of this fallacy. By virtue of his office, every judge, ever officer of the law, is supposed and pronounced to be profoundly versed in the science of the law. In the science of the law as it *is*, however, and not in that very different thing, the science of the law as it *ought to be*. Now the proposal in question has for its real object, the bringing of the law as it is somewhat closer to the law as it ought to be. But that is one of those things for which the great dignitary of the law is sure to be at all times unprepared: – unprepared to join in any such design, everything of the sort having been at all times contrary to his interests, unprepared to so much as form any judgment concerning the conduciveness of the proposal to its object, it being never to his interest to consider such measures seriously.

A mind that from the beginning has been applying its whole force to finding the most effectual means of making a profit from the imperfections in the legal system; a mind to which in consequence the profit to be gleaned from these sources of affliction has been all along an object of complacency, and affliction itself an object of indifference; a mind which has throughout the whole course of its career been receiving a corresponding bias and distortion; – such a mind cannot with reason be expected to exert itself with much alacrity or facility in a track so opposite and new. For the quiet of his conscience, if, at the outset of his career, it were the fortune of such a man to have a conscience, he will naturally have been feeding himself with the notion that, if there is anything amiss, in practice it cannot be otherwise. This being granted – that suffering to a certain amount cannot but take place, whatever profit can be extracted from it is thus fair game, and as such, belongs of right to the first discoverer among persons duly qualified.

The wonder would not be great if an officer of the military profession should exhibit some awkwardness, for a time at least, if forced to act as a surgeon's assistant. To inflict wounds requires one sort of skill, to dress and heal them requires another. Telephus is the only man on record who possessed an instrument by which wounds were with equal dispatch and efficiency both made and healed.[1] But the race of Telephus is extinct; and as for his spears, if ever any of them found their way into Pompeii or Herculaneum, they still remain among the ruins.

Unfortunately in cases of this sort, were the ability to form a judgment ever so complete, the likelihood of co-operation would not thereby be increased. For none are so completely deaf as those who will not hear; none are so completely unintelligent as those who will not understand. Call upon a chief justice to concur in a measure for giving possibility to the recovery of a debt, the recovery of which is in his own court rendered impossible by costs which partly go into his own pocket. (As well might you call upon the Pope to abjure the errors of the Church of Rome!) If not hard pressed, he will maintain a prudent and easy silence. If hard pressed, he will let fly a volley of fallacies: he will play off the argument based on the imputation of bad motives, and tell you of the profit expected by the party by whom the bill was framed. If that be not sufficient, he will transform himself into a witness giving evidence before a committee, and then, after multiplying himself into the number of members necessary to hear and report upon the evidence, he will make a report accordingly. And it will be to the effect that when in any town a set of tradesmen have obtained a judgment for the recovery of a debt of less than

[1] Bentham errs in thinking that the spear belonged to Telephus, King of Mysia, who according to legend was wounded by the Pelian Spear of Achilles through error. An oracle said, "The wounder shall heal"; whereupon some rust was scraped from the spear by Ulysses and made into a plaster which worked the cure. – Ed.

five pounds without incurring the accumulated expenses which are always the price of justice in his court, then they were probably guilty of perjury.

Sec. 2. The Self-trumpeter's Fallacy

By this name it is not intended to designate those occasional impulses of vanity which lead a man to display or overrate his pretensions to superior intelligence. Against the self-love of the man whose altar to himself is raised on this ground, rival altars, from every one of which he is sure of discouragement, raise themselves all around.

But there are certain men in office who, in the discharge of their functions, arrogate to themselves a degree of probity which is supposed to exclude all imputations and all inquiry. Their assertions are to be deemed equivalent to proof; their virtues are guarantees for the faithful discharge of their duties; and the most implicit confidence is to be reposed in them on all occasions. If you expose any abuse, propose any reform, they set up a cry of surprise, amounting almost to indignation, as if their integrity were questioned or their honor wounded. With all this they dexterously mix up intimations that the most exalted patriotism, honor, and perhaps religion, are the only sources of all their actions.

Such assertions must be classed among fallacies, because (1) they are irrelevant to the subject under discussion; (2) the degree to which the predominance of social or disinterested motives is commonly asserted or insinuated it, by the very nature of man, rendered impossible; and (3) the sort of testimony thus given affords no legitimate reason for regarding the assertion in question to be true. For such an assertion is no less completely in the power of the most profligate than in that of the most virtuous of mankind; nor is it less in the interest of the profligate man to make such assertions. Be they ever so completely false, he sees himself exposed to not the slightest danger of punishment at the hands of the law or of public opinion.

For ascribing to any one of these self-trumpeters the smallest possible particle of that virtue which they so loudly profess to possess, there is no more rational cause than for looking upon this or that actor as a good man because he acts well the part of Othello, or bad because he acts well that of Iago. On the contrary, the interest he has in seeing what may be done by such means, is more decided and exclusive than in the case of the man of real probity and social feeling. The virtuous man, being what he is, has the chance of being looked upon as such; whereas the self-trumpeter in question, having no such ground of reliance, sees his only chance in the conjoined effect of his own effrontery, and the imbecility of his hearers.

These assertions of authority, therefore, by men in office who would have us estimate their conduct by their character, and not their character by their conduct, must be classed among the political fallacies. For if there be any one maxim in politics more certain than another, it is that no possible degree of virtue in the governor can render it expedient for the governed to dispense with good laws and good institutions.[2]

[2] Madame de Staël says that in a conversation which she had in St. Petersburg with the Emperor of Russia, he expressed his desire to better the condition of the peasantry, who are still in a state of absolute slavery. Upon which the female sentimentalist exclaimed, "Sire, your character is a constitution for your country, and your conscience is its guarantee." His reply was, "If that were so, it would never be more than a happy accident." *Dix années d'exil,* 313.

CHAPTER VI

Laudatory Personalities

Ad amicitiam.

PERSONALITIES OF THIS CLASS are the opposites, and in some respects the counterparts of vituperative personalities, which will be treated at the commencement of the next book. The object of vituperative personalities is to effect the rejection of a measure on account of the alleged bad character of those who promote it: "The persons who propose or promote the measure are bad, therefore the measure is bad, and ought to be rejected." The object of laudatory personalities is to effect the rejection of a measure on account of the alleged good character of those who oppose it: "The measure is rendered unnecessary by the virtues of those in power; their opposition is a sufficient authority for its rejection."

The argument indeed is little else than an extension of the self-trumpeter's fallacy. In both of them, authority derived from the virtues or talents of the persons lauded is advanced as superseding the necessity of all investigation. "The measure proposed implies a distrust of the members of His Majesty's Government; but so great is their integrity, so complete their disinterestedness, so uniformly do they prefer the public advantage to their own, that such a measure is altogether unnecessary. Their disapproval is sufficient to warrant opposition. Precautions can only be needed where danger is apprehended; here, the high character of the individuals in question is an ample guarantee against any ground of alarm."

The panegyric goes on increasing in proportion to the dignity of the functionary thus exalted. Subordinates in office are the very models of assiduity, attention, and fidelity to their trust; ministers, the perfection of probity and intelligence; and as for the highest magistrate in the state, no adulation is equal to the description of his various merits.

There can be no difficulty in exposing the fallacy of the argument attempted to be deduced from these panegyrics. (1) They have the common character of being irrelevant to the question under discussion. The measure must be extraordinary if a right judgment cannot be made concerning its merits without first estimating the character of the members of the government. (2) If the goodness of the measure be sufficiently established by direct arguments, the reception given to it by those who oppose it will form a better criterion for judging their character, than their character, inferred from the places which they occupy, will be for judging the goodness or badness of the measure. (3) If this argument be good in any one case, it is equally good in every other; and the effect of it, if admitted, would be to give to the persons occupying for the time being the offices in question, an absolute and universal veto upon every measure not agreeable to their inclinations. (4) In every public trust, the legislator should, for the purpose of prevention, assume the trustee disposed to break his trust in every imaginable way in which the breach of it would be to his personal advantage. This is the principle on which public institutions ought to be formed; and when it is applied to all men universally, it is injurious to none. The practical inference is to oppose to such possible breaches of trust every bar that can be opposed consistently with the power that is requisite to the efficient discharge of the trust. Indeed, these arguments, drawn from the supposed virtues of men in power, are opposed to the first principles on which all laws proceed. (5) Such allegations of individual virtue are never supported by specific proof and are hardly ever susceptible of specific disproof. Such disproof, if offered, could not be admitted, for example, in either house of parliament. If attempted elsewhere, the punishment would fall, not on the unworthy trustee, but upon him by whom the unworthiness had been proved.

PART THE SECOND

FALLACIES OF DANGER

The subject of which is Danger in various shapes, and the object, to repress discussion altogether, by exciting alarm.

CHAPTER I

Vituperative Personalities

Ad odium.

TO THIS CLASS BELONGS a cluster of fallacies so intimately connected with each other, that they may first be enumerated and some observations made upon them as a group. The fallacies that belong to this cluster are: (1) Imputation of bad design, (2) Imputation of bad character, (3) Imputation of bad motive, (4) Imputation of inconsistency, (5) Imputation of suspicious connections, and (6) Imputation founded on an identity of name.

Of all the fallacies belonging to this class, the common characteristic is the endeavor to draw aside attention from the *measure* to the *man*, in such a way as to cause the latter's badness to be imputed to the measure he supports, or his goodness to his opposition. It is charged that, in bringing forward or supporting the measure in question, the person accused has a bad design; therefore the measure is bad. He is a person of bad character; therefore the measure is bad. He is actuated by a bad motive; therefore the measure is bad; he has fallen into inconsistencies; therefore the measure is bad. He is on a footing of intimacy with this or that person, who is a man of dangerous principles and designs, or has been seen more or less frequently in his company, or has professed or is suspected of entertaining some opinion which the other has professed, or has been suspected of entertaining; therefore the measure is bad. He bears a name that was borne at a former period by a set of men now no more, by whom bad principles were entertained, or bad things done; therefore the measure is bad.

In these arguments thus arranged, a sort of anti-climax may be observed: the fact intimated by each succeeding argument being suggested in the character of the evidence for the one preceding it, and the conclusion being accordingly weaker and weaker at each step. The second is a sort of circumstantial copy of the first, the third of the second, and so on. If the first argument is inconclusive, the rest fall at once to the ground.

Exposure

There is varied evidence of the futility of this class of fallacies: of the improbity of their utterers, and the weakness of their acceptors. In the first place comes that general character of irrelevancy which belongs to these along with other fallacies. Next comes their complete inconclusiveness. Whatsoever be their force as applied to the worst measure ever imagined, they would be found to apply with little less force to the best measure that can be imagined.

Among 658 or any such large number of persons taken at random, there will be people of all characters. If the measure is a good one, will it become bad because it is supported by a bad man? If it is bad, will it become good because it is supported by a good man? If the measure is really expedient, why not at once show that it is so? Your producing these irrelevant and inconclusive arguments in place of direct ones, though not sufficient in itself to prove that the measure you thus oppose is a good one, nevertheless *contributes* to proving that you yourself regard it as a good one.

Sec. 1. Imputation of Bad Design

The measure in question is not charged with being a bad one. The bad design imputed does not consist in the design of carrying this measure, but some other measure which is thus, by necessary implication, charged with being a bad one. Here, then, four things remain to be proved: (1) That the design of bringing forward the supposed bad measure is really entertained; (2) That this design will be carried into effect; (3) That the measure will actually prove to be a bad one; and (4) That, but for the presently proposed measure, the supposed bad one would not be carried into effect.

But on what ground rests the supposition that the supposed bad measure will, as such a consequence, be carried into effect? The persons by whom, if at all, it will be carried into effect will be either the legislators for the time being or of some future contingent time. As for the legislators of the present day, observe the character and frame of mind which this oratory imputes to them: " Give not your sanction to this measure; for though there may be no particular harm in it, yet, if you do sanction it, the same man by whom this measure is proposed, will propose to you others that will be bad; and such is your weakness that, however bad they may be, you will lack either the discernment necessary to enable you to see them in their true light, or the resolution to enable you to vote against measures, of the mischief of which you are fully convinced." The imbecility of the persons thus addressed in the character of legislators and judges, and their consequent unfitness for their situations, such, it is manifest, is the basis of this fallacy.

Sec. 2. Imputation of Bad Character

The inference meant to be drawn from an imputation of bad character is either to cause the person in question to be considered as entertaining a bad design, or about to bring forward future contingent and pernicious measures, or simply to destroy any persuasive force with which his opinion is likely to be attended. In this last instance, it is another modification of the Fallacy of Distrust, of which more will presently be said.

In proportion to the degree to which a man suffers these instruments of deception to operate upon his mind, he enables bad men to exercise over him a sort of power, the very thought of which ought to cover him with shame. Allow such an argument the effect of a conclusive one, and you put it into the power of any man to draw you at pleasure away from the support of any measure which in your own eyes is good, or to force you to support any and every measure which in your own eyes is bad. It is good? The bad man embraces it, and you reject it. Is it bad? The bad man vituperates it, and that suffices for driving you into its embrace. You split upon the rocks, because he has avoided them; you miss the safe harbor, because he has steered into it.

Give yourself up to any such blind antipathy, and you are no less in the power of your adversaries than by a correspondingly irrational sympathy and obsequiousness you might put yourself in the power of your friends.

Sec. 3. Imputation of Bad Motive

The proposer of the measure, it is asserted, is actuated by bad motives, from which it is inferred that he entertains some bad design. This again is no more than a modification of the Fallacy of Distrust; and one of the very weakest, because (1) motives are hidden in the human breast, and (2) if the measure is beneficial, it would be absurd to reject it on account of the motives of its author.

But what is peculiar to this particular fallacy, is the falsity of the supposition on which it is grounded, namely — the existence of a class or species of motives to which the epithet " bad " may be with propriety applied. What constitutes a motive is the eventual expectation either of some pleasure, or exemption from pain. Inasmuch as there is nothing good in itself but pleasure, or exemption from pain, it follows that no motive is bad in itself, though every kind of motive may, according to circumstances, occasion good or bad actions, and motives of the dissocial sort may aggravate the mischief of a pernicious act. But if the act itself to which the motive gives birth — if, for instance, in the proposed measure there is nothing pernicious — then it is not in the motive's being of the dissocial or self-regarding class that makes the act a bad one. Upon the influence and prevalence of motives of the self-regarding class depends the preservation, not only of the species, but of each individual belonging to it. When a man beholds the prospect of personal advantage in any shape whatever from the introduction of a measure, say a pecuniary advantage as being the most ordinary and, speaking critically, the most gross, it is certain that the contemplation of this advantage must have had some share in causing the conduct he pursues. It may even have been the only cause. The measure itself being by supposition not pernicious, is it the worse for this personal advantage? On the contrary, it is so much the better. For of what stuff is public advantage composed but of private and personal advantage?

Sec. 4. Imputation of Inconsistency

Admitting the fact of the inconsistency, the most that it can amount to in the character of an argument against the proposed measure is the affording of a presumption of bad design or bad character on the part of the proposer or supporter of the measure. Of the futility of that argument, a view has already been given; and this, again, is a modification of the Fallacy of Distrust.

That inconsistency, when pushed to an extreme degree, may afford all too conclusive evidence of a sort of relatively bad character is hardly to be denied. If, for example, personal interest inclining him against the measure on a former occasion, arguments have been urged by the person in question against the measure, while on the present occasion, personal interest now inclining him the opposite way, arguments are urged by him in its favor. In each case if no notice of the inconsistency is taken by the person himself, its operation to his prejudice will naturally be considered stronger than if he gives a more or less satisfactory account of the circumstances occasioning the shift of opinion.

But be the evidence with regard to the cause of the change what it may, no inference can be drawn from it against the measure unless it be that such inconsistency, if proved, may weaken the persuasive force of the opinion of the person in question as an authority; and in what respect and degree such an argument is irrelevant has already been demonstrated.

Sec. 5. Imputation of Suspicious Connections

Admitting the alleged badness of character of the alleged associate, the argument now in question will stand on the same footing as the four preceding ones, the weakness of which has already been exposed, and will constitute only one more branch of the Fallacy of Distrust. But before it can stand on a par even with those weak ones, these ulterior points remain to be established: (1) the badness of character of the alleged associate, (2) the existence of a social connection between the person and his supposed associate; and (3) that the influence exercised on the mind of the person in question is such that in consequence thereof he will be induced to introduce and support mischievous measures which otherwise he would not have introduced or supported.

As to the first two of these three supposed facts, their respective degrees of probability will depend upon the circumstances of each case. In private life the force of the third presumption is established by daily experience; but in the case of a political connection it loses a great part, and sometimes the whole, of its force. Few indeed are the political measures, concerning which men of all characters, men of all degrees in the scale of probity and improbity, may not be seen on both sides. The mere need of information respecting matters of fact is a cause capable of bringing together, in a state of apparent connection, some of the most opposite characters.

Sec. 6. Imputation Founded on Identity of Name

This fallacy is distinguished from the last preceding by the fact that in this case between the person in question and the obnoxious persons by whose opinions and conduct he is supposed to be influenced, neither personal intercourse nor the possibility of personal intercourse can exist. In the former case, his measures were to be opposed because he was connected with persons of bad character; in the present instance, because he bears the same name as persons now no more, but who, in their own time, were the authors of pernicious measures.

Now community of name does not imply community of interest. It is only occasionally the sign, not the efficient cause, of community of interest. What have the Romans of the present day in common with the Romans of early times? Do they aspire to recover the empire of the world? [1]

But when evil designs are imputed to men of the present

[1] Words written something more than a century before the imperial ambitions of Benito Mussolini had their brief day. — Ed.

day on the ground that evil designs were entertained and prosecuted by their namesakes in times past, whatever may be the community of interest, one circumstance should never be out of mind. That is, the gradual melioration of character from the most remote and barbarous down to the present times, the consequence of which is that in many particulars the same ends which were formerly pursued by persons of the same name are not now pursued, or not by the same bad means. If this observation pass unheeded, the consequences may be no less mischievous than absurd: that which *has* been, is unalterable. If this fallacy be suffered to influence the mind and determine human conduct, whatever degree of depravity has been imputed to preceding generations bearing the obnoxious name, whatever opposition has been manifested towards them or their successors — must continue without abatement to the end of time. " Be my friendship immortal, my enmity mortal " is the sentiment that has been so warmly and justly applauded in the mouth of a sage of antiquity.[2] But the present fallacy would maintain the baneful influence of enmity forever.

It is in matters touching religious persuasion, and to the prejudice of certain sects, that this fallacy has operated with the greatest and most pernicious effect. In England, particularly, against measures for the relief of the Catholics, it has been argued: " Those of our ancestors who, professing the same branch of the Christian religion as that which you now profess, and hence distinguished by the same name, entertained pernicious designs that for some time showed

[2] In Livy, *Histories,* XL, 46; *Vulgatum illud, quia verum est, in proverbium venit: Amicitias immortales, mortales inimicitias debere esse.* (There is an old saying, which, from its truth, has become proverbial, that friendships should be immortal, enmities mortal). Cicero expresses a similar idea in *Pro Rabirio Postumo* 12:32: *Neque me vero paenitet mortales inimicitias, sempiternas amicitias habere.* (Indeed, I do not regret having mortal enmities, but enduring friendships.) — Ed.

themselves in pernicious measures. Therefore you, entertaining the same pernicious designs, would now, had you but power enough, carry into effect the same pernicious measures. They, having the power, destroyed by fire and faggot those who, in respect of religious opinions and ceremonies, differed from them; therefore you, had you but power enough, would do likewise."

Upon this ground, in one of the three kingdoms (Ireland), a system of government continues which does not so much as profess to have in view the welfare of the majority of the inhabitants — a system of government in which the interest of the many is avowedly, and so long as the government lasts, intended to be kept in a state of perpetual sacrifice of the interest of the many to that of the few. In vain is it urged that the above inferences, drawn from times and measures long since past, are completely belied by the universal experience of the present. In the Saxon kingdom, in the Austrian empire, in the vast and ever-flourishing empire of France, though the sovereign is Catholic, whatever degree of security the government affords is possessed alike by Catholics and Protestants. And in vain is it observed, and truly observed, that the Church of England continued her fires after the Church of Rome had discontinued hers.[3] It is only in the absence of interest that experience can hope to be regarded, or reason heard. In the character of sinecurists and over-paid placemen, it is to the interest of the members of the English government to treat the majority of the people of Ireland on the double footing of enemies and subjects; and such is the treatment which is in store for them to the extent of their endurance.

Sec. 7. Cause of the Prevalence of this Class of Fallacies

Whatever the nature of the several instruments of deception

[3] Under James I, when, for being Anabaptists or Arians, two men were burnt at Smithfield.

by which the mind is liable to be influenced, the degree of success they enjoy depends ultimately upon one common cause – the ignorance and mental imbecility of those upon whom they operate. In the present instance, besides this ultimate cause or root, they find a sort of intermediate cause in the human propensity to save exertion by resting satisfied with authority.

Besides, nothing but laborious application, and a clear and comprehensive intellect, can enable a man on any given subject to employ successfully relevant arguments drawn from the subject itself. To employ personalities, neither labor nor intellect is required. In that sort of contest the most idle and most ignorant are quite on a par with, if not superior to, the most industrious and the most highly-gifted individuals. Nothing can be more convenient for those who would speak without the trouble of thinking: the same ideas are brought forward over and over again, and all that is required is to vary the turn of expression. Close and relevant arguments have very little hold on the passions, and serve rather to quell than to inflame them, while in personalities there is always something stimulating, whether on the part of him who praises or him who blames. Praise forms a kind of connection between the party praising and the party praised, and vituperation gives an air of courage and independence to the party who blames.

Ignorance and indolence, friendship and enmity, concurring and conflicting interest, servility and dependence – all these conspire to give personalities the ascendancy they so unhappily maintain. The more we lie under the influence of our own passions, the more we rely on others being affected in a similar degree. A man who can repel these injuries with dignity may often convert them into triumph: "Strike me, but hear," says he; and the fury of his antagonist redounds to his own discomfiture.

CHAPTER II

The Hobgoblin Argument, or "No Innovation"

Ad metum.

Exposition

THE HOBGOBLIN WHOSE eventual appearance is denounced by this argument is *Anarchy*, which tremendous spectre has for its forerunner the monster *Innovation*. The forms in which this monster may be denounced are as numerous and varied as the sentences in which the word innovation can be used.

"Here it comes!" exclaims the barbarous or unthinking servant in the hearing of the affrighted child, when, to rid herself of the burden of attendance, such a servant does not scruple to employ an instrument of terror, the effects of which may continue throughout life. "Here it comes!" is the cry; and the hobgoblin is rendered all the more terrifying by the suppression of its name.

Of a similar nature, and productive of similar effects, is the political device here exposed to view. As an instrument of deception, it is generally accompanied by personalities of the vituperative sort. Imputation of bad motives, bad designs, bad conduct and character are ordinarily cast upon the authors and advocates of the supposedly obnoxious measure, while the very term employed is such as to beg the question in dispute. Innovation is made to mean *bad* change, presenting to the mind, besides the idea of change, the proposition either that change in general is a bad thing, or at least that the sort of change in question is a bad change.

Exposure

This is one of the many cases in which it is difficult to render the absurdity of the argument more glaring than it is upon the face of the argument itself. For whatever reason it affords for looking upon the proposed measure as about to be mischievous, it affords the same reason for entertaining the same opinion about everything that exists at the present time. To say that all new things are bad is as much as to say that all things are bad, or in any event that all were bad at their commencement. For of all the old things ever seen or heard of, there is not a single one that was not once new. Whatever is now *establishment* was once *innovation*.

He who on this ground condemns a proposed measure, condemns in the same breath the very things he would be most averse to be thought to disapprove. He condemns the Revolution, the Reformation, the assumption made by the House of Commons of a part in the penning of the laws in the reign of Henry the Sixth, the institution of the House of Commons itself in the reign of Henry the Third, – all these he bids us regard as sure forerunners of the monster Anarchy, but particularly the birth and first efficient agency of the House of Commons, an innovation in comparison with which all others, past or future, are for effectiveness, and hence for mischievousness, but as grains of dust in the balance.

Sec. 1. Apprehension of Mischief from Change, What Foundation It Has in Truth

One thing which gives a sort of color to the use of this fallacy is the fact that it can scarcely ever be found without a certain grain of truth adhering to it. Supposing the change in question to be one which cannot be effected without the interposition of the legislature, even this circumstance is sufficient to attach to it a certain amount of mischief. The words necessary to commit the change to writing cannot be put in that form without labor, bringing a proportional quantity of vexation to the head employed in it. When disseminated by the press, as it always must be before it can be productive of whatever effect is aimed at, it becomes productive of further vexation and expense. Here, then, is so much unavoidable mischief, which even the most salutary and indispensable change cannot fail to produce, besides the factitious and avoidable mischief which may be added by circumstances. This is the *minimum* of mischief which accompanies every change; and in this minimum of mischief we have the minimum of truth contained in this fallacy, protecting it against a flat and undiscriminating denial.

It is seldom, however, that the whole of the mischief, with its corresponding portion of truth, is confined within such narrow bounds. Wherever any portion, great or small, of the aggregate mass of the objects of desire: wealth, power, dignity, or even reputation, whether in possession or in remote prospect, must pass, in consequence of the change, out of any hand or hands that are not willing to part with it (either without compensation or with insufficient compensation), we have, in the quantity of vexation uncompensated, so much mischief beyond dispute.

In some such cases the party called upon to make the sacrifice will feel that his opposition to the proposed change has a reason; and when and if such uncompensated injury is presented to view, it belongs not to the account of fallacies. But when the alleged damage will not, even in his own view of it, bear the test of inquiry, he will betake himself to the general fallacy in place of specific argument. He will set up the cry of " Innovation! Innovation! " hoping by this watchword to bring to his aid all whose sinister interests are connected with his own, and which impel them to say, and the unreflecting multitude to believe, that the change in question is one in which the mischief is not outweighed by a preponderant mass of advantage.

Sec. 2. Time the Innovator-General, a Counter-Fallacy

Among the stories current in the profession of law is that of an attorney who, when his client applied to him for relief from a forged bond, advised him, as the shortest and surest course, to forge a release. Thus, as a shorter and surer course than that of attempting to make men aware of the imposture, this fallacy has now and then been met by what may be termed its counter-fallacy: "Time itself is the arch-innovator." The inference is that the proposed change, branded as it has been by the odious name of innovation, is in fact no change at all: its sole effect being either to prevent a change, or to bring the matter back to the good state in which it formerly was. This counter-fallacy, if such it may be termed, has no such pernicious consequences as may be indicated by that name. Yet it deserves the name of fallacy, because it has no specific application to the particular measure in hand, and may on that score be set down as irrelevant. It also, by a sort of implied concession and virtual admission, gives color and countenance to the fallacy which it opposes, admitting by implication that if the name of change did properly apply to the proposed measure, the latter might on that single account with propriety be opposed.

A few words, then, are sufficient to strip the mask from this fallacy. No specific mischief, as likely to result from the measure, is alleged. If it were, the argument would not belong under this head. What is alleged is nothing more than that some mischief, without regard to the amount, will be among the results of the measure. But this is no more than can be said of every legislative measure that ever did pass or ever can pass. If it is to be ranked as an argument, it is an argument that involves in one common condemnation all political measures whatsoever, past, present, and to come, in all places as well as in all times. Delivered from the mouth of an old woman beguiling by her gossip the labors of the spinning-wheel in her cottage, such a notion might pass for simple and ordinary ignorance; delivered from the exalted station of a legislative house or judicial bench, if it can be regarded as sincere, it is a mark of drivelling rather than of ignorance.

But it may be said, " My meaning is not to condemn all change, all new institutions, all new laws, all new measures, but only violent and dangerous ones, such as that which is now being proposed." The answer is, if you do not draw or attempt to draw any line, you pass condemnation indiscriminately upon all change. Draw such a line, and the reproach of insincerity or imbecility shall be withheld. Draw your line, but remember that whenever you draw it, or so much as begin to draw it, you give up this argument.

Alive to possible and imaginable evils, dead to actual ones, eagle-eyed to future contingent evils, blind and insensible to all existing ones — such is the character of the mind to which such a fallacy as this can really have presented itself as an argument possessing the smallest claim to notice. Such a mind is blind to evils such as these: that by the denial and sale of justice, anarchy, insofar as it concerns nine-tenths of the people, is actually by force of law established; that to question the fitness of great characters for their high stations is in one man a crime, while to question their fitness so that their motives remain unquestioned is legal; that the crime of libel remains undefined and indistinguishable, while the liberty of the press is defined to be the absence of that security which would be afforded to writers by the establishment of a licenser; that under a show of limitation, a government shall be in fact an absolute one, while pretended guardians are really accomplices, and at the nod of a minister by a regular trained body of votes, black shall be declared white; miscarriage, success; mortality, health; disgrace, honor; and notorious imbecility, consummate skill. To such a mind these, with other evils boundless in extent and number, are either not seen to be in existence, or felt to be such. In such a mind, the horror of innovation is as really a disease as any to which the body in which it is seated is exposed. In proportion as a man is afflicted with it, he is the enemy of all the good, no matter how urgent, which remains to be done. Nor can he be said to be completely cured of it until he shall have learned on such occasions, and without repugnance, to take general utility for the general end, and to judge whatever measures are proposed in the character of means more or less conducive to that end.

Sec. 3. Sinister Interests in Which This Fallacy Has Its Source

Could the wand of that magician be borrowed at whose potent touch the emissaries of his wicked antagonist threw off their several disguises, and made instant confession of their real characters and designs; could a few of those ravens by whom the word " Innovation! " is uttered with a scream of horror, and the approach of the monster Anarchy denounced; could they be touched with it, we should then learn their real character, and have the true import of their screams translated into intelligible language.

1. I am a lawyer, one of them would be heard to say, a fee-fed judge who, considering that the money I lay by, the power I exercise, and the respect and reputation I enjoy, depend upon the undiminished continuance of the abuses of the law, the factitious delay, vexation, and expense with which the few who have money enough to pay for a chance at justice are loaded, and by which the many who have not the money, are cut off from that chance — I take this method of deterring men from attempting to alleviate those torments in which my comforts have their source.

2. I am a sinecurist, cries another, who, being in receipt

of 38,000 pounds a year, public money, for doing nothing, and having no more wit than honesty, have never been able to open my mouth to pronounce an articulate sound for any other purpose; yet, hearing a cry of " No sinecures! " am come to join in the shout of " No innovation! Down with the innovators! " in the hope of drowning out, by these defensive sounds, the offensive ones which chill my blood and make me tremble.

3. I am a contractor, cries a third, who, having bought my seat that I may sell my votes; and in return for them, being in the habit of obtaining with the most convenient regularity a succession of good jobs, now foresee, in the prevalence of innovation, the ruin and destruction of this established branch of trade.

4. I am a country gentleman, cries a fourth, who, observing that from having a seat in a certain assembly a man enjoys more respect than he did before, on the turf, in the dog-kennel, and in the stable, and having tenants and other dependents enough to seat me against their wills for a place in which I am detested, and hearing it said that if innovation were suffered to run on unopposed, elections would come in time to be as free in reality as they now are in appearance and pretense; – I have left for a day or two the cry of " Tally-ho! " and " Hark forward! " to join instead in the cry of " No Anarchy! " " No Innovation! "

5. I am a priest, says a fifth, who, having proved the Pope to be Anti-Christ to the satisfaction of all orthodox divines whose piety prays for the cure of souls, or whose health has need of exoneration from the burden of residence; and having read, in my edition of the Gospel, that the apostles lived in palaces, which innovation and anarchy would cut down to parsonage-houses; though grown hoarse by screaming out " No reading! " " No writing! " " No Lancaster! " and " No Popery! " – for fear of coming change, I am here to add what remains of my voice to the full chorus of " No Anarchy! " " No Innovation! "

CHAPTER III

Fallacy of Distrust, or What's at the Bottom?

Exposition

THIS ARGUMENT MAY BE considered as a particular modification of the No-Innovation argument. An arrangement has been proposed, so plainly beneficial and at the same time so manifestly innocuous, that no prospect presents itself of bringing to bear with any effect the cry of "No Innovation!" Is the anti-innovationist mute? No; he has this resource: in what you see as yet, he says, there may perhaps be no great mischief; but depend upon it, in the quarter from whence these proposed innocuous arrangements come, there lurk *more behind them* of a very different complexion. If these innocuous ones are suffered to pass, others of a noxious character will succeed without end, and will be carried likewise.

Exposure

The absurdity of this argument is too glaring to be susceptible of any considerable illustration from anything that can be said about it.

1. In the first place, it begins with a virtual admission of the propriety of the proposed measure considered in itself; and thus, containing within itself a demonstration of its own futility, it cuts from under it the very ground on which it endeavors to stand. Yet from its very weakness, it is apt to derive for the moment a certain degree of force. By the monstrosity of its weakness, a feeling of surprise, and thereupon of perplexity, is likely to be produced; and as long as this feeling continues, the difficulty of finding an appropriate

answer continues with it. For, to that which is itself nothing, says a man, what answer can I possibly find?

2. If two measures, G and B, were both brought forward at the same time, G being good and B bad, then rejecting G because B is bad would be quite absurd enough; and at first view a man might be apt to suppose that absurdity could go no further. But the present fallacy does in effect go much further. Two measures, brought on the carpet together, both of them unobjectionable, are to be rejected, not for anything that is amiss with either of them, but for something which may possibly be found amiss in some other or others, that nobody knows of, and of which the future existence, without the slightest ground, is to be assumed and taken for granted.

In the field of policy as applied to measures, this vicarious reprobation forms a counterpart to vicarious punishment in the field of justice as applied to persons. The measure G, which is good, is to be thrown out because, for aught we can be sure of, some day or other it may happen to be followed by some other measure B, which may be a bad one. Just as a man A, against whom there is neither evidence nor charge, is to be punished because, for aught we can be sure of, sometime or other there may be some other man who will have been guilty.

If on this ground it is right that the measure should be rejected, so ought every other measure that ever has been or can be proposed. For of no measure can anybody be sure that it may not be followed by some other measure or measures of which, when they make their appearance, it may be said that they are bad. If, then, the argument proves anything, it proves that no measure ever ought to be carried, or ever ought to have been carried; and that therefore all things that can be done by law and government, and hence law and government themselves, are nuisances.

This policy is exactly that which was attributed to Herod in the extermination of the innocents; and the sort of man by whom any argument of this sort would be employed is the sort of man who would have acted as Herod did, had he been in Herod's place. But think, not only what sort of man he must be who can bring himself to employ such an argument, but moreover, what sort of men they must be to whom he can venture to propose it with the hope of making any impression. "Such drivellers," says he to them in effect, "are you, so sure of being imposed upon by anyone who will attempt it, that you do not know the difference between good and bad. When at the suggestion of this or that man you have adopted any one measure, good or bad, then let that same man propose any number of other measures, and whatever their character, ye are such idiots and fools, that without looking at them yourselves, or vouchsafing to learn their character from others, you will adopt them in a lump." Such is the compliment wrapped up in the use of this sort of argument.

CHAPTER IV

Official Malefactor's Screen, or "Attack Us, You Attack Government"

Ad metum.

Exposition

THE FALLACY HERE IN QUESTION is employed almost as often as persons use expressions of condemnation or censure in speaking of the persons by whom, or of the system according to which, the business of government is conducted. The fallacy consists in affecting to consider such condemnation or censure as being, if not in design, at least in tendency, pregnant with mischief to government itself. "Oppose us, you oppose Government." "Disgrace us, you disgrace Government." "Bring us into contempt, you bring Government into contempt; and anarchy and civil war are the immediate consequences." Such are the forms which this fallacy assumes.

Exposure

Only let this notion be acceded to, and all persons now partaking or likely to partake of the business and profit of misrule in any of its shapes must be allowed to continue without disturbance. All abuses, future as well as present, must continue without remedy. The most industrious laborers in the service of mankind will experience the treatment proper to those to whose dissocial or selfish nature the happiness of man is an object of aversion or indifference. Punishment, or at least disgrace, will be the reward of the most exalted virtue; perpetual honor, as well as power, the reward of the most pernicious vices. Punishment will be, not for him who commits a crime, but for him who complains of it. This is true of the English law of libel today, providing the criminal is of a certain rank in the state, and the mischief of his crime to a certain degree extensive enough.

As long as the conduct of the business of government contains anything amiss in it, as long as anything about it could be made better, as long, in a word, as it continues to be short of a state of absolute perfection – so long will there be no other mode of bringing it nearer to perfection, no other means of cleansing it of the most mischievous abuses with which government can be defiled, than the indication of such points of imperfection as at the time exist, or are supposed to exist in it. These points of imperfection will always be referable to one or the other of two heads: either to the conduct of some individual in some department of government, or to the state of the system of administration. But neither in the system nor in the conduct of the person in question can any imperfections be pointed out without producing aversion or contempt toward such system or person to a degree proportional to the apparent importance and extent of the alleged imperfection. In effect, this fallacy is merely a mode of intimating that no abuse ought ever to be reformed, that nothing ought to be uttered in relation to the misconduct of any person in office which might produce any sentiment of disapprobation.

In this country at least, few if any persons aim at any such object as the bringing into contempt of any of those offices on the execution of which the maintenance of the general security depends, such as king, member of parliament, or judge. As to the person of the king, if the maxim, "The king can do no wrong," be admitted in both its senses, there can be no need of imputing blame to him, unless by way of defense against the imprudence or improbity of those who, by groundless or exaggerated eulogies on the personal character of the individual monarch on the throne, seek to extend his power, and to screen from scrutiny the misconduct of his agents.

But in the instance of any other office but the kingship, to reprobate everything, the tendency of which is to expose the office to hatred or contempt, is to reprobate everything that can be said or done either in the way of complaint against the past or for the purpose of preventing future transgressions. To reprobate everything the tendency of which is to expose the office to hatred or contempt, is to reprobate everything that can be said or done towards pointing out the need of reform, no matter how much needed, in the constitution of the office.

If in the constitution of the office with respect to mode of appointment or remuneration there is anything that tends to give to persons placed in it an interest in opposition to their official duty, or to give an increased facility to the effective pursuit of any such sinister interest, then everything that tends to expose such sinister interest, or such facility, contributes, it may be said, to bring the office itself into contempt. That under the existing system of judicature, as far as concerns its higher seats, the interest of the judge is, throughout the whole field of his jurisdiction, in a state of constant and diametrical opposition to his line of duty; — that it is to his interest to maintain undiminished, and as far as possible to increase, every evil opposite to the ends of justice, such as uncertainty, delay, vexation, and expense; — that giving birth to these evils has at all times been more or less an object with every judge (the present ones excepted, of whom we say nothing) who ever sat on a Westminster hall bench, and that under the present constitution of the office it would be weakness to expect at the hands of a judge anything better; — that of the above-mentioned evils endured by the people of this country only a very small part is to be regarded as the natural and unavoidable lot of human nature; — all these are propositions which have already been demonstrated in this work, and in the belief of which the writer has been confirmed by the observations of nearly sixty years

— propositions of the truth of which he is no more able to entertain a doubt than he is of his own existence.

But in expressing these sentiments, has the writer any such wish as to see the authority of judges enfeebled and exposed to effectual resistance? Or the authority of any established judicatory? Or of any one occupant of any such judicial seat? No; the most strenuous defender of abuse in every shape would not go further than he in wishes, and upon occasion in exertion, for the support of such authority.

For preventing, remedying or checking transgression on the part of members of government, or preventing their management of the business of government from becoming completely arbitrary, however, the nature of things affords no other means than those which have a tendency to lower either the managing heads, or the system, or both, in the affection and estimation of the people. When this effect is produced to a high degree, it may be termed bringing them into hatred and contempt. But it is far from being true that a man's aversion or contempt for the hands by which the powers of government are exercised, or the system under which they operate, is the same as aversion or contempt for government itself. What in consequence of such contempt or aversion he desires, is not that there should be no hands at all to exercise these powers, but that such hands might be better regulated; not that the powers should not be exercised at all, but that they should be better exercised; not that in their exercise no rules at all should be observed, but that the rules observed should be a better set of rules.

All government is a trust; every branch of government is a trust, and has been immemorially acknowledged so to be. It is only by the magnitude of the scale that public trusts differ from private trusts.

I complain of the conduct of a person in the character of domestic guardian having the care of a minor or insane person. In so doing, do I say that guardianship is a bad institution? Does it enter into the head of anyone to suspect me of so doing?

I complain of an individual in the character of a commercial agent, or assignee of the effects of an insolvent. In so doing, do I say that commercial agency is a bad thing? Or that the practice of vesting in the hands of assignees or trustees the effects of an insolvent for the purpose of their being divided among his creditors is a bad practice? Does any such conceit ever enter into the head of man, as that of suspecting me of so doing?

I complain of an imperfection in the state of the law relative to guardianship. In stating this supposed imperfection in the state of the law, do I say that there ought to be no law on the subject? Or that no human being ought to have any such power as that of guardian over the person of any other? Does it ever enter the head of any human being to so much as suspect me of entertaining such an idea, not to mention endeavoring to cause others to entertain it?

Nothing can be more groundless than to suppose that the disposition to pay obedience to the laws by which security in respect to person, property, reputation and condition in life is afforded, is influenced by any such consideration as that of the fitness of the several public functionaries for their respective trusts, or even of the system of rules and customs under which they act. The chief occasions upon which a member of the community is called upon to manifest his obedience are two: the payment of taxes, and submission to orders of courts of justice. The first of these is a habitual practice; the second is an occasional and eventual one. But in neither instance is any variation in the person's disposition to obedience produced by any increase or diminution in the good or ill opinion he entertains toward the official persons who carry on the business of those departments of government, or toward the systems under which they act.

Were the business of government carried on ever so much

worse than it now is, it is still from the power of government that each man receives whatever protection he enjoys against both foreign and domestic adversaries. Therefore what produces his own disposition to obedience, and his wish to see others obey, is not his respect either for the persons by whom or the system according to which the powers are exercised, but his regard for his own security. Were it even his wish to withhold his own obedience, that wish would be altogether ineffectual unless and until he could be joined by many others of a like disposition: a state of things which could only arise from a common sense of overwhelming misery, and not from the mere utterance of complaints against the government. There is no freedom of the press, no power to complain, in Turkey; and yet of all countries it is the one in which revolts and revolutions are the most frequent and the most violent.

Here and there a man of strong appetites, weak understanding, and stout heart excepted, it might be affirmed with confidence that even the most indigent and most ignorant in any society would not be foolish enough to desire a complete dissolution of the bonds of government. In such a state of things, whatever a man might expect to grasp at the moment, he would have no assured hope of keeping. Were he ever so strong, his strength, he could not but see, would avail him nothing against a momentarily confederated multitude; nor in one part of his field against a swifter individual ravaging the opposite part; nor during sleep against the weakest and most sluggish. Let him suppose himself entered into an association with others for mutual security against such continually impending disasters, and he would then find himself living again under some sort of government.

Even the comparatively few who prefer depredation to honest industry as the source of their subsistence are no less dependent for their wretched and palpitating existence than the honest and industrious are for theirs, on that general security to which their bad practices create exceptions. Be the momentary object of his rapacity what it may, what no one of them could avoid is the proposition that it could not exist for him any further than it is secured against others.

So far is it from being true that no government can exist consistently with the exposure of defects in its administration; no good government can exist without such exposure. Unless by open and lawless violence, there can be no hope or chance of beneficial change in government except by lowering in the estimation of the people the hands by which its powers are exercised, if unfit, or the system of management under which they act, if ill-constructed. Since there is no sufficient reason for ascribing even to the worst-disposed persons any wish so foolish as that of seeing the bonds of government entirely dissolved, and since the best-disposed have no other means of reform save bringing unfit officials into general disesteem; there cannot be a more unfounded imputation, or viler artifice, if it be artifice, or grosser error, if it be error, than that which infers from the disposition or even the endeavor to lessen in the estimation of the people their existing rulers any such wish as that of seeing the bands of government dissolved.

In producing a local or temporary debility in the action of the powers of the natural body, in many cases, the honest and skilful physician beholds the only means of curing it; and it would be as reasonable to infer a wish to see the patient perish, from the act of the physician in prescribing a drug, as to infer a wish to see the whole frame of government destroyed or rendered worse, from the act of a statesman who lowers the reputation of an official whom he regards as unfit.

Insofar as a man's feeling and conduct are influenced and determined by what is called public opinion, and that opinion runs in conformity with the dictates of the principles of general utility, then in proportion to the value set upon reputation and the degree of respect entertained for the community at large, his conduct will be the *better*, the more completely the quantity of respect he enjoys is dependent upon the goodness of his behavior; and it will be the *worse*, the more completely the quantity of respect he is sure of enjoying is independent of it. Thus the portion of respect which the people at large are in the habit of bestowing upon the individual who holds any office may, as long as their habit continues, be said to be attached to the office, just as certain emoluments. But as it is with emolument, so it is with respect. The greater the quantity of it a man is likely to receive independently of his good behavior, the less good, in proportion to the degree of influence which the love of reputation exercises upon his mind, is his behavior likely to be. It this be true, then it is to the interest of the public that the portion of respect which, along with the salary, is habitually attached to any office should be as small as possible.

But while it is in the interest of the public that the remuneration received by each of its trustees in the shape of respect should be as completely dependent as possible upon the goodness of his behavior in the execution of his trust, it is also in the interest of the trustee himself that whatever portion of the good things of this world he receives upon any score should be as great as possible, since by good behavior neither respect nor anything else can ever be earned by him except through sacrifices of some sort or other, particularly in the shape of ease.

Whatever, therefore, the official position occupied by the person in question, it is to his interest that the quantity of respect habitually attached to it should be as great, and at the same time as securely attached to it as possible. And from the point of view from which he is by his personal and sinister interest led to consider the subject, the point of perfection will not be reached until the quantity of respect he receives by virtue of mere possession of the office is as great as the nature of the office permits. Assuming that, at all times, the quantity of respect received is completely independent of the goodness of his behavior in office: — just as great, in the event of his making the worst use, as if he had made the best use of the powers belonging to it. To this purpose, among others, will be directed whatever influence his will can exert upon other wills, and whatever influence his understanding can exert upon other understandings.

If, for example, his office be that of a judge, then, by the influence of will upon will, it will seldom be in his power to compel men by force to bestow upon him the sentiment of respect; but he may restrain men from saying or doing any of those things, the effect of which would cause others to bestow upon him less respect than they would otherwise. If, being a judge of the King's Bench, any man has the presumption to question his fitness for such high office, he may punish him for so doing by fine and imprisonment. If a Lord Chancellor, he may prosecute him before a judge, by whom a disposition to attach such punishments to such offenses has been demonstrated by practice.

When it comes to the influence of understanding upon understanding, that which depends upon the exertions of an official (as distinct from the hold of the office itself upon the understanding of the people), consists in giving utterance and circulation in the most impressive manner possible to this fallacy, together with a few others closely connected with it.

Upon the boldness and readiness with which the personnel and system of government may be spoken ill of, depends the difference between arbitrary and limited government — between a government in which the great body of the people have, and one in which they have not, a share.

What the members of the governing body would undoubtedly most desire is that no one should endeavor to lower them in the estimation of the public unless they had truly been guilty of want of probity or weakness of judgment or want of appropriate talent. Unfortunately such a state of things is plainly (need it be said?) an impossible one. Admit no accusations at all, and you may and you will exclude all unjust ones. Admit just ones, and you must admit unjust ones along with them; there is no help for it. One of these two evils being necessarily to be chosen, the question is, which is the lesser? Shall we admit all such imputations, and thereby some unjust ones; or shall we exclude all such imputations, and thereby some just ones?

I answer without difficulty: the admission of unjust imputations is, beyond comparison, the lesser of the two evils. If you exclude all unjust imputations, and with them all just ones, then the only check by which the career of public deterioration can be stopped being thus removed, both hands and system will grow continually worse until they arrive at the extreme of despotism and misrule. The rulers will grow worse because there is nothing to counteract the separate and sinister interest to which they are constantly exposed; and the system will grow worse, it being all along the interest and within the power of the hands themselves to make it so.

Admit just imputations, although along with them you admit some unjust ones, and so slight is the evil as scarcely to deserve the name. For, along with unjust imputations, are not defenses admitted? In respect to both motives and means, have not the defendants in any such case, beyond all comparison, the advantage of the complainants? As far as motives are concerned, the principle of self-preservation acting upon those attacked is stronger than the cause which disposes their attackers. While as for means, the office-holder is always in a position to use the resources of his office for the purpose of engaging defending advocates.

Let it not be said: "This is a persecution to which an honorable man ought not to be exposed — a persecution so intolerable to some men as to deprive the public of the benefit of their services." A notion to any such effect can hardly be advanced with a straight face. That censure is the tax imposed by nature upon eminence is the A B C of commonplace. Who can doubt that exposure to such imputations is among the inevitable appendages of office? If we were discussing an office which in no shape whatever had any rewards or allowances annexed to it, or a situation into which men were pressed, then the observation would have a better foundation. But in the class of office here in question, there is no such situation.

A self-contradiction is involved in the observation itself. The subject of which so morbid a sensibility is predicated is said to be an honorable man. But to any man to whom the attribute honorable can with truth and justice be applied, such sensibility cannot be attributed. The man who will not accept an office except on condition that his conduct in it shall remain exempt from all imputation, does not intend that his conduct shall be what it ought to be. The man to whom the idea of being subject to those imputations to which he sees the best of men exposed, is intolerable – such a man is in his heart a tyrant. To become one in practice, he needs nothing except to be seated on one of those thrones or benches in which, by the appearance of chains made for show rather than for use, a man is enabled with greater dignity as well as safety to act the part of tyrant, and glut himself with vengeance.

To a man who accepts a commission in the civil sphere it is not less evident that by so doing he exposes himself to imputations, some of which may happen to be unjust, than it is to a man who accepts a commission in the military that by so doing he exposes himself to be shot at. And with about equal truth, that is – none at all – it might be said that an honorable man will not accept a commission in either of these spheres, except on condition of being protected from imputations or bullets.

In such circumstances it is unlikely that a public man

will have to labor under an unjust imputation in the long run. Insofar as anything of the sort takes place, evil does in truth exist; but even so, the evil will not be unaccompanied with good operating in compensation for it. On the part of men in office, it contributes to maintain the habit of considering their conduct as exposed to scrutiny, to keep up in their minds that sense of responsibility on which goodness of conduct depends, and in which good behavior finds its chief guarantee. On the part of the people at large, it serves to keep alive the expectation of witnessing such attacks, the habit of looking out for them, and, when any such attack does come, it prevents the added hardship which attaches to such an infliction when it is unprecedented or rare.

When, in support of such imputations, false facts are alleged, the act of him who makes such false allegations not only ought to be regarded as pernicious, but ought to be, and is, consistently with justice and utility, punishable. Such charges should be punishable even when advanced through temerity without consciousness of their falsity, and more so when they are accompanied by consciousness of their dishonesty. But by a sort of law, of which the protection of high-placed official delinquency is at least the effect, if not the object, the above important distinction is carefully overlooked: and whenever to the detriment of the reputation of a man, especially if he be a man in office, a fact which has been asserted or insinuated with more or less confidence turns out to be false, the existence of dishonest consciousness, whether or not it really exists, is assumed.

A general propensity to scrutinize the conduct of men who are trustees and agents for the people is a useful propensity, even though it risks the casting upon them of imputations which are more or less unmerited. It is conducive to good behavior on their part. And for the opposite and corresponding reason, the habit of general praise, of praise without specific grounds, is a mischievous propensity, being conducive to bad behavior on their part.

Render all such endeavors hopeless, and you will take from a bad state of things all chance of becoming better. Allow to all such endeavors the freest range, and you do no injury to the best state of things imaginable. For no matter what facilities the adversaries of the existing state of things have for lowering it in the estimation of the people, its friends have equal or greater facilities for keeping and raising it up.

Under the English constitution, at any rate, the most strenuous defenders of the existing set of managing hands, as well as of the existing system of management, are not backward in representing an opposition as being no less necessary among the springs of government than the regulator in a watch.[1] But in what way does an opposition act, or can it act, but by endeavoring to lower either the managing hands or the system of management in the estimation of the people? And from a watchmaker's putting a regulating spring into the watch he is making, it would be just as reasonable and fair to infer that his intent is to destroy the watch, as, from the circumstance of a man's seeking to lower in the estimation of the people the hands or the system of management, to infer a desire on his part to destroy the government.

Under the English constitution, as we have seen, the more independent the authority of the government is of all public esteem for its officials, the better for the stability and prosperity of the state. If on each occasion public authority depended upon the degree of esteem in which the officials were held by the majority of the people, that power might become much too strong at one time, and much too weak at

[1] More's *Observations*, 77–78. Ed. Note: The full title is *Observations upon Anthroposophia Theomagica and Anima Magica by Alazonomastix Philalethes* (1650). Henry More, (1614–1687) an Anglican theologian, was one of the Christian Platonists at Cambridge.

another. Among the peculiar excellences of the English constitution is the fact that the existence of the government, and even its good conduct, depends to a less degree than any other monarchy upon the personal qualifications of the monarch, and the place he occupies in the estimation of his people. If the character of the chief ruler were perfect in every respect, then all checks upon his power would be a nuisance. On the other hand, under a constitution providing for checks upon that power, the stronger and more efficient such checks are, the worse the personal character of the chief ruler may be without any fatal disturbance in the business of government.

When an abuse exists, and some alteration is desirable, it is usually impossible to bring such a change about without lowering in the estimation of the people the persons who refuse to make the change. Suppose the latter to be assured of possessing, in the event that they veto all change, as high a place in the estimation of the people as they previously held, then anything which might be done by them to further a proposed change would be an effect without a cause. For all or most of them have, in their personal capacities, little to gain and much to lose by any change which might be proposed.

True, it may be said, to be remedied an imperfection must be pointed out. But what we complain of as dangerous to government is not the indication of such imperfections with their proposed remedies, but the way in which they are apt to be pointed out, the heat and the violence with which such indications are accompanied. This we object to, not merely as dishonest, but as unwise, as tending to irritate the very persons at whose hands the remedy is sought.

To this complaint, the answer is as follows:

1. Whatever terms may be the most decorous and allegedly the best adapted to the obtaining of the relief desired,

it is not possible to describe them beforehand in such a way that a man could satisfy himself as to what terms will be considered exposed to, and what exempt from censure.

2. The true cause of irritation is not in the terms of the proposal but its substance. Hence the greatest irritation will be produced by that mode of application which appears most likely to lead to its adoption, and the least irritation will be caused, no matter what the terms in which it may be couched, by that mode of application which affords the fairest pretense for non-compliance.

3. Since the imperfection in question is one the advantages of which are enjoyed by a few, while the interest of the many, each taken individually, in its removal is comparatively small and remote, great difficulty is commonly encountered by anyone who tries to persuade the many to assemble a sufficient degree of pressure to operate upon the ruling powers with effect. On the part of the many, the natural interest in the matter being commonly weak, it takes additional aids to bring it into effective action. Strong arguments, no matter how strong they may be, will hardly be sufficient. For at best they can amount to no more than an indication of an interest which has already been shown to be weak. In addition to the utmost strength of which the argument is susceptible, then, strength of expression will also be necessary, or at least it will be regarded as necessary, and as such employed. But in proportion as this strength of expression is employed, the presentation of the argument stands exposed to those charges of heat, violence, and acrimony, the use of which it is the pretended object of the critic to prevent.

4. It is only when the proposed change will be conducive to, or at least not repugnant to the interest of the ruling powers addressed, that a simple statement of the alleged imperfection and its proposed remedy can with reason be expected to operate upon them with effect. But the fact

is that repugnance on their part, to a degree more or less considerable, is what on every such occasion ought in reason to be expected. If the imperfection in question deserves the name of *abuse*, then these ruling powers have, by the supposition, a special profit arising from the abuse, and consequently a special interest in its preservation and defense. Even if there be no such special interest, there exists in that quarter at all times, and in more shapes than one, a general and constant interest by which officials are rendered mutually averse to such applications. In the first place, in addition to their ordinary labors, they find themselves called upon to undertake a course of extraordinary labor which it was not their design to undertake, and for which some or all of them may feel themselves only indifferently prepared and qualified. In the next place, to the extent of the task imposed upon them, they find the business of government taken out of their hands. To that same extent their conduct is determined by a will which did not originate among themselves. And if, the proposed measure being carried into effect, the promoters of it should obtain reputation, respect, and affection, the result would inflict a blow upon the interest of their pride.

CHAPTER V

Accusation-Scarer's Device, or "Infamy Must Attach Somewhere"

Ad metum.

Exposition

THIS FALLACY CONSISTS in representing the imputation of calumny as necessarily and justly attaching to the man who, having made a charge of misconduct against anyone possessed of political power or influence, fails to produce evidence sufficient for conviction. Its manifest object is, as far as possible, to secure impunity to every shape of crime and transgression on the part of persons in office, by placing impediments in the path of possible accusers, and by holding out to the latter in case of failure, the prospect not only of disappointment, but of disgrace.

Exposure

" Infamy must attach somewhere." A dictum to this effect is ascribed to the Right Honorable George Canning, on the occasion of the debates in the inquiry into the conduct of the Duke of York in his office of commander-in-chief.[1]

In principle, an insinuation to this effect has unlimited application. It applies not only to all charges against persons possessed of political power, but with more or less force to all criminal charges against any persons whatever, and even

[1] The inquiry resulted in the enforced retirement of Frederick Augustus, Duke of York, second son of George III, on March 18, 1809, in consequence of his relations with Mrs. Mary Ann Clarke, who was convicted of profiting by her intimacy with the duke to extract money from officers by promising to recommend them for promotion. At the time George Canning (1770–1827) was Secretary of State for Foreign Affairs. — Ed.

to all the litigants on both sides of a civil case. If taken as a general proposition applying to all public accusations, nothing can be more mischievous as well as fallacious. Supposing the charge in question unfounded, it may have been made in bad faith, or by temerity only, or it may have been perfectly blameless. It is only in the case of a charge made in bad faith (with consciousness of its injustice) that infamy can properly attach to the one who makes it. A charge that is really groundless may have been honestly believed to have been well-founded, that is, it may have been believed with a sort of provisional credence, sufficient for the purpose of justifying an investigation.

But a charge may be perfectly groundless without attaching the smallest particle of blame upon him who brings it forward. Suppose him to have heard from one or more persons representing themselves as eye-witnesses, a story which *in toto* or perhaps only in important circumstances, should prove to be false and mendacious. How is the person who hears it, and acts accordingly, to blame? What sagacity can enable a man, in advance of legal investigation, a man who has no power to insure correctness or completeness in this sort of extra-judicial testimony, to guard against deception in such a case? Mrs. C. states to the accuser that the Duke of York knew of the business, stating a conversation as having passed between him and herself on the occasion. Suppose all that to be perfectly false, how was it possible for one in the accuser's situation to be apprized of its falsity?

The tendency of this fallacy is to prevent by intimidation all true charges whatever from being made, and so to secure impunity to delinquency of every description.

But the conclusion that because the testimony of a witness is false in one particular or on one occasion, it must therefore be false *in toto*, or more particularly that because it is false on some extra-judicial occasion, it must therefore be incredible upon judicial examination, is quite unwarranted. If such an argument were consistently and universally applied, no evidence at all ought ever to be received, or at least to be believed; for where was ever the human being of full age, by whom the exact line of truth had never in any instance been departed from in the whole course of his life?

The fallacy consists, not in pointing out instances of falsehood or inconsistency as lessening the credibility of a witness, but in regarding them as conclusive. Such errors do not warrant the turning of a deaf ear to everything else the witness may have to say. Suppose that falsehood has been uttered by the witness under the pressure of some strong and manifestly falsehood-inciting interest; be it so. Does it follow that falsehood will on every occasion — on the particular occasion in question — be uttered by him without any such incitement? Under the pressure of terror, the Apostle Peter, when questioned as to whether he was one of the adherents of Jesus, then in the situation of a prisoner just arrested on a capital charge, denied his being so. In so doing, he uttered a wilful falsehood, and thrice repeated it within a short space of time. Does it follow that the testimony of the apostle ought not on any occasion to have been considered capable of being true? If any such rule were consistently pursued, what judge who had ever acted in the profession of advocate, could with propriety be received in the character of a witness?

With respect to the object of the charge, accusations, whether made in court or at the bar of public opinion, so far from being less serious when made against a public rather than a private individual, are incomparably more serious. For in case of the truth of the accusation, the mischief is greater, and the demand for appropriate censure as a check is correspondingly increased. On the other hand, in case of non-delinquency, the mischief to the groundlessly-accused individual is less. Power, in whatever hands it is lodged, is almost sure to be more or less abused. The checks on power, in all their shapes, as long as they do not defeat the good purposes for which the power has been given, can never be too strong.

That against a man who has done nothing wrong, it is not desirable, whether his situation be public or private, that an accusation should have been preferred, and that he should have been subjected to the danger, alarm, and other shapes of evil attached to it, is too plainly true to be worth saying. But a public accusation, even supposing that it turns out to be groundless, is not altogether without its use. The evil it produces is not altogether without compensation: for by the alarm that it keeps up in those breasts which harbor a disposition to delinquency, it acts as a check, and contributes to the prevention and repression of wrong-doing. The mischief of an unfounded accusation against a public man is less than one against a private man; and the public man possesses, in the advantages attached to his office, a fund of compensation which the private man does not enjoy. Apprized as he ought to be of the enmity and envy to which his office exposes him, and not the private man, he ought to be proportionably prepared to expect it, and to be less sensibly affected by it when it comes.

PART THE THIRD
FALLACIES OF DELAY

The subject of which is Delay in various shapes; and the object, to postpone discussion, with a view of eluding it.

CHAPTER I

The Quietist, or "No Complaint"

Ad quietem.

Exposition

A NEW LAW OR MEASURE being proposed as the remedy for some incontestable abuse or evil, an objection is frequently raised as follows: "The measure is unnecessary; nobody complains of the disorder which your measure proposes to remedy. Now men are notoriously far from slow to complain, even when they have no cause for complaint, and especially under governments which admit of complaints. They are much less slow where any just cause for complaint exists." The argument amounts to this: Nobody complains, therefore nobody suffers. It constitutes a veto on all measures of precaution or prevention; and it goes on to establish a maxim for legislation, which is directly opposed to the most ordinary prudence in everyday life: that is – it enjoins us to build no parapets to a bridge until the number of accidents has raised a universal clamor.

Exposure

This argument would have more plausibility than it has, if there were any chance of complaints being attended to, and if the silence of those who suffer did not rise from despair occasioned by observing the fruitlessness of former complaints. The expense and vexation of collecting and addressing complaints to Parliament being great and uncertain, a complaint will ordinarily not be made without adequate expectation of relief. But how can any such expectation be entertained by anyone who is in the slightest degree acquainted with Parliament as at present constituted? Members who are independent of and not responsible to the people can have very few and very slight motives for listening to complaints, the redress of which would affect their own sinister interests. Again, how many complaints are repressed by the fear of attacking powerful individuals, and incurring resentments which may prove fatal to the complainant!

The most galling and oppressive of all grievances is that complicated mass of evil which is composed of the uncertainty, delay, expense, and vexation in the administration of justice. All but a comparatively minute proportion of it is factitious, as being the work originally of the man of law, and latterly, in part of its superstructure, of the man of finance. Its extent is such that, of the whole population, there is not one individual who is not at every moment of his life exposed to suffering under it, and there are few advanced in years who, in some shape or other, have not actually been sufferers from it.

By the price which has been put upon justice, or what goes by that name, a vast majority of the people, to some such proportion as nine-tenths or nineteen-twentieths, are altogether bereft of the opportunity of putting in for a chance at it. To those to whom, instead of being utterly denied any sort of chance at it, justice is sold, it is sold at such a price that to the poorest who can pay it at all, it is utter ruin, and even to the richest, a matter of serious and sensible inconvenience.

In comparison with this one scourge, all other political scourges put together are feathers. And, as compared with the income tax, even if the latter amounted to nine-tenths instead of one-tenth, a further addition to it would be a positive relief alongside the affliction produced by the sum assessed upon law proceedings. For the income tax falls upon none but the comparatively prosperous, and increases in proportion to their ability to sustain it, whereas the tax upon law proceedings falls exclusively upon those who are laboring under affliction — under that sort of affliction which, as long as it lasts, operates as a perpetual blister on the mind.

Here, then, is a matter of complaint for every British subject who breathes. Here injustice, oppression, and distress are all extreme. Yet complaint there is none. Why? Because by unity of sinister interest, and consequent confederacy between lawyer and financier, relief is rendered hopeless.

CHAPTER II

Fallacy of False-Consolation

Ad quietem.

Exposition

A MEASURE HAVING BEEN PROPOSED which has for its object the removal of some abuse — some practice the result of which is a mass of suffering greater than the harvest of enjoyment reaped from it by the few — this argument consists in pointing to the general condition of the people in this or that other country, in order to show that their condition, either in the particular respect in question or on the whole, is not so felicitous as, notwithstanding the abuse, it is in the country for which the reform is proposed.

"What is the matter with you? What would you have?" Look at the people there, and there; think how much better off you are than they are. Your prosperity and liberty are objects of envy to them. Your institutions are the models which they endeavor to imitate."

Now assuredly it is not the intention here to label with the name of fallacy the disposition to keep the eye of preference turned toward the bright side of things, especially when no prospect of special good suggests the opposite course. It is only when a particular suffering, produced as it appears by an assignable and assigned cause, has been pointed out as existing, and a man whose duty it is to relieve afflictions to the best of his ability, instead of attending to it himself, or inviting the attention of others to it, employs his exertions in turning his eyes or those of others to any other quarter in preference, that such action affords just ground for censure, and deserves to be listed among the fallacies.

Exposure

The depravity as well as fallaciousness of this argument can scarcely be exhibited in a stronger or truer light than by the name, " False-consolation," that is here used to characterize it.

1. Like all other fallacies upon this list, it is nothing to the purpose.

2. In his own case, no individual would accept it. Take any one of the orators by whom this argument is tendered, or any of the sages on whom it passes for sterling, and let any one of his tenants propose to pay him in his own coin with an observation concerning the general wealth and prosperity of the country in his mouth instead of a half-year's rent in his hand – will it be accepted?

3. In any court of justice, or any action for damages, did it ever occur to learned ingenuity to use the device of pleading assets in the hands of a third person, or of the whole country, in bar to a demand? What the largest wholesale trade is to the smallest retail, so much and more in point of magnitude is the relief commonly sought for at the hands of the legislator as compared to that commonly sought for at the hands of the judge. In the same ratio, and even more, is the injustice aimed at when this argument is employed in the seat of legislative power, as compared to the injustice that would be committed by using it in a court of law.

No country is so wretched, so poor in every element of prosperity as not to supply material for this fallacy. Even if the prosperity were ever so much greater than it is at present – take for the country any country whatever, and for the present time any time whatever – neither the injustice of this argument, nor its absurdity, would be in the smallest degree diminished.

It can never be employed seriously and pointedly in the character of bar to any measure of relief or improvement.

Suppose a bill brought in for converting an impassable road anywhere into a passable one. Would any man stand up to oppose it who could find nothing better to urge against it than the multitude and goodness of the roads we have already? No; when an argument so palpably inapplicable is offered as a serious bar to the measure in hand, it can only be for the purpose of creating a diversion. The hope is to turn aside the minds of men from the subject really in hand to a picture which may by its beauty engross the attention of the assembly, and make them forget momentarily for what purpose they came together.

CHAPTER III

Procrastinator's Argument, or "Wait a Little, This is Not the Time"

Ad socordiam.

Exposition

THE EXPRESSIONS THAT MAY BE GIVEN to the instrument of deception here brought to view are various to an indefinite degree; but in its nature and conception nothing can be more simple. Under this head belongs every form of words by which, in speaking of a proposed measure of relief, an intimation is given that the time at which the proposal is made, whenever it may be, is too early for the purpose. And this assertion is made without any proof being offered of its truth, such as, for instance, the lack of requisite information, or the need of some preparatory measures.

Exposure

This is the sort of argument which we so often see employed by those who, being actually hostile to a measure, are afraid or ashamed of being seen to be so. They pretend, perhaps, to approve of the measure; they only differ as to the proper time to bring it forward. But only too often their real wish is to see it defeated forever.

This constitutes in legislation the same sort of quirk which in judicial procedure is called a plea in abatement. And it has the same object, being never employed but on the side of a dishonest defendant, whose hope it is to obtain ultimate impunity and triumph by overwhelming his injured adversary with despair, impoverishment, and lassitude.

Any serious refutation would be ill bestowed upon so frivolous a pretense. The objection exists in the will, and not in the judgment of the objector. " Is it lawful to do good on the sabbath day? " was the question put by Jesus to the official hypocrites. Which is the properest day to do good? Which is the properest day to remove a nuisance? Answer, the very first day a man can be found to propose the removal of it; and whosoever opposes the removal of it on that day, will, if he dare, oppose its removal on every other.

The doubts and fears of the parliamentary procrastinator are the conscientious scruples of his prototype the Pharisee; and neither the answer nor the example of Jesus has succeeded in removing those scruples. Rest assured that whatever he finds too soon today, tomorrow he will also find too soon, if not too late.

Now it is true that occasionally an observation of this sort may be made by a friend to the measure in question, not as a fallacy, but as an expedient of unhappily necessary prudence. Whatever it may be some centuries hence, up to now the fault of the people has been, not groundless clamor against imaginary grievances, but insensibility to real ones. Not insensibility to the effect, the evil itself (for that, were it possible, far from being a fault, would be a happiness), but to the cause, the system or course of misrule. Thus it has come about that, throughout a vast proportion of the field of legislation, in regard to the grievances complained of, it has been true that the time for bringing forward a measure of effectual relief has not arrived. Why? Because the people, although groaning under the effect, have been prevented by the artifice and hypocrisy of their oppressors from entertaining any tolerably adequate conception of the cause. Hence they would at that time regard either with indifference or with suspicion the healing hand that came forward with the only true and effectual remedy. Thus it is, for example, with that Pandora's box of grievance and misery, the contents of which are composed of the evils opposite to the ends of justice.

CHAPTER IV

Snail's-Pace Argument, or "One Thing at a Time! Not too Fast! Slow and Sure!"

Ad socordiam.

Exposition

THE PROPOSED MEASURE OF REFORM requiring that a number of operations be performed successively or at short intervals, the fallacy here in question consists in holding up to view the idea of graduality or slowness as characteristic of the course which wisdom would dictate. As additional recommendations, the eulogistic epithets *moderate* and *temperate* are often used, with the implication that in proportion as the pace recommended by the word *gradual* is quickened, such an increased pace will justly incur the censure expressed by the opposite epithets: immoderate, violent, precipitate, extravagant, intemperate.

Exposure

This fallacy is neither more nor less than a contrivance for making out of a mere word an excuse for leaving undone an indefinite multitude of things which the arguer is convinced, and cannot forbear acknowledging to himself, ought to be done.

Suppose that there are half a dozen abuses which equally and with equal promptitude stand in need of reform. This fallacy requires, that without any assignable reason save that which is contained in the pronouncing or writing of the word "gradual," all but one or two of them shall remain untouched. Or suppose that six operations must be performed in order that some one of the abuses should be effectually corrected. To save the reform from the reproach of being violent and intemperate, and to secure for it the praise of graduality, moderation, and temperance, you insist that, of these half-a-dozen necessary operations, some one or two only shall be talked of and proposed to be done. One of them is to be embodied in a bill to be introduced at this session if it be not too late (which you contrive that it shall be), and another at the next session, which time being come, nothing more will be said about the matter, and there it will end. For this abandonment, no one reason that will bear looking at can be cited for the sidetracking of the five measures laid upon the shelf, but only an unmeaning assemblage of three syllables, the word "gradual."

A law suit which, to do full justice to it, might require six weeks, or six days, or six minutes in one day, has been made to last six years. In order that your caution and your wisdom may not be questioned, by a first experiment reduce the time to five years; then if that succeeds, in another parliament (should it be in the humor, which it is hoped it will not) reduce it to four years; then again to three years; and if it should be the good fortune of your grandchildren to see it reduced to two years, they may think themselves well off, and admire your prudence.

Nine-tenths of the people stand excluded from all hope of justice — to which in every eye but that of the plunderer and oppressor, rich and poor have an equal right — by the load of expense that has been heaped up. You propose to reduce this expense. The existence of the evil is admitted, and the nature of the remedy admits of no doubt. But by the magic of the three syllables *grad-u-al*, you will limit the remedy to a reduction of about one-tenth of this expense. Some time afterwards you may reduce it another tenth, and so on until, in about two centuries, justice may, perhaps, become generally accessible.

Importance of the business — extreme difficulty of the

business — danger of innovation — need of caution and circumspection — impossibility of foreseeing all consequences — danger of precipitation — everything should be gradual — one thing at a time — this is not the time — great occupation at present — wait for more leisure — people well satisfied — no petitions have been presented — no complaints heard — no such mischief has yet taken place — stay until it has taken place — such is the prattle which the magpie in office who, understanding nothing, understands that he must have something to say on every subject, and shouts it out to his audience as a substitute for thought.

Transfer the scene to domestic life, and suppose a man who, his fortune not enabling him without running into debt to keep one race-horse, has been for some time in the habit of keeping six. To shift to this private theater the wisdom and benefit of the gradual system, what you would recommend to your friend would be something like this: — Spend the first year in considering which of your six horses to give up; the next year, if you can satisfy yourself which one it shall be, give up one of them. By this sacrifice, the sincerity of your intention and your reputation for economy will be established; which done, you need think no more about the matter.

One source of delusion in arguments consists in giving an improper extension to some metaphor. It would be a service to the cause of truth if some advocate of the gradual system would let us into the secret of the metaphor he has in view, and give us an idea of some physical disaster caused by precipitation. A patient killed by too rapid bleeding, a chariot dashed in pieces by runaway steeds, a vessel capsized by carrying too much sail in a squall — all these images presuppose a degree of haste which, if pursued by the proposers of a political measure, would at once be apparent, and their obvious and assignable consequences would afford unanswerable arguments against them.

Nevertheless cases are not wanting in which a dilatory course may be consented to or even proposed by a friend of a reform measure. Suppose a dozen distinct abuses in the seat of legislative power, each abuse having a set of members interested in its support. If you attack the whole body at once, all these parties will join together to a certainty, and oppose you with their united force. Attack the abuses one by one, and it is possible that you may have but one of the parties, or at least less than all of them, to cope with at a time. To each branch of the public service belongs a class of officials, each of which has its sinister interest, the source of the mass of abuses on which it feeds. In the person and power of the universal patron, the fountain of all honor and of all abuse, all those sinister interests are joined and embodied in one. This is a branch of science in which no man is ever deficient. It is understood to perfection, even by him to whom nothing else ever was or ever can be clear.

If there be any case at all in which graduality may well be consented to with some reasonable prospect of advantage, it is one in which, without such consent, nothing whatever could be done. Under the existing system, even where good intention is not altogether wanting, so extreme is the timidity and apprehension of legislators, that without assurance of extreme slowness, no concurrence to a proposal for setting one foot before another at even the slowest pace, would be obtainable at all. The only pace at which such people can be persuaded to move is that which a traveler would take when journeying in a pitch-dark night over a road broken and slippery and edged on each side with precipices. Time is requisite for quieting timidity. Why? Because time is requisite for instructing ignorance.

Sec. 1. Lawyers: Their Interest in the Employment of This Fallacy

In proportion to the magnitude of their respective shares

in the general fund of abuse, the various fraternities interested in the support of abuses have each of them their interest in exploiting this as well as all the rest of the list of fallacies. But it is the fraternity of lawyers who, if they have not decidedly the most to gain by the dexterous management of this or other fallacies, have had the greatest quantity of practice and have derived the greatest degree of dexterity in the management of it.

Since judicial processes require reflection, and the greater the complication of the case, the greater the degree and length of the reflection required, lawyers have succeeded in establishing a general impression of a sort of proportion in quantity as well as a necessary connection between delay and attention to justice. Not that, in fact, a hundredth part of the established delay has actually originated in a regard for justice. But for want of sufficient insight into the impossibility of a regard for justice on the part of persons highly placed in terms of power, the men of the law have been unhappily only too successful in propagating the above impression. And it is, perhaps, to the prevalence of this error that the snail's-pace fallacy is indebted, more than to any other cause, for its dupes. Be that as it may, it is certainly true that in no track of reform has the slow rate of progress, which it is the object of this fallacy to secure, been adhered to with greater effect than in the law. To exemplify the truth of this observation, one need only look at the titles in the Statute Book. There one will see an abuse so monstrous that, on the part of the judicial hands by which it was manufactured, the slightest doubt of its mischievousness was impossible, yet generation after generation groaning under this abuse, and at length when the support of the abuse is deemed no longer practicable, comes at length a remedy. And what remedy? Never anything better than a feeble palliative.

CHAPTER V

Fallacy of Artful Diversion

Ad verecundiam.

Exposition and Exposure

THE DEVICE HERE IN QUESTION may be explained by the following directions or recipe for its manufacture and application: When a measure is proposed which on any account whatever it suits your interest or your humor to oppose at the same time that, because of its undeniable utility, you find it inadvisable to condemn directly, hold up some other measure which will present itself to the minds of your hearers as superior in order of importance. Your language, then, will be: Why that? (meaning the measure already proposed) Why not this? (mentioning some other which it is your hope to render more acceptable) By this means you will create a diversion, and turn aside from the obnoxious measure the affections and attention of the audience.

There is one case in which such a maneuver does not deserve the name of fallacy. That is where the pursuit of the first measure proposed would really operate as a bar or obstacle to another and more beneficial measure that is in competition with it. Where the measure first proposed, however, is of unquestionable utility, and you oppose it merely because it is adverse to your own sinister interest, you must not suggest any other measure of reform in its place unless every conceivable form of opposition by argument is considered hopeless. A measure altogether irrelevant and foreign to the purpose may be used to gain the time and attention that is necessary for the passage of the desired legislation; but such a move involves a risk of accomplishing little toward the diminution of the abuse in question. In this role of irrelevant counter-measure, any accidental business whatever may be made to serve, as long as it can be made to preoccupy a sufficient portion of the disposable time and attention of the legislators upon whose votes its passage or defeat depends.

Supposing the necessity for a relevant counter-measure to exist, and you have accordingly introduced it. Then the first thing to be done is to stave off the undesirable moment of its passage for as long as possible. According to the established usage, you give notice of your intention to propose a measure on the subject. It is of too great importance to be framed and enacted in the same year or session. You accordingly announce your intention for the next session. When the next session comes, the measure is of too great importance to be brought on the carpet at the beginning of the session. At that period it is not yet mature enough. If it is not advisable to delay any longer, you bring it forward just as the session closes. Time is thus gained, and without any decided loss of reputation; for what you undertook to do, has to the letter been performed.

When the measure has once been brought up, you have to choose between operations for delay and for rejection. Operations for delay have a manifest title to preference, for as long as their effect can be made to last, they accomplish their object, with no sacrifice either of design or of reputation. The extreme importance and extreme difficulty of the proposal are the themes on which you blow the trumpet, and which you need not be afraid of not hearing sufficiently echoed by others. When the treasury of delay has been exhausted, you must again choose between trusting to the chapter of accidents for the defeat of the measure, or trying to engage some friend to propose its rejection. But you will be unfortunate indeed if you can find no tolerably plausible opponents except among your friends specially commissioned for the purpose, for a kind of confidence more or less dangerous must in that case be reposed.

On the whole, however, you must be singularly unfortunate or unskilful, if by the counter-measure of diversion any considerable reduction of the abuse or imperfection should, in spite of your utmost endeavors, be effected, or any shred of reputation sacrificed that you need care about.

PART THE FOURTH
FALLACIES OF CONFUSION

The object of which is, to perplex, when discussion can no longer be avoided.

CHAPTER I

Question-Begging Epithets

Ad judicium.

BEGGING THE QUESTION, or *petitio principii,* is a fallacy that is very well known even to those who are not conversant with the principles of logic. In answer to a given question, the party who employs this fallacy contents himself by simply affirming the point in debate. Why does opium occasion sleep? Because it is soporiferous.

Begging the question is one of the fallacies enumerated by Aristotle. But Aristotle did not point out what it will be the object of this chapter to expose, namely – that the mode of using the fallacy with the greatest effect and the least risk of detection is by the employment of a single question-begging name.

Exposition and Exposure

Among the names employed to designate objects in the field of moral science, there are some by which the object is presented singly, unaccompanied by any sentiment of approbation or disapprobation, such as: desire, labor, disposition, character, habit, and so on. As compared to the two sorts of names which we are about to mention, these may be termed *neutral.*

There are other names to which the idea of general approbation is habitually attached, such as: industry, honor, piety, generosity, gratitude, and so on. These are termed *eulogistic* or laudatory. There are still others to which the idea of general disapprobation is habitually attached, such as: lust, avarice, luxury, covetousness, prodigality, and so on. These may be termed *disparaging* or vituperative.

Among the pains, pleasures, desires, emotions, motives, affections, propensities, dispositions and other moral entities, some, but very far from all, are furnished with names of all three sorts; some with none but eulogistic epithets; and others, and in a greater number, with none but those of a disparaging cast. By names I mean here, of course, single-worded names; for by words, take but enough of them, anything may be expressed.

It seems reasonable to think that originally all terms expressive of any of these objects were neutral. By degrees they acquired, some of them a eulogistic, some a disparaging cast. This change extended itself as the moral sense, if so loose and delusive a term may on this occasion be employed, advanced in growth.

But to return to the fallacy: its use neither requires nor so much as admits of being taught. A man falls into it only too naturally by himself, and the more naturally and freely, the less he is restrained by any such sense as that of shame. The great difficulty is to unlearn it. And our humble endeavor in the case of this, as of so many other fallacies, is by teaching it to unteach it.

In speaking of the conduct, behavior, intention, motive, or disposition of this or that man, if he is one who is indifferent to you, and if you care not whether he is well or ill thought of, you will employ the *neutral* term. If he is a man whom you wish to recommend to favor, especially a member of your own party, you will employ the *eulogistic* term. But if he is a man whom it is your aim to consign to aversion and contempt, you will employ the *disparaging* term.

To the proposition of which it is the leading term, every such eulogistic or disparaging epithet, secretly as it were, and in general insensibly, slips in another proposition of which the same leading term is the subject, and the assertion of praise or blame is the predicate. The person, act, or thing in question is *or* deserves to be, or is *and* deserves to be, an object of approbation or of disapprobation.

The proposition thus asserted is commonly one which requires proof. But when this fallacy is committed, the proposition is one that is not true, and cannot be proved. And when the person who employs the fallacy is conscious of its deceptive tendency, his object is, by employing the artifice of the question-begging name, to cause that to be taken for true which is not so.

By appropriate eulogistic and disparaging terms many sorts of misrule find justifying arguments that are conclusive in all too many eyes. Take, for example, the following eulogistic terms:

1. In war, *honor* and *glory*.

2. In international affairs, *honor, glory,* and *dignity.*

3. In finance, *liberality.* It is always at the expense of unwilling contributors that this virtue (for so it is listed by Aristotle) is exercised. For the word *liberality, depredation* may, in perhaps every case and without impropriety, be substituted.

4. In the higher levels of all official departments, *dignity,* though not in itself depredation, operates as a pretense for, and hence as a cause of *depredation.* Wherever you see *dignity,* you may be sure that money is requisite for the support of it; and that, insofar as the dignitary's own money is regarded as insufficient, public money raised by taxes imposed upon all other individuals, on the principle of

liberality, must be found to supply it. Exercised at a man's own expense, liberality may or may not be a virtue, according to the circumstances. Exercised at the expense of the public, it can never be anything better than a vice. Exercised at a man's own expense, whether or not it is accompanied by prudence and beneficence, it is at any rate disinterested. Exercised at the expense of the public, it is pure selfishness. It is, in a word, depredation; since money, or money's worth, is taken from the public in order to purchase for the liberal man respect, affection, gratitude with its eventual fruits in the shape of services of all sorts: in a word – reputation, power.

When you have a practice or a measure which you wish to condemn, find some more general name within the meaning of which the obnoxious practice or measure cannot be denied to be included. This should be a name to which you, and those whose interests and prejudices you have espoused, have contrived to annex a certain degree of unpopularity, so much so that it has become a bad name.

Take, for example, *improvement* and *innovation*. To pass censure on anything called an improvement would be too bold, and would even seem to be verging upon self-contradiction and nonsense. But *improvement* means something new, and so does *innovation*. Now happily for your purpose, *innovation* has contracted a bad name. It now means something new which is new and bad at the same time. Improvement means something new and good at the same time; and therefore, if the thing in question is good as well as new, innovation is not the proper name for it. Since the idea of *novelty* was the only idea originally attached to the word innovation, and the only one directly expressed in its etymology, you may well venture to employ the word innovation, since no man can readily convict that name of being an improper one on the face of it.

With the epithet thus chosen for the purpose of passing condemnation, the man who claims his measure is an improvement is not likely to be well satisfied; but that was to be expected. What you want is a pretense which your partisans can lay hold of for the purpose of giving a colorable warrant for passing upon the improvement that censure which you are determined and they, if not determined, are disposed to pass upon it.

The potency of this instrument of deception is most deplorable. It is only in recent years that its nature has been exposed, and the need and the extreme difficulty of such exposure have been equally made manifest. In every part of the field of thought and discourse, the effect of language depends upon the principle of association: the associations formed between words and those ideas of which they have become the signs. But in no small part of the field of discourse, one or the other of the two reciprocally correspondent and opposite affections — the amicable and the hostile — expressed by approbation and disapprobation — are associated with a word by a tie little less strong than that by which the object in question is associated with its name.

To do away completely with the effect of this fallacy, and render all minds without exception at all times insensible to it, seems scarcely possible. Even to diminish it must be a work of time. But in proportion as its effect on the understanding, and hence on the temper and conduct of mankind, is diminished, the good effect of such exposure will become manifest.

By such of these passion-kindling epithets as are of the eulogistic cast, comparatively speaking, no bad effect is produced. But by those which are of the disparaging cast, prodigious is the mischief caused, when considered from the moral point of view. By a single word or two of this complexion, what hostility has been produced! How intense its feeling! How wide its range! How full of mischief, in all imaginable shapes, its effects! [1]

[1] As an instance remarkable enough, though not for mischievousness, yet in respect to the extent and importance of the effects produced by a single word, note Lord Erskine's defense of the Whigs, avowedly produced by the application of the disparaging word *faction* to that party in the state. Ed. Note: The great forensic reputation of Thomas Erskine, first Baron Erskine (1750–1823) carried him briefly to the Lord Chancellorship in the Grenville ministry of 1806.

CHAPTER II

Impostor Terms

Ad judicium.

Exposition

THIS FALLACY IS SIMILAR TO the one which has just been exposed, but it is applied chiefly to the defense of things which under their proper names are manifestly indefensible. Instead, therefore, of speaking of such things under their proper names, the sophist has recourse to some name which, along with the indefensible object, includes some other, generally an object of favor. For instance, persecutors in matters of religion have no such word as persecution in their vocabularies; *zeal* is the word by which they characterize all their actions.

For the employment of this fallacy, two things are requisite: (1) a fact or circumstance which, under its proper name, and seen in its true colors, would be an object of censure, and which it is therefore necessary to disguise; and (2) the name which the sophist employs to conceal what would be deemed offensive, or even to bespeak a degree of favor for it by the aid of some happier accessory.[1]

[1] The device here in question is not peculiar to politicians. It may perhaps be clarified by an example drawn from private life. The word *gallantry* is employed to denote either of two dispositions which, although not altogether without connection, may either of them exist without the other. In one of these senses, it denotes the disposition on the part of the stronger sex to testify on all occasions towards the weaker sex those sentiments of respect and kindness by which civilized existence is so strikingly and happily distinguished from the life of savages. In the second sense, it is, in the main, synonymous with *adultery*, yet not so completely synonymous (as indeed words rarely are) but that, in addition to this sense, it presents an accessory and collateral one.

Having acquired from the habit of being employed in the other

Exposure

Example: Influence of the Crown

The sinister influence of the crown is an object which, if it were given a peculiar and distinctive name, would find perhaps but few defenders, but which, as long as no other name than *influence* is applied, will rarely meet with indiscriminate reprobation. *Corruption,* the term which, in the eyes of those to whom this variety of influence is an object of disapprobation, is the appropriate and only single-worded term capable of being employed to express it, and is a term of the disparaging cast. It cannot therefore be possibly employed by anyone who does not intend to join in the condemnation of the above practice. He is therefore obliged to

sense a eulogistic cast, it serves to give to the act or habit or disposition which in this sense it is employed to present, something of that eulogistic cast in place of the disparaging coloring suggested by its proper name. Whatever act a man regards himself as being known to have performed, he will not, in speaking of it, make use of any term which has a tendency to call forth any sentiment of disapprobation of the act or the agent by whom it has been performed. To the word *adultery,* an effect more or less unpleasant to every man is attached by the use of language. Whenever it is necessary to refer to an act of this obnoxious description, he will naturally be on the lookout for a term which presents it with an accompaniment, not of reproach, but rather of approbation. This approbation would not, in general, have accompanied it, were it not for the other meaning which the word is also employed to designate. Such a term he finds in the word *gallantry.*

There is a sort of man who, whether or not he is ready to commit any act or acts of adultery, would gladly be thought to have been habituated to the commission of such acts. But even this sort of man would neither be found to say of himself, "I am an adulterer"; nor would he be pleased to have it said of him, "He is an adulterer." But to have it said of him that he is a man of gallantry – that epithet the sort of man in question would regard as a compliment, by the sound of which he would be pleased and flattered.

find some term which will incontestably apply to the practice in question, and will be of the eulogistic or at least of the neutral class. To one or another of these classes belongs the term *influence.*

Under this term *influence,* when the crown is spoken of as possessing it, are included two species of influence. One of them is such that the removal of it could not be considered as desirable by anyone without an utter reprobation of the monarchical form of government, or as possible without its utter destruction. The other species is such that in the opinion of many persons its complete destruction or removal would if possible be desirable; and that, though its complete removal would not be practicable consistently with the continuance of monarchical government, yet the diminution of it to such a degree that the remainder would not have any practically pernicious effects, would not be impracticable.

It is upon the distinction between the influence of *will upon will* and that of *understanding upon understanding* that the utility or noxiousness of influence depends. To the influence of understanding upon understanding, by whomever exercised, on whomever exercised, and whenever exercised, the freest range ought to be left. It should be left, even if exercised by the crown, and on the representatives of the people. Not that this influence may not be productive of mischief to any amount, but that because, without this influence, scarcely any good can be accomplished, and also because, when it is left free, disorder cannot present itself without leaving the door open at least for the entrance of the remedy. The influence of understanding upon understanding is, in a word, none other than the influence of human reason — a guide which, like other guides, is liable to miss its way, or even dishonestly to recommend a wrong course, but which is the only guide of which the nature of the case is susceptible.

Under the British constitution, the principal and leading

part of the management of the public business belongs to the crown, and it is only by the influence of understanding upon understanding, or by the influence of will upon will, that anything can be done by anyone except by the immediate application of physical force. For the execution of the ordinary mass of duties belonging to the crown, the influence of will upon will is necessary, as long as it is exercised by the proper persons. This species of influence is necessary to be exercised upon all persons to whom the crown gives *orders*, for it is only by virtue of this sort of influence that orders, as distinct from mere suggestions or rational arguments, can be productive of any effect.

In all the instances so far cited, the use of influence may rightly be regarded as *legitimate*. The case in which the epithet *sinister* may be applied to the influence of the crown is one in which the person on whom the influence of will upon will is exercised is either a member of parliament or possessed of an electoral vote with reference to a seat in parliament. The ground of the charge is simply this: that insofar as the influence is effective, the will professed to be pronounced is not in truth the will of him whose will it professes to be, but rather the will of him in whom the influence originates, and from whom it proceeds. So much so that, if every member of parliament without exception in each house were under the influence of the crown, the monarchy, instead of being the limited sort of monarchy it professes to be, would be in effect an absolute one. It would not even remain in form a limited one any longer than it happened to be the pleasure of the monarch that it should continue so to be.

Under such circumstances, whatever law is acceptable to the crown, will not only be introduced but carried. No law that is not acceptable to the crown will be so much as introduced. Every judgment and every inquiry will be made or not made as the crown desires. Let misconduct of the servants of the crown, any or all of them, be in every imaginable shape ever so enormous, no application that is not acceptable to the crown will ever be made for their removal, meaning no such application at all. Raised to the pitch of this extreme case, there are few men in the country who would withhold the name of sinister influence.

Now it is undeniable that there are many members of parliament upon whom this sort of influence — of will upon will — is exerted. No man can be in the possession of any desirable position from which he is removable without its being exerted upon him. Say rather, without its exerting itself upon him, for no act or express intimation of will on the part of any person is necessary to produce the full effect of such influence in that situation.

Here, then, is the grand question in dispute. In the opinion of some, not the least particle of that sort of influence of will upon will exercising itself from the crown upon a member of parliament, or at any rate upon the elected representatives of the people in the House of Commons, is necessary; not the least particle is in any way beneficial; and not the least particle, insofar as it is operative, can be other than pernicious. In the language of those by whom this opinion is held, every bit of such influence is sinister influence, corrupt or corruptive influence, or, in one word, corruption.

There are others in whose opinion, or at any rate in whose language, such influence is not only innocuous but beneficial, and not only beneficial but absolutely necessary to the maintenance of the constitution in a good and healthful state. To this number must naturally be supposed to belong all those on whom this obnoxious species of influence is actually exercising itself.

CHAPTER III

Vague Generalities

Ad judicium.

Exposition

VAGUE GENERALITIES COMPREHEND a numerous class of fallacies resorted to by those persons who, in preference to the most particular and specific expressions which the nature of the case in question permits, employ others which are more general and indeterminate. An expression is vague and ambiguous when it designates, by one and the same name, an object which may be good or bad according to the circumstances. If, in the course of an inquiry concerning the qualities of such an object, that sort of expression is employed without a recognition of the distinction, the expression operates as a fallacy.

Take for example the terms *government, laws, morals,* and *religion.* The genus comprehended in each of these terms may be divided into two species, the good and the bad. For no one can deny that there have been and still are in the world, bad governments, bad laws, bad systems of morals, and bad religions. The bare circumstance, therefore, of a man's attacking government or law, morals or religion, does not of itself afford the slightest presumption that he is engaged in anything blameable. If his attack is directed only against that which is bad in each, his efforts may indeed be productive of any amount of good. This essential distinction the defender of abuse takes care to keep out of sight, and boldly imputes to his antagonist the intention to subvert all government, laws, morals, or religion.

But it is in the form of insinuation, rather than of direct assertion, that this argument is most commonly brought to bear. Propose anything with a view to the improvement of existing practice in relation to government at large, to the law, or to religion, and he will treat you to an oration on the utility and necessity of government, of law, or of religion. To what end? To the end that you will draw the inference which he desires you to draw: – that what is proposed has in its tendency something which is prejudicial to one or another or all of these objects of regard. Of the truth of the intimation thus conveyed, had it been made in the form of a direct assertion, some proof might naturally have been expected. By a direct assertion, a sort of notice is given to the reader or hearer to prepare himself for something in the shape of proof. But when nothing is asserted, nothing is on the one hand offered, and nothing is on the other expected, to be proved.

Exposure

Sec. 1. Order

Among the several cloudy expressions which have been commonly employed as cloaks for misgovernment, there is none more conspicuous in this atmosphere of illusion than the word *order*. This word is in a peculiar degree adapted to the purpose of a cloak for tyranny, for *order* is more extensive than law, or even than government. But, what is still more material, it has a eulogistic cast; whereas the words *government* and *law* still remain tolerably neutral in spite of the praise bestowed upon them in the lump. In this respect they are closer to the words *constitution* and *institutions*.

Thus, whether a measure or arrangement be a mere transitory measure or a permanent law, if it be a tyrannical one, be it ever so tyrannical, in the word *order* you have a term not only wide enough but in every respect better adapted than any other in the language to serve as a cloak for it. Suppose any number of men meeting together for the purpose of obtaining a remedy for the abuses they are suffering, and destroyed by a speedy death or a lingering one. What nobody can deny is, that by their destruction, *order* is maintained. For the worst order is as truly order as the best. Accordingly, a clearance of this sort having been effected, suppose in the House of Commons a Lord Castlereagh, or in the House of Lords a Lord Sidmouth,[1] to stand up and insist that, by a measure so undeniably prudential, order was maintained, with what truth could they be contradicted? And who is there who would have the boldness to assert that order ought not to be maintained?

To the word *order* add the word *good,* and the strength of the checks, if any, thus applied to tyranny would be little if at all increased. By the word *good* no other idea is brought to view but that of the sentiment of approbation of the person using the term. Good order is that order, be it what it may, of which it is my wish to be thought to approve.

Take the state of things under Nero, under Caligula. With just as indisputable propriety might the word *order* be applied in those instances as to the present state of things in Great Britain or in the American United States. What in the eyes of Napoleon Bonaparte was good order? That which it had been his pleasure to establish.

By the qualification *social,* the subject *order* is perhaps rendered somewhat less fit for the use of tyrants, but not much. The word *social* may indeed mean a state of things favorable to the happiness of society; but it may also mean anything having a place in society. No great addition to the happiness of society was ever supposed to be made by the war which, in Roman history, is known as the social war. Yet it was none the less a social one.

[1] Until 1821, Lords Castlereagh and Sidmouth were the leaders of the majority in their respective houses. Robert Stewart, Viscount Castlereagh (1739–1821) reached the zenith of his career at the Congress of Vienna, where he represented Great Britain in 1815. Henry Addington, Viscount Sidmouth (1757–1844) entered parliament in 1784, was elected speaker in 1789, and became home secretary in 1813. – Ed.

Whenever any suggestion is made that would lessen the sacrifice of the interest of the many to that of the few, *social* is the adjective which is used to designate the *order* of things to which the measure is pronounced hostile. By any subtraction from the mass of factitious delay, vexation, and expense out of which lawyers' profit is made to flow; by any lessening of the volume of needless and worse-than-useless emolument to office, with or without pretense of service rendered; by any addition to the quality or quantity of service furnished in return for such emolument; by every endeavor to persuade the people to place their fate at the disposal of any other agents than those in whose hands breach of trust is certain, and due fulfilment of it morally and physically impossible; — by all these, *social order* is said to be endangered, and threatened with destruction.

Proportionate to the degree of clearness with which the only true and justifiable end of government is held up to view in any public discourse, is the danger and inconvenience to which those rulers are exposed who, for their own particular interest, have been engaged in a habitual departure from that only legitimate and defensible course. Hence it is that, as compared to the words *order, maintenance of order*, the use of such words as *happiness, welfare, well-being*, vague as they are, is not altogether free from danger to such rulers. And when the description of the end is made still more determinate and instructive, as in the phrase *greatest happiness of the greatest number*, the danger and inconvenience to misgovernment, its authors and its instruments, becomes still more distressing and alarming. For then, men are referred to a rule whereby to measure the goodness or badness of a government, that is as simple and universally intelligible a standard as the multiplication table. By pointing men's attention to this end, and by the clearness of the light cast upon it, the importance of such words as *order*, which by their obscurity substitute for offensive light the useful and agreeable darkness, is more and more apparent.

Sec. 2. Establishment

In the same way again, *establishment* is a word used to protect the bad parts of establishments. It does so by charging all those who wish to remove or alter them with the wish to subvert all establishments, or all good establishments.

In the church establishment, the bad parts are: (1) Quantity and distribution of payment — its inequality creates opposing faults, both excess and deficiency. The excessive part calls men off from their duty, and, as in lotteries, tempts an excessive number of adventurers. The deficiency deters men from engaging in their duty, and renders them unable to perform it as it ought to be performed. (2) Mode of payment, such as tithes, a tax on food. This discourages agricultural improvements, and occasions dissensions between the minister and his parishioners. (3) Forms of admission, which compel insincerity, and are subversive of morality. As to purely speculative points it does not matter which side a man embraces, as long as he is sincere. But it is highly mischievous that he should maintain even the right side, where there happens to be any, when he is not sincere.

Sec. 3. Matchless Constitution

The constitution has some good points. It also has some bad ones. It gives facility, and, until radical reform shall have been accomplished, security and continual increase to waste, depredation, oppression, and corruption in every variety of shape and in every department.

Now in their own names respectively, waste, depredation, oppression, and corruption cannot be toasted. Gentlemen would not cry out: "Waste forever! Depredation forever!

Corruption forever!" But "The constitution forever!" This a man may cry, and does cry, and makes a merit of it.

The use of this instrument of rhetoric is at least as old as Aristotle. Equally old is the recipe for making it. For Aristotle himself has given it; and of how much longer standing the use of it may have been, it might baffle the sagacity of a Mitford [2] to determine. How sweet are gall and honey! How white are soot and snow!

Matchless constitution! There's your sheet-anchor! There's your true standard! Rally round the constitution, that is — rally round waste, rally round depredation, rally round oppression, rally round corruption, rally round election terrorism, rally round imposture — imposture on the hustings, imposture in the honorable House, imposture in every court of law.

Connected with all this boasting and toasting is a theory such as a Westminster or Eton boy of the sixth form, aye, or his grandmother, might be ashamed of. For among those who are the loudest in decrying theory, whenever any attempt is made at reasoning, some silly sentimental theory may almost always be found. The constitution, why must it not be looked into? Why is it that under pain of being *ipso facto* convicted of anarchism, we must never presume to look at it except with our eyes shut?

Because it was the work of our ancestors, of legislators, few of whom could so much as read, and those few having nothing before them that was worth reading. First theoretical presupposition: *wisdom of barbarian ancestors.*

And when from their ordinary occupation, the cutting of one another's throats, or those of Welshmen, or Scotchmen, or Irishmen, they could now and then steal a holiday, how did they employ it? In cutting Frenchmen's throats in order

[2] William Mitford (1744–1827) published his *History of Greece* in five quarto volumes from 1784 to 1810, and it remained the standard work until the time of Grote.— Ed.

to get their money. This was active virtue; leaving Frenchmen's throats uncut was indolence, slumber, inglorious ease. Second theoretical presupposition: *virtue of barbarian ancestors.*

Thus fraught with habitual wisdom and habitual virtue, they sat down and devised; and setting before them the best ends, and pursuing those best ends by the best means, they framed in outline — at any rate — they planned and executed our matchless constitution — the constitution as it stands, and may it forever stand!

Planned and executed? On what occasion? On none. At what place? At none. By whom? By nobody.

At no time? Oh, yes, says everything-as-it-should-be Blackstone. Oh, yes, says Whig after Whig. Anno Domini 1660; it was then that it was in its perfection, about fourteen years before James the Second mounted the throne with a design to govern in politics as they do in Morocco, and in religion as they do in Rome: to govern without parliament, or in spite of parliament.

What then says the only true theory, that which is uniformly confirmed by all experience? That on no occasion, in no place, at no time, and by no person possessing any adequate power, has any such end as the establishing the greatest happiness of the greatest number been hitherto entertained. And on no occasion has there been any endeavor on the part of any such person, or any wish for any happiness other than his own and that of his own connections, or any care about the happiness or security of the subject many, any further than his own happiness has been regarded as involved in it.

Among men of all classes, from the beginning of historic time, there has been a universal struggle on the part of each individual for his own security and the means and instruments of his own happiness, for money, for power, for reputation natural and factitious, for constant use and incidental vengeance. In the course of this struggle, under favorable circumstances connected with geographical situation, this and that little security has been caught at, obtained, and retained by the subject many as against the conjoined tyranny of the monarch and his aristocracy. No plan was pursued by anybody at any time. The good that became established, as well as the bad which remained, were alike the result of this universal scramble, carried on in the storm of contending passions as opportunity favored. At each period, some advantages were gained which in former periods were lost, and others which had never been gained.

Since the only regular and constant means of security is the influence exercised by the will of the people on those politicians who in the same breath admit and deny themselves to be their agents, and since the corruptive influence of the ruling few, the servants of the monarchy and the members of the aristocracy, increases with every passing day, the whole state of things grows every day worse and worse, and will continue to do so until even the forms of parliament are regarded as a useless encumbrance; and pure despotism, unless arrested by radical reform, takes the sceptre without disguise. While the debris of waste and corruption is continually accumulating, and while the avalanche composed of it is steadily rolling on, it seems absolutely impossible for things to continue long in their present state. Three varieties of government contend for the ultimate result: despotic monarchy undisguised, representative democracy under the form of monarchy, and representative democracy under its own form.

In this, as in every country, the government has been as favorable to the interests of the ruling few, and hence as unfavorable to the general interests of the subject many, or in one word as *bad*, as the subject many have persuaded themselves to suffer it to be. No abuse has been parted with except under a sense of necessity; no remedy has been applied except under similar pressure. But under the influence of circumstances in a great degree peculiar to this country, the ruling few have found themselves at times under the necessity of sacrificing this or that abuse, of instituting or tolerating this or that remedy.

Thus it has been thanks to the contest between the Whigs and the Tories that the liberty of the press, the foundation of all other liberties, has been suffered to grow up and continue. But this liberty of the press is not the work of intentional institution; it is not the work of law; what there is of it exists not by means of the law, but in spite of it. It is all of it contrary to law. By law there is no more liberty of the press in England, than in Spain or Morocco. It is not the constitution, it is not the force of law that we have to thank for it. It is rather the weakness of the law. It is not the Whigs that we have to thank for it, any more than it is the Tories. The Tories, that is, the supporters of monarchy, would destroy it, once assured of their never being in a condition to have need of it. The Whigs would destroy it with equal readiness, or concur in destroying it, provided they possessed that same comfortable assurance. But this has never been in their power; and to that impotence we are indebted for the zeal of both parties in behalf of the liberty of the press, and the support they have given to the people in the exercise of it. Without this arm they could not fight their battles; without this trumpet they could not call the people to their aid.

Such corruption was not the work of design in the head of any original framer of the constitution. But were this said without any further explanation, it might be thought to be implied that the constitution *was* the work of design — the whole, or the chief part of it — originally in some one head. The evil consequence of such a notion would be that, such a design being infinitely beyond the wisdom and virtue of any man of the present time, a planner would be sought in the most distant age that could be found. Thus the ancestor-wisdom principle would be the ruling principle of the search, and it would be fruitless and endless.

But the non-existence of any determinate design in the formation of the British constitution can be proved from history. The House of Commons is the characteristic and vital principle. In the year 1258 the first germ was planted by Simon de Montfort, Earl of Leicester, a foreigner and a rebel. In this first call to the people there was no better nor steadier design than that of obtaining momentary support for the rebellion.[3] The practice of seeing and hearing deputies from the lower orders before money was to be taken out of their pockets having thus sprung up, in the next reign Edward the First saw his convenience in conforming to it. From this time until the reign of Henry the Sixth, instances in which laws were enacted by kings, sometimes without consulting commons, sometimes without consulting them or lords, are not worth looking up.

Henry the Sixth's was the first reign in which the House of Commons had really a part in legislation. Until then, they had had no part in the penning of any laws; no law was penned until after they were dissolved. Here then, as late as about 1450 (between 1422 and 1458) the House of Commons as a branch of the legislature was an innovation. Until then, *constitution* (if the House of Commons be a part of it) there was none. Parliament? Yes; consisting of king and lords, *legislators*; and deputies of commons, *petitioners*. Even of this aristocratic parliament the existence was precarious. Indigence or weakness allowed its occasional reproduction; greater prudence and good fortune would have sufficed to throw it into disuse and oblivion — a mere possibility, like

[3] Simon de Montfort (*ca.* 1200–1265) with the Earl of Gloucester headed the opposition in the "Mad Parliament" of Oxford in 1258, and provided for parliamentary control of the triumvirate which he set up in 1264.— Ed.

the obsolete legislative bodies of France and Spain. All this while, and down to the time when the re-assembling of parliaments was imperfectly secured by indeterminate laws occasioned by the temporary nature of supplies of money and the constant cravings of royal paupers, if the constitution had been a tree, and both houses branches, either or both of the latter might have been lopped off, and the tree remained a tree still.[4]

After the bloody reigns of Henry the Eighth, and Mary, and the too short reign of Edward the Sixth, comes that of Elizabeth, who openly made a merit of her wish to govern without parliament. Members presuming to think for themselves, and to speak as they thought, were sent to prison for repentance. After the short parliaments produced in the times of James the First, and Charles the First, by profusion and distress, came the first long parliament.

Where is now the constitution? Where the design? Where the wisdom? The king having tried to govern without lords or commons, failed; the commons having extorted from the king's momentary despair the act which converted them into a perpetual aristocracy, tried to govern without king or lords, and succeeded. In the time of Charles the Second, there was no design but the king's design, which was that of arbitrary government through the instrumentality of a seventeen-year-long parliament. As yet, for the benefit of the people, no design was possible except in the seat of supreme power; and *there* it was hardly to be expected of human nature.

[4] Between Henry the Third and Henry the Sixth (1258 to 1422) it is true that there were frequent acts ordaining annual and even oftener-than-annual parliaments. (See Christian on Blackstone). Still these were but vague promises, made only by the king with two or three petty princes. The commons were not legislators, but petitioners who never saw until after enactment the acts to which their assent was recorded.

The circumstances to which the cry of matchless constitution is to a great degree indebted for its pernicious efficiency is that there has been one instance in which the assertion contained in it has proved incontrovertibly true. Until the American colonies threw off the yoke and became independent states, no political state possessing a constitution equalling or approaching theirs in goodness, was anywhere to be found.

But from its comparative goodness no well-grounded argument could at any time be afforded against any addition that could be made to its intrinsic worth. Suppose that persons happier than myself are not to be found anywhere; what reason is there for my forbearing to make myself as much happier than I am at present as I possibly can?

This pre-eminence is therefore nothing to the purpose. It is, moreover, every day growing less and less, so that while men keep on vaunting this spurious substitute for positive goodness, sooner or later it will vanish altogether. The supposition always is that it is the same on one day as on another. But never for two days together has this been true. Since the revolution took place it has never been for two days the same; every day it has been worse than the preceding. For by every day, in some way or other, addition has been made to the quantity of the matter of corruption by which the effect of the only efficient cause of good government, the influence of the people, has been lessened.

A pure despotism may continue in the same state from the beginning to the end of time; and by the same names the same things may always be signified. But a mixed monarchy such as the English never can continue to be the same. The names may continue in use for any length of time; but by the same names the same state of things is never signified for two days together. Since the quantity of the matter of corruption in the hands of the monarch grows every day greater and greater, so does the amount of practice in its application, and the skill with which it is applied, as well as the patience and indifference with which its application is witnessed. Hence the comparative quantity of influence wielded by the people, and the security it affords, grows every day less and less.

While the same names continue to be used, no difference in the things signified is ever perceived, except by the very few who, having no interest either in being themselves deceived or in deceiving others, turn their attention to the means of political improvement. Thus it was that with stupid indifference or acquiescence the Roman people sat still while their constitution, a bad and confused mixture of aristocracy and democracy, was converted into a pure despotism.

With the title of representatives of the people, the people behold a set of men meeting in the House of Commons, originating the laws by which they are taxed, and concurring in all the other laws by which they are oppressed. Only in proportion as these their nominal representatives are actually chosen by the people, and, in case of their betraying their trusts, are removable by them, can such representatives be of any use. But, with a small number of exceptions – too small to be on any one occasion capable of producing any visible effect – these pretended representatives are neither removable, nor have they been chosen by them. If, instead of a House of Commons and a House of Lords, there were two Houses of Lords, and no House of Commons, the ultimate effect would be just the same. If it depended on the vote of a reflecting man whether, instead of the present House of Commons, there should be another House of Lords, his vote would be in the affirmative. The existing delusion would then be dissipated completely, and the real state of the nation would be visible to all eyes. A great deal of the time and trouble which is now expended in those debates which are still suffered for the purpose of keeping the delusion alive would be saved.

Even now, no man can be found so insensible to shame as to affirm that any real representation exists. But there is, it is claimed, a *virtual* one; and with this those persons are satisfied who think it worth their while to maintain the delusion, together with those who are, or appear to be, deluded. If those who are so well satisfied with a virtual representation which is not real, would only be equally well satisfied with a virtual receipt of taxes on the one hand, and a virtual payment of taxes on the other, all would be well. But this unfortunately is not the case. The payment of taxes is only too real, while the falsity of the ground on which their exaction is even pretended to be justified, representation, is a matter of such incontestable verity and universal notoriety that to assert its existence is a cruel mockery.

Sec. 4. Balance of Power

In general, those by whom this phrase has been used have not known what they meant by it. It has had no determinate meaning in their minds. Should any man ever find for it such a determinate meaning, it will be this — that of the three branches into which the aggregate powers of government are divided under the English constitution, it depends upon the will of each to prevent the other two from doing anything, that is, from giving effect to any proposed measure. It is easy to see the evil of this arrangement, for one sure effect of it is, that whatever in the judgment of any one of the three branches is contrary to its own sinister interest, will not be done. At the same time, notwithstanding the supposed security, whatever measure is supposed by all three of them to be conducive to their aggregate interests will be carried into effect, no matter how plainly it may be contrary to the universal interest of the people. No abuse in which all three have an interest will ever be removed; and no improvement in the prevention of which any one of them has an interest will ever be made.

The fact is, that wherever in this connection the word *balance* is employed, the sentence is mere nonsense. By the word balance in its original import was meant a pair of scales. By a derived meaning in arithmetic it signifies the sum by which the aggregate on one side of an account exceeds the aggregate on the other side. But the meaning at present under discussion does not correspond with either of these. In fact the idea would be better conveyed by the word *equipoise*: meaning two bodies so connected that when one is in motion, the other will move in proportion. But neither is actually in motion, since they weigh exactly the same. And since the object of the figure of speech in this instance is not to give, but to prevent, a clear view of the matter, a nonsensical expression serves better than a significant one. The subject is thrown into confusion, and the mind's eye in its endeavors to see into it are bewildered; and that is what is wanted.

It is by a series of simultaneous operations that the business of government is carried on. It works by a series of actions; and when the actions cease, the body politic, like the natural body, is at an end. But a balance holding two equal weights does not move. To have action, the weights must be made unequal, and then they will no longer be in equipoise.

In the illustration in question, instead of the two weights in a common pair of scales, there are said to be three which are supposed to be antagonistic to one another. But this is not in itself a conclusive objection to the metaphor, since, from one and the same fulcrum or fixed point you might have three scales hanging with weights in them.

But the fallacy often assumes a more elaborate shape. " The constitution is composed of three forces which, antagonizing each other, cause the business of government to be carried on in a course which is different from that in which it would be carried on if it were directed solely by any one. The course which results is the product of the joint influence of all three, each contributing in the same proportion to the final result." This is the image of the composition and resolution of forces. It is not as familiar as that of the balance, but it is free from the former's absurdity. On the whole, however, the matter will not be found to be much mended by its use.

In proportion as the business of government is well conducted, it is uniformly carried on in a direction tending toward a certain end: the greatest happiness of the greatest number. In proportion as they are well conducted, the operations of all the agents concerned will tend toward the same end. Now in the case in question, there are three forces, each supposedly tending to a certain end. But take any one of these forces and the direction in which it acts: suppose it acting alone, undisturbed, and unopposed. The end in view will be attained by it. Now add another of these forces acting in exactly the same direction. The same end will be attained, only so much sooner; and so again if you add the third force. But if the direction in which the second force acts be supposed to be ever so little different from the direction in which the first force is headed, then the greater the difference, the further will the aggregate or compound force be from the exact attainment of that end.

But in the present illustration, how is it with the three forces? So far from their all tending to a single end, the end that each is seeking is as opposite to that end as possible. It is true that among the three forces, that relation really prevails by which a sort of compromise is produced: the ultimate direction taken is not exactly the same as it would have been if any one of the three forces had acted alone, and clear of the influence of both of the others. But with all this complication, what is the direction taken by the whole machine?

One which carries it to an end almost opposite to that which a single force would reach.

In plain language, here are two bodies of men, and one individual more powerful than the two bodies put together, say three powers in all — each busily pursuing its own interest, each interest a little different from the two others, and not only different from, but opposite to, the interest of the greatest number of the people. Of the substance of the people, each gets for itself and devours as much as it can. Each of them, were it left alone, would be able to get more of that substance than it does at present. But in its endeavors to get that more, it finds itself counteracted by the two others. Each therefore permits the two others to help themselves to their respective shares; and thus it is that harmony is restored.

Nevertheless there is one instance in which the image of a balance of forces may be employed with propriety, namely — in international law and international relations. Supposing it to be attainable, what is meant by a balance of forces or balance of power is in that field a legitimate object, beneficial to all the parties concerned. What is that object? It is, in one word, *rest* or *peace*, the absence of all hostile action, together with the absence of all coercion exercised by one of the parties over another: that rest which is the fruit of mutual and universal independence. Here then, as between nation and nation, the result of well-balanced forces is peace and prosperity.

But has the state of rest brought about by balance the same prosperous result internally? No; on the contrary; the consequence of universal rest in the body politic, as in the natural body, is death. No action on the part of the officers of government, no money collected; no money, no subsistence; no subsistence, no service; no service, and everything falls to pieces. Anarchy takes the place of government; government gives way to anarchy.

Returning to the metaphor of the composition of forces,

suppose that they are: the power of the monarch, the power of the House of Lords, and the power of the people. Then one-third would be engaged in promoting the interest of the people, and two-thirds in sacrificing it. Of every three hundred pounds of taxes raised upon the whole people, one hundred would be applied to their use, and the other two hundred to the use of the two confederative powers, the king and the House of Lords.

This state of things would not be very advantageous to the majority of the people, and not very conducive to good government. But it would be more conducive to good government than is the real state of things, and to a prodigious degree. For what is the real state of things? The power mentioned above as the power of the people, is actually the power of the monarch and the power of the House of Lords, together with that of the rest of the aristocracy, under another name.

Sec. 5. Glorious Revolution

This is a Whig's cry. A revolution for the people? No; but, what is much better, a revolution for the Whigs — the revolution of 1688. There is your revolution: the only one that should ever be thought of without horror. A revolution for discarding kings? No; only a revolution for changing them. There would be some sense in changing kings, for there would be something to be got by it. When their forefathers of 1688 changed James for William and Mary, William got a good slice of the cake, and they got the rest among them. If, instead of being changed, kings were discarded, what would the Whigs get by it? Nothing; they would lose not a little. They would lose their seats, unless they really sat in them and did the business they were sent to do; and then they would lose their case.

The real uses of the revolution of 1688 were: the putting to an end of the tyranny, political and religious, of the

Stuarts: — the political tyranny, governing without parliament, and forcing the people to pay taxes without even so much as a show of consenting to them through their chosen deputies; the religious tyranny, forcing men to join in a system of religion which they believed not to be true. But the deficiencies of the revolution were: — leaving the power of governing, and especially that of taxing, in the hands of men whose interest it was to make the amount of the taxes excessive, and to exercise misrule in a great variety of other ways.

As far as by security given to all, and hence by a check applied to the power of the crown, the particular interest of the leaders of the aristocracy in the revolution promised to be served, such security was established and such a check was applied. But where security could not be afforded to the whole community without trenching upon the powers of the ruling few, there it was denied. Freedom of election as against the despotic power of the monarch was established; freedom of election as against the disguised despotism of the aristocracy, Tories and Whigs together, remained excluded.

CHAPTER IV

Allegorical Idols

Ad imaginationem.

Exposition

THE USE OF THIS FALLACY is the securing of respect to persons in public office independently of their good behavior. It is in truth only a modification of the preceding fallacy of Vague Generalities. It consists in the substituting for men's proper official label the name of a fictitious entity to whom, by customary language, the attribute of excellence has been attached.

Examples: (1) *Government,* for members of the governing body; (2) *The law,* for lawyers; and (3) *The church,* for churchmen. The advantage is that it obtains more respect for them than would otherwise be bestowed upon the class under its correct name.

Exposure

1. *Government* – in its proper sense, in which it designates the set of operations for carrying on the public business, it is true, and it is universally acknowledged, that almost everything valuable to man depends upon it: security against evil in all shapes, from external adversaries as well as domestic. 2. *The law* – meaning the execution of the law. It is by this that men receive whatever protection they are afforded against domestic adversaries and disturbers of their peace. By *government – law – the law,* are therefore brought to view the most natural and worthy objects of respect and attachment within man's sphere; and for conciseness and ornament (not to mention deception) the corresponding fictitious entities are feigned, and are represented as being constantly occupied in the performance of the above-men-

tioned all-preserving operations. As to the real persons so occupied, if they were presented in their proper character, whether collectively or individually, they would appear clothed in their actual qualities, good and bad together. But, as presented by means of this allegorical contrivance, they are decked out with all their good and acceptable qualities, and divested of all their bad and unacceptable ones.

Under the name of the god Aesculapius, Alexander the impostor, his self-constituted high priest, received to his own use the homage and offerings addressed to the god. Within comparatively recent years the word *government* has obtained a latitude of import which is in a peculiar degree adapted to the sinister purpose here in question. From being abstract, its meaning has become, as the phrase is, concrete. From signifying the system in all its parts taken together, it has come to denote the whole assemblage of the individuals employed in the carrying on of the system, those who for the time being happen to be members of the official establishment, and of these more particularly, and even exclusively, the ones who are members of the administrative branch. To designate either that branch of the system or the members belonging to it, the language had already furnished the word *administration*. But that word would not have suited the purpose of this fallacy; accordingly, for the proper word administration the too ample and hence improper word government has been substituted, probably by a mixture of design and accident, by those who have had an interest in turning it to account.

This impropriety of speech being thus happily and successfully established, the fruits of it are gathered every day. Point out an abuse, point to this or that individual deriving a profit from the abuse, and up will come the cry: "You are an enemy of government!" Then, with a little news in advance, "Your endeavor is to destroy government!" Thus you are a Jacobin, an anarchist, and so forth. And the greater the pains you take for causing government to fulfill its professed ends to the greatest possible perfection, the greater the pains which will be taken to persuade those who wish, or who are content to be deceived, that you desire and endeavor to destroy it.

3. *The church* — is an expression particularly well adapted to the purpose of this fallacy. To the elements of confusion which it shares with government and law, it adds others which are proper to itself. Some of the meanings which are indifferently attachable to the word are: (1) Place of worship; (2) Inferior officers engaged by government to take a leading part in the ceremonies of worship; (3) All the people considered as worshippers; (4) The superior officers of government by whom the inferior mentioned above are engaged and managed; and (5) The rules and customs respecting these ceremonies.

The use of this fallacy to churchmen is the securing to them of a share of coercive power. Their sole public use and even their original destination is serving the people in the capacity of instructors in a branch of learning now more thoroughly learned without them than with them (that is, from unordained Methodists, Quakers, and others). In the phrase "Church and State," churchmen are represented as superior to all non-churchmen; by "Church and King" they are represented as superior to the king. Fox and Norfolk were struck off the list of privy counselors for drinking a toast "To the sovereignty of the people;" [1] the reduction would be greater if all were struck off who have ever drunk a toast "To Church and King."

According to Bishop Warburton, the people in the char-

[1] At a dinner of the Whig Club at the Crown and Anchor tavern on January 24, 1798, the Duke of Norfolk gave the toast, and was dismissed from his lord lieutenancy in consequence. Charles James Fox repeated the toast at a dinner held early in May, and on May 9, 1798, his name was erased from the privy council.— Ed.

acter of the Church, meeting with all themselves in the character of the State, agreed to invest the expounders of the sacred volume with a large share of the sovereignty. Against this system, the lawyers, their only rivals, were estopped from pleading its seditiousness in bar. In Catholic countries, the churchmen who compose holy mother church possess one beautiful female by whom the people are governed in the field of spiritual law, within which has been enclosed as much as possible of profane law. But by Protestants, on holy mother church the title of Whore of Babylon has been conferred; they recognize no holy mother church. In England the churchmen, or a large portion of them, compose two *Almae Matres Academiae,* kind Mother Academies or Universities.

The object and fruit of all this ingenuity is the protection of all the abuses and imperfections which attach to this part of the official establishment. The church being so excellent a being, none but a monster can be an enemy or foe to her. To each and every question having in view some reform or improvement in the official establishment, the answer is one and the same: "You are an enemy to the Church, monster, anarchist, Jacobin, leveller, and so on."

Suppose that one asks such questions as these: 1. What does this part of the official establishment do, except give further explanation to one book, of which more explanation has been given already than the longest life would suffice to hear? 2. Does this not presuppose a people incapable of being taught to read for themselves? 3. Would the book be not more read if each person, being able to read, had it constantly by him to read all through, than by their being at liberty some of them to go miles to hear small parts of it? 4. Should not the same rules apply to the connection between reward and service in the church as are observed in profane affairs. Can a man serve a place without being there? In

Scotland, where there is less pay, is not residence more general, and clerical service more abundant and efficient?

Answer: "Enemy of the church, and, if English-bred — Apostate!"

In Scotland, does any evil arise from the absence of bishops? In the House of Lords, any good? Is not non-attendance in the House of Lords more general even than non-residence elsewhere? And is not such non-attendance felt rather as a relief than as a grievance?

Answer: "Enemy of the church!"

In Ireland, what is the use of Protestant priests to Catholics who will neither hear nor see them, and to whom they are known as plunderers? By such exemption from service, is not the value of Irish preferment actually increased? In eyes not less religious than gracious, is not the value of religion inversely as the labor, as well as directly as the profit? Is not this estimate the root of those scruples, by which oaths imposed to protect Protestantism from being oppressed are employed to secure to it the pleasure of oppressing?

Answer: "Enemy of the church!"

CHAPTER V

Sweeping Classifications

Ad judicium.

Exposition

THE DEVICE OF THOSE who employ sweeping classifications as a fallacy is that of ascribing to an individual object (person or thing) the properties of another object, only because both are ranked in the same class by being designated by the same name. By its nature, this fallacy is equally applicable to undeserved eulogy as well as undeserved censure; but it is more frequently used for the purpose of censure, since its efficiency is greater in that direction.

Exposure

Example 1. *Kings — The crimes of kings*

In the heat of the French Revolution, when the lot of Louis XVI was standing between life and death, among the means employed for bringing about the catastrophe that ensued, was the publication of a multitude of inflammatory pamphlets, one of which had for its title "The Crimes of Kings."

Kings being men, and all men standing exposed to those temptations by which some of them are led into crime, material could hardly be wanting for a book so entitled. And if there are some crimes to the temptation of which men thus elevated stand less exposed than the inferior orders, there are others to which, perhaps, that elevation renders them but the more prone. But on the above occasion, the object of the pamphlet was probably to set up this syllogism: All criminals ought to be punished; all kings are criminals, and Louis XVI is a king; therefore Louis XVI ought to be punished.

Example 2. *Catholics — Cruelties of Catholics*

Not long ago, in the course of a controversy over whether that part of the community which is composed of persons of the Catholic persuasion ought or ought not to be kept any longer in a state of degradation, a book made its appearance under the title of "The Cruelties of Catholics." The object of the publication was to keep Catholics still debarred from any relief from the oppressions under which they labor. Justice will not be done to the complexion of this argument, and to the mind that could bring it forward, unless an adequate conception is formed of the practical consequences to which it would lead.

To all Catholics of the present and all future time will be attributed whatever cruelties and other enormities were committed in former times by persons who were called by the same indefinitely comprehensive name. Whatever harsh treatment, therefore, this argument warrants the bestowing upon these their namesakes of the present era, the same argument will continue to justify as long as there remains a single individual who may truly be characterized by the same name.

Be they what they may have been, the barbarities of the Catholics of former times have their limits. But the barbarity of this abhorrer of Catholic barbarities has, in respect of the number of his intended victims, no limits other than those of time. The barbarity of the man who, to put an end to the cruelties of kings, did what he could to extirpate the class of kings, was, comparatively speaking, confined within a narrow range. All Europe could hardly have supplied his scaffold with a dozen victims. But after crushing as many millions of the vermin whom his piety and his charity had marked out for sacrifice, the zeal of this abhorrer of Catholic cruelties would have been in the condition of the tiger depicted by a traveler in Southern Africa, as lying breathless with fatigue amid a flock of antelopes.

By the same injurious device the painter of the crimes of kings might no less conclusively have proved the necessity of crushing the English form of the Protestant religion, and of consigning to the fate of Louis XVI its present head. For by order of King James the First, two men whose misfortune it was not to be able to form, in relation to some inexplicable points of technical theology, the same conception that was entertained, or professed to be entertained, by the royal ruler and instructor of the people, were burnt alive. Now the present sovereign George the Fourth not only bears in common with James the First the two different titles, Protestant of the Church of England, and King of Great Britain, but is actually of the same blood and lineage with that royal and triumphant champion of local orthodoxy.

If, indeed, in the authentic and generally received doctrines of the religion in question, there were anything which compelled its professors to burn or otherwise destroy or ill-treat all or any of those who differed from them, and if by any recent overt act an adherence to those dissocial doctrines had appeared in practice, then just ground would be afforded for whatever measures of security were deemed necessary to safeguard other men from the effects of such doctrines and practices. But by no doctrines of their religion are Catholics compelled to burn or otherwise ill-treat those who differ from them, any more than James the First was compelled by the doctrines of the Church of England to burn those poor Anabaptists.

If in Ireland, where three-fourths or more of the population is composed of Catholics, no ill-treatment has within the memory of man been bestowed by Catholics as such upon Protestants as such, while in the same country so much ill-treatment has been bestowed by each of these persuasions upon the other on other accounts, it may be said that it is because the power of so doing with impunity is not in Catholic hands. But in countries where the Catholic religion is the predominant religion, and in which, at the same time as in our islands, barbarity on the score of heresy was exercised by Catholics according to law, and to the most conspicuous degree, no instance of such barbarities has occurred for a long course of years. Even in Spain, I have been assured by persons fully informed, no instance of a capital execution for any offense against religion has taken place within the last twenty-two or twenty-three years. And in the capital of Mexico, a gentleman of distinction from this country was recently conducted into every apartment of the prison of the Inquisition by the Grand Inquisitor himself, for the purpose of being assured by ocular demonstration of the non-existence of any prisoner within its walls.

CHAPTER VI

Sham Distinctions

Ad judicium.

Exposition

THE NATURE OF THIS DEVICE may be explained by the following directions for the use of it. When any existing state of things has too much evil in it to be defensible *in toto,* or proposals for amending it are too plainly necessary to be rejectible *in toto,* the evil and the good being nominally distinguished from each other by two corresponding and opposite terms, eulogistic and disparaging, but without any real, determinate difference between the two, you declare your approbation of the good by its eulogistic name, thus reserving to yourself the advantage of opposing the same thing under its disparaging name, and *vice versa* with respect to disapprobation of the evil.

Exposure

Example 1. *Liberty and Licentiousness of the Press*

Understanding by the press every instrument employed or employable for the diffusion of human discourse by visible signs, we find that it has two distinguishable uses, moral and political. The moral use consists in whatever check it may prove capable of opposing to misconduct in private life; the political, to similar misconduct in public life. It must do this by directing against the persons to whom such misconduct is imputable, a more or less considerable portion (according to the nature of the case) of disapprobation and consequent ill-will.

If no check at all were opposed to such conduct by means of the press, the sorts not prohibited and punished by law would range uncontrolled. The political effect of such exemption from control would be power uncontrollable, or despotism at the hands of those who happen to exercise the functions of government. This would even extend to those forms of conduct which were punishable by law, since by delay, vexation, and expense, abused individuals would be prevented from demanding the prosecution of the guilty.

At the same time, on the other hand, the press cannot be altogether free, lest on the pretense of exposing conduct that has actually taken place, it may wrongly impute to this or that individual some misconduct that did not take place. Insofar as any such imputation happens to be false, the effects of the liberty of the press will be of an evil cast, and the disparaging name of *licentiousness* will naturally be invoked.

Here then is a dilemma, two evils between which a choice must absolutely be made. Leave to the press its perfect liberty, and along with the just imputations, which alone are the useful ones, will come, and in an unlimited proportion, unjust imputations, from which evil is liable to arise. But to him whose wish it really is that good morals and good government should prevail, the choice need not be so difficult as at first sight it may seem to be.

Let all just imputations be buried in utter silence, and what you are sure of is this: that misconduct in every part of the field of action, moral and political, public and private, will range without control — free from all that sort of control which can be applied by the press, and not by anything else. On the other hand, let all unjust imputations find through this channel an unobstructed course, still there is neither the certainty of the same amount of evil — the personal suffering threatened — nor in general any near approach to it. When it is open to accusation, the very same channel is not less open to defense. If by accident that is not the case, it constitutes a different and distinct evil, for which is required a different and distinct remedy.

He therefore who has truth on his side will have all that advantage which it is the nature of truth to confer. Is that advantage an inconsiderable one? On the contrary supposition is founded whatever is done in the reception and collection of judicial evidence, and in the administration of whatever goes by the name of justice.

In the meantime, if there be any arrangement by which the door may be shut against unjust imputations without incurring to an equal amount that sort of evil which is liable to result from the exclusion of just ones, then so much the better. But unless and until such arrangement shall have been devised and carried into effect, the tendency and result of all restrictions having for their object the abridging of the liberty of the press cannot but be evil on the whole.

To shut the door against such imputations as are either unjust or useless, leaving it open at the same time to such as are just and useful, would require a precise, determinate, correct, and complete definition of the term by which the abuse, the improper use, the (supposedly) preponderantly pernicious use of the press is to be characterized. This definition would have to be established by those in whom the supreme power of the State is vested. No such definition has ever been given, nor can such a definition be reasonably expected at the hands of any person so situated, since the act of establishing it would curtail their power and prejudice their interest.

While this necessary definition remains unestablished, they remain free to continue and to increase the abuses and misgovernment by which their interests are at present advanced. And until that definition is given, every disclosure by the press of any abuse from the practice of which they derive any advantage is *licentiousness.* The *liberty* of the press is only such disclosure as will occasion them no apprehension of inconvenience.

No such definition can be given but at their expense —at

the expense of their arbitrary power of misconduct in the affairs of government, their power of sacrificing the public to their own private interest. Should the line ever be drawn, then it will be true that licentiousness may be opposed without opposing liberty. But while it remains undrawn, opposing licentiousness means opposing liberty.

This being understood, what is the nature of the device here in question? It consists in employing the sham approbation given to the species of liberty here in question under the name of *liberty*, as a mask or cloak for the real opposition given to it under the name of *licentiousness.* It is in the licentiousness of the press that the judge pretends to see the downfall of that government, the very corruption of which he is himself upholding by inflicting upon all within his reach the punishments which have been provided by his predecessors for the suppression of all those disclosures by means of which the abuses by which he profits might be checked.

Example 2. *Reform, temperate and intemperate*

For the designation of that species or degree of political reform which is meant to be represented as excessive or pernicious, the language affords no single-worded name like *liberty.* To make the nominal (and pretended real) distinction, recourse must therefore be had to epithets, such as violent, intemperate, outrageous, theoretical, speculative, and so forth.

If a man indulges himself in the practice of reprobating reform in terms thus vague and comprehensive with the aid of the subterfuge provided by these disparaging epithets, without designating the species or degree of reform to which he objects by any more particular or determinate word, you may in general venture to conclude that it is not to any particular species or degree that his real disapprobation and intended opposition confines itself, but that it extends to every species or degree of reform which he thinks would be effective in correcting the existing abuses. For, between all abuses whatever, there exists a connection; and between all persons who see any advantage to themselves in any abuse whatever, there exists in point of interest a close and sufficiently understood connection, as has already been intimated. No one abuse can be corrected without endangering the existence of every other abuse.

Suppose a person inwardly determined to prevent the adoption of any reform, but convinced that it is necessary or advisable to present the appearance of a desire to contribute to reform. Using the device or fallacy here in question, he will represent that which goes by the name of reform as distinguishable into two species: one of them a fit subject for approbation, the other for disapprobation. The class which he professes to approve he will characterize by some epithet of the eulogistic cast, such as moderate or temperate or practicable. To the other of these two nominally distinct species he will, at the same time, attach an epithet of the disparaging cast, such as violent, intemperate, extravagant, outrageous, theoretical, speculative, and so forth.

Thus, then, in profession and to all appearances, there are in his conception of the matter two distinct and opposite species of reform, to one of which his approbation, and to the other his disapprobation, is attached. But the species to which his approval is attached is actually an *empty* species, one in which no individual is, or is intended to be contained. The species to which his disapproval is attached is, on the contrary, a crowded species, a receptacle into which the whole contents of the genus reform are intended to be included.

CHAPTER VII

Popular Corruption

Ad superbiam.

Exposition

THE ARGUMENT OF THIS FALLACY may be expressed in the following terms: — The source of corruption is in the minds of the people. So rank and extensively seated is that corruption, that no political reform can ever have any effect in removing it.

This was an argument brought forward against parliamentary reform by William Windham[1] in the House of Commons, and by him insisted upon with great emphasis. He was among the disciples, imitators, and cooperators with Edmund Burke, that Burke to whom the subject many were the swinish multitude — swinish in nature, and therefore apt to receive the treatment given to swine. In private life, that is, in their dealings with their immediate associates, especially those of their own class, many of these haters and calumniators of mankind at large, are not unamiable. But seduced by that sinister interest which they have in common, they encourage in one another the anti-social affection where it operates upon the most extensive scale. If, while thus encouraging himself in the hating and contemning the people, a man of this cast finds himself hated by them, the fault is surely more in him than in them. And whatever it may happen that he suffers at their hands, he has only himself to blame.

[1] William Windham (1750–1810) was Secretary at War in 1794 and again in 1804. A dignified and commanding figure in the House, he opposed parliamentary reform at the same time that he urged reform of the Army.— Ed.

Exposure

This fallacy consists in giving to the word *corruption,* when it is applied to the people, a sense altogether indeterminate. All that is distinctly expressed is the distaste of the speaker towards the persons spoken of, imputing to them a bad moral character or cast of mind without giving any intimation of its particular nature. It is the result of a thick confusion of ideas, whether it be sincere, or affected for the purpose.

In a parliamentary election each voter acts as a trustee for himself and for all the rest of the community in his exercise of the suffrage. Now if he is precluded from the possibility of promoting his own particular interest to the prejudice of the remainder of the universal interest by the manner in which his vote is cast (as by ballot), then the only interest of his which he has any prospect of promoting by his vote is his share of the universal interest. And for doing this, he sees before him no other possible means except voting for the candidate who is likely to render the most service to the universal interest.

No matter how small his share in the universal interest may be in his eyes, it will still be sufficient to turn the scale when there is nothing in the opposite scale. This emptiness of the opposite scale is supposed to be made as certain as can be by the secrecy of the ballot. Thus the voter's estimate of the value to him of his share in the universal interest will only have to be large enough to overcome his aversion to labor, or love of ease. He will then repair to the polling place and vote for the candidate who, in his eyes, is likely to do most service to the universal interest. If his estimate is too small, he will fail to cast his vote; and though he will do no good to the universal interest, he will do it no harm.

Thus it is that, under a properly-devised system of election procedure, the least benevolent set of men, supposing them equal in self-regarding prudence, will render as much service to the universal interest as the most benevolent. And by " least benevolent " is meant, if anything is meant, the " most corrupt."

But, on the other hand, if the system of election is so arranged that it enables a man to promote his own separate interest, then it is notorious that no ordinary portion of benevolence in the shape of public spirit will be sufficient to prevent breaches of trust from being committed on all sides.

The word " corruption," then, has no determinate and intelligible application to the subject many to which it has been exclusively applied. But to the class of the ruling few, it has a perfectly intelligible application: one that is as clear as the existence of the sun at noon-day. Pretending to be, all of them, chosen by the subject many, when only a small proportion of them are chosen in that manner, the ruling few profess to act as trustees who are bound to support the interest of the subject many. Instead of so doing, being bribed by one another under the ruling *one,* and with money exacted from the subject many, they act in constant breach of their trust, serving in all things their own particular and sinister interests. By so doing they sacrifice that interest of the subject many, which, together with that of the ruling few, composes and constitutes the universal interest. Applied to such conduct, the words *corrupt, corruption, corruptors, corruptionists* assuredly lack nothing in the way of intelligibility.

A circumstance which renders this fallacy especially insidious and dangerous, is a sort of obscure reference made by it to the doctrine of original sin as set forth in the 39 articles of the Church of England. It is not necessary on this occasion to explore the religious bearings of the doctrine. The field here in question is that of politics; and, applied to this area, the fallacy would lay the axe to the root of all government. It would do so, not only to political remedies, but to all other remedies against that preponderance of self-regarding interest over social interest and affection, which is essential to man's existence, but which, for the creation and preservation of political society and man's well-being in it, has to be checked by a force formed within itself. It tends to the exclusion of all laws, and particularly of all penal laws, since it holds that what is amiss cannot be remedied by the infliction of punishment applied to such crimes as those against fair and honest elections.

By employing this fallacy, a man affords himself a double gratification. He gratifies his own anti-social pride and insolence; and he affords his argument a promise of effectiveness by feeding the same appetites in the breasts of his auditors, whom he sees to be bound to him by a common sinister interest. Out of the very sink of immorality, in truth, is this fallacy drawn: from a sentiment of hatred and contempt, not only for all one's fellow-countrymen, but supposedly for all mankind.

" So bad are men in themselves, that no matter how badly they are treated, they cannot be treated worse than they deserve to be. Of a bad bargain, says the proverb, make the best; of so bad a crew, let us make the best for ourselves. No matter what they may suffer, they deserve it." If Nero had thought it worth his while to look around for a justification, he could not have found a more pat one than this. For it is an argument which, while it harmonizes completely with the worst passions of the worst of men, screens its true nature in some measure from the better men, by the cloud of confusion in which it wraps itself.

In regard to corruption and incorruption, vice and virtue, how then stands the plain and real truth? That there is the most corruption in the ruling few, because in their hands has been the power of serving their own private and sinister interest at the expense of the universal interest. And in so doing they have, in the design and with the effect of making instruments of one another for the accomplishment of that perpetual aim, been the disseminators of vice and corruption. That there has been least of vice and corruption in the subject many, because they have not been so much affected by sinister interest, and have thus been left free to pursue the course pointed out to them, partly by men who have found a personal interest in giving their conduct a universally beneficial direction, and partly by discerning and uncorrupted men, lovers of their country and mankind, who have not had their generous affections overpowered by any particular self-regarding interest.

Nearly akin to the cry of popular corruption is the following common exhortation: "Instead of reforming others, instead of reforming your betters, instead of reforming the state, the constitution, the church, everything that is most excellent — let each man reform himself, let him look at home, he will find there enough to do, and what is within his power, without looking abroad and aiming at what is out of his power, and so on." Language to this effect may at all times be heard from anti-reformists, and always, as the tone of it manifests, accompanied with an air of triumph, the triumph of superior wisdom over shallow and presumptuous arrogance.

One feature which helps to distinguish it from the cry of popular corruption is the tacit assumption of incompatibility between the operation condemned and the operation recommended. When closely examined, it will be seen that no assumption could be more groundless. But it is certain that if every man's time and labor is exclusively employed in the correcting of his own personal imperfections, no part of it can be employed in the endeavor to correct the imperfections and abuses of government. Thus the mass of those imperfections and abuses will go on, never diminishing, but perpetually increasing, along with the torments of those who suffer by them and the comforts of those who profit by them; which is exactly what is wanted.

CHAPTER VIII

Observations on the Seven Preceding Fallacies

IN THE SEVEN PRECEDING FALLACIES and in others of similar nature, the device resorted to is uniformly the same, and consists in avoiding the question in debate by substituting general and ambiguous terms in the place of clear and particular names. In other fallacies the argument advanced is generally irrelevant, but argument of some kind they do contain. In these fallacies there is no argument at all; there are words and voices and nothing else.

To find the only word that will suit his purpose, the defender of corruption is obliged to make an ascent in the scale of generalization, to soar into the region of vagueness, until he arrives at a word whose extensiveness of import enables him to confound thought by confounding language. Thus he may without immediate fear of detection defend with a fair chance of success an object which he would have no hope of defending under its proper and peculiar name.

When of two terms, one generic and the other a specific term included under it, the specific term alone is proper, then to substitute the generic term for it is to be ambiguous, and to commit error and deception. Opposed to this "aërial" mode of argument is that known and designed by the name of *close reasoning*. Now in proportion as a man's mode of reasoning is close (always supposing his intention to be honest), he employs for the designation of every object he wishes to indicate, the most exact and particular expression he can find. He does his best to find language which will distinguish his object as clearly as possible from what is not to his purpose and what he does not wish to bring into view. In proportion as a man is desirous of contributing to the welfare of the community, and at the same time is skilled in the means which most certainly and directly lead to the attainment of that end, he will look out for that plan of nomenclature and classification in designating each proposed measure, by which the degree of its conduciveness or repugnancy to that end may be the more easily and correctly judged.

Thus in regard to offenses, he will not be content with the generic term applicable to all of them, but he will find and assign to each type of offense a name which will show the relation which it bears to the other types, and the place which it occupies in the aggregate assemblage of such obnoxious acts. He will employ a classification by which the several *modes* in which wounds are inflicted upon the general welfare are made perceptible, such as: (1) Offenses against individuals other than oneself; (2) Against a man's self; (3) Against this or that particular class of the community; and (4) Against the whole community without distinction.[1]

For the opposite reason, in proportion as a man is desirous of promoting his own personal or any other private interest to the sacrifice of the general welfare, he will employ for the designation of proposed measures that plan of nomenclature and classification which will mask as effectually as possible the real tendency of the measure which he proposes to support. In the English law under the principle of arrangement which until comparatively recent times was the only one, and which is still the predominant one, offenses were classified as treasons, felonies unclergyable, felonies clergyable, *premunires*, and misdemeanors. Such were the groups into which offenses were thus huddled together, that their classical names gave not the slightest intimation of the nature of the mischief included under each.

By the first four of these five names what is designated

[1] See *Traités de Législation*, Vol. I, 172. *Classification des délits.*

is not the offense itself, but the treatment given to the offender by way of punishment for committing it. By the fifth name, not even that much is indicated: it is the miscellaneous class of punishable offenses that are not included in any of the other classes.

What is the cause of a scheme or arrangement that is so incompatible with clear thinking and useful instruction? Its creation may be traced to one source; its continuance to another. So great is its antiquity that, for its creation, the weakness of the public intellect presents an adequate cause. The origin of treason and felony – terms imported at the Norman conquest with the rest of the nomenclature of the feudal system – is lost in the darkness of barbarism. Religion in the form of a perversion of Christianity gave birth after a long and hard labor to the distinction between clergyable and unclergyable. Religion by a still further perversion gave birth to *premunires* in the reign of Edward the Third.

For the designs of those whose interest it is that misrule should be perpetuated, and hence that the useful information by which it might be put to shame, and, in time, to flight, should be suppressed as long as possible, nothing could be more serviceable than this primeval imbecility. Under these class-names in general, and particularly under felony, acts of any description are capable of being classified with equal propriety, or rather with equal absence of propriety. These include acts which are altogether free from any of those mischievous consequences which alone warrant the punishment of offenders who commit them. Thus offenses which are actually clear of any really mischievous quality have been created, and still continue in existence, in convenient abundance.

By this contrivance the open tyranny of the lawyer-led legislator, and the covert tyranny of the law-making judge are placed at the most perfect ease. The keenest eye cannot descry the felonies which are destined to be created by the touch of the sceptre upon the pattern of the old. The liveliest imagination cannot portray to itself the innocuous acts destined to be fashioned or swollen into felonies. Analogous to this ancient English system is the one lately contrived by the legislators of France and their forced imitators in Germany. *Faute, contravention, délit, crime,* are classes rising one above another to a climax of severity. But all of them are designative, and loosely so, rather of the treatment to which the offender is subjected at the hands of the judge, than of the sort of act which deserves the treatment, much less of its grounds or justifying reasons in terms of the quality and quantity of the mischief involved.

Lawyer-craft in alliance with political tyranny may be identified as the source of this confusion in the English case; lawyer-craft in subjection to political tyranny in the French case. In England it is to the interest of the man of law that the rule of action should remain in a state of as general uncertainty and unintelligibility as possible. As law-advisor and advocate, he wants to continue to be master of men's purses by the simple expedient of pronouncing on every occasion the suitable legal jargon. As judge, he wants to continue to be master of a man's purse, his reputation, his condition in life, and even of life itself; and all to as complete a degree, and with as little odium and suspicion as possible. This is the state of things which it always has been, and always will be the interest of the man of law to perpetuate; and this is the state of things which he has hitherto been able to continue, and which accordingly does continue to exist to this day.

In France, where the man of law is not the ally of the politician but his slave, that which the politician strives to keep out of the view of the citizen is not what the law *is*, but rather what the law *ought to be*. Having brought the rule of action within a compass the narrowness of which, in respect of the quantity of words used, has never been equalled, the tyrant of France has displayed, by this one act of charity, a quantity of merit ample enough in itself to cover no inconsiderable portion of his sins. But nevertheless the examples of vague generalities afforded by such a code are sufficiently striking. For it provides at the top a set of classes so boundless in their extent that they are capable without impropriety of including almost any object on which it might be convenient to stamp the factitious label desired. Noxiousness of any specific sort is a quality which it is not in the power of despotism to communicate to any act; but it is only too easy for the supreme power to cause persons committing an act to undergo such and such a punishment.

Here then are so many instances in which the turn of the man in power not being capable of being served, or at least so well served, by giving an object its most particular and proper name, one of more general and extensive import is employed for the purpose of deception. This makes possible an exercise of power which, under its correct name, would have been seen to be improper and mischievous, and would hence have been dissipated.

CHAPTER IX

Anti-Rational Fallacies

Ad verecundiam.

Exposition

WHEN REASON IS FOUND or supposed to operate in opposition to a man's interests, his endeavor will naturally be to render the faculty itself, and whatever issues from it, an object of hatred and contempt. As long as a government tolerates any sort of abuse from which its members derive a profit and in the continuance of which they consequently have an interest, if reason is against them, they will to the same extent be against reason.

Instead of reason we might here use the word *thought.* Reason is a word that implies not merely the use of the faculty of thinking, but the right use of it. But sooner than fail of its object, sarcasm is directed not merely at reason, but against all thought, as if there were something about thought itself which rendered its exercise incompatible with useful and successful living.

Some examples of this fallacy are:

1. Sometimes a plan whose adoption would be contrary to the official person's interests is without more ado pronounced a *speculative* one. By this observation all need of rational and deliberate discussion, such as objections that the end proposed is not a fit one, or that the means are unfit means, is considered as being superseded. To the word speculative may be added or substituted a number of synonymous terms, such as: *theoretical, visionary, chimerical, romantic, utopian.*

2. Sometimes the following distinction is taken, and a concession made: the plan is good in *theory,* but would be

bad in *practice*. That is to say, its being good in theory does not hinder its being bad in practice.

3. Sometimes, as if in consequence of further progress made in the art of irrationality, the plan is pronounced to be *too good to be practicable*; and furthermore its being as good as it is, is thus represented as the very cause of its being bad in practice.

4. In short, such is the perfection at which this art has at length attained, that the very circumstance of a plan's being susceptible of being called a *plan* has been gravely offered as a circumstance sufficient to warrant its rejection with hatred, or even more galling in the eyes of the millions, with contempt. Listen to Mr. Brougham[1] on the subject of parliamentary reform in 1810: "Looking at the House of Commons with these views, my object would be to find out its chief defects and to attempt the remedy of these *one by one*. To propose no *system, no great project,* nothing which pretended even to the name of a *plan,* but to introduce in a temperate and conciliatory manner . . . one or two separate bills."

Yet that is the way in which the members of parliament must be addressed if a man is to have any chance of doing anything with them. And it will continue to be so until by radical reform the house is purged of a class of men characterized by the most complete ineptitude for their positions. Indeed, to find their level, one must descend, on the scale of probity and intellectual ability, to a point below that of the very dregs of the people. Oh what a picture is here drawn of them, and by how experienced a hand! How cutting, yet

[1] Henry Peter Brougham (1778–1868), later Baron Brougham and Vaux, entered parliament in 1810, and broke with Bentham in 1818. Nevertheless Halévy regards Brougham, who reached the Lord Chancellorship in 1830, as none the less Bentham's "disciple, his spiritual son." Elie Halévy, *The Growth of Philosophic Radicalism,* 264, 510.

how unquestionably just, the perhaps unintended, or perhaps intended satire. To avoid awakening the real terrors of some and the sham terrors of others, all consistency, all comprehensive acquaintance with the field of action must be abjured. When idolatry in all its forms shall have become extinct, and the words *wise ancestors* are no longer an instrument of deception, but a by-word, with what scorn will not ancestors such as these be looked back upon by their posterity?

Exposure

Sec. 1. Abuse of the Words Speculative, Theoretical, etc.

It is the abuse of these epithets which constitutes a fallacy; and such abuse occurs whenever, in a serious speech, and without the allegation of any specific objection, such an epithet applied to the measure is exhibited as a sufficient reason for rejecting it.

What is altogether beyond dispute is that many a measure has been proposed to which this class of epithets is justly applicable. But a man's ideas must be woefully indistinct, or his vocabulary deplorably scanty, if he cannot contrive to intimate what, in his view, there is bad about a measure without employing an epithet the effect of which is to bring into contempt the very operation of thinking itself.

The fear of theory has, to a certain extent, its foundation in reason. There is a general propensity in those who adopt this or that theory to push it too far. They are prone to set up a general proposition which is not true until certain exceptions have been noted, without any of those exceptions, and to pursue it, without regard to them, into instances in which it is false, fallacious, and repugnant to reason and utility. The propensity to push theory too far is acknowledged to be almost universal.

But what is the just inference? Not that theoretical

propositions, that is, those of considerable extent, should because of their extent be regarded as false *in toto*; but only that in the particular case inquiry should be made whether, supposing the proposition to be a general rule generally true, this may not be a case which, to keep things within the limits of truth, reason, and utility, should be regarded as an exception.

Every man's knowledge is, in its extent, proportioned to the extent as well as the number of those general propositions of the truth of which, they being true, he has the persuasion in his own mind. In other words, the extent of his theories comprises the extent of his knowledge. And if, indeed, his theories are false, then, in proportion as they are extensive, he is all the more deeply steeped in ignorance and error.

But from the mere circumstance of its being theoretical, the falsehood of a proposition is inferred by these enemies-to-knowledge as if it were a necessary consequence. This is about as sensible as inferring, as the necessary consequence of a man's speaking, that what he says is false.

One would almost think that in the process of thinking there was something wicked, or at least unwise. Everybody seems to feel or to fancy the necessity of disclaiming it. " I am not given to speculation." " I am no friend to theories." Speculation, theory, what are they but *thinking*? Can a man disclaim speculation, can he disclaim theory, without disclaiming thought as well? If those words do not mean thought, they mean nothing; for unless they call for a little more thought than ordinary, theory, speculation, mean nothing at all.

To escape from the imputation of meditating destruction to all mankind, a man, it would seem, must disclaim everything that raises him above the level of a beast. A plan proposes a wrong end; or, the end being all right, it proposes a wrong set of means. If this be what a man means, why can he not say so? Would not what he says then have somewhat more meaning, be a little more consistent with the principles of common sense, with common honesty, than saying of it that it is theoretical, that it is speculative?

Sec. 2. Utopian

The epithet *utopian* would seem to be rightly applied when felicitous results are represented as about to take place in the event of the adoption of a proposed plan, when no causes adequate to the production of such effects are to be found in it. In Sir Thomas More's romance, in which the epithet has its origin, a felicitous state of things is announced by the very name. Considering the age in which he lived, even without adverting to the brand of religion of which he was so honest and pertinacious an adherent, we may rest assured that the institutions stated by him to have been productive of the effect, had actually, taking them altogether, very little tendency to produce it.

Such, in general, is likely enough to be the case with the portion of political felicity exhibited in any other romance. And hence the epithet *romantic* is likely enough to be well applied to any political plan which comes to the notice of the public in any such literary vehicle. Causes and effects being alike at the command of this species of poet in prose, the credit for any felicitous event is as easily ascribed to *uninfluencing circumstances,* or even to *obstacles,* as to actual *causes.*

If the established state of things, including the many varieties of abuse interwoven in it, were anything like what its undiscriminating defenders represent it as being, namely – a system of perfection, then it might properly be referred to as a utopia. For it would be in truth a felicitous result flowing from causes not having it in their nature to be productive of any such effects, but having it in their nature to be productive of just the contrary effects.

In every department of government, say the advocates of

reform, abuses and imperfections are abundant, because the persons who exercise the powers of government have been placed in such circumstances, partly by their own artifice, partly by the supineness of the people, that abuse is a source of profit to themselves. Under such circumstances, if any expectation were really entertained, that by their hands any considerable reduction in the sum total of abuse will ever be made, to no other expectation could the charge of utopianism be with more propriety applied. Effects so produced would not only be produced absolutely without a cause, but in the face of irresistible obstacles.

But in that same system there has all along been preserved by the many, a faculty every now and then exercised, although much too seldom and too weakly, of creating more or less uneasiness in the minds of their rulers without any great inconvenience or danger to themselves. In that state of things there is nothing of utopianism, for it is a matter of universally notorious fact; and in this faculty on the part of the many who suffer by abuses, of creating uneasiness in the bosoms of those who profit by them – in this invaluable, and, except in America, unexampled faculty, rests the only chance, the only source of hope for the future.

Sec. 3. Good in Theory, Bad in Practice

Even in the present stage of civilization it is rare that reason, looking toward the end in view, determines a matter of government; and the cause is the existence of so many institutions which are adverse to the only proper end – the greatest happiness of the greatest number – since they favor the interest of the ruling few. Custom, blind custom, established under the dominion of that separate and sinister interest, is the guide by which most governmental operations are conducted. Insofar as the interest of the governed many has appeared to the governing few to coincide with their own separate interests, it has been pursued; but insofar as it has appeared to be incompatible with those interests, it has been neglected or opposed.

One consequence of this is, that when by accident a plan comes on the carpet which does aim at the only legitimate end of government, if it departs in ever so slight a degree from the beaten track of custom, the practical man, the man of routine, does not know what to make of it. Its goodness, if it be good, and its badness, if it be bad, are equally removed from his sphere of observation. If it be conducive to the end, that is more than he can see, because the end is one at which he has never been accustomed to aim. He has not been used to inquiring, concerning any plan that is proposed, what its proper end is, and whether it is suited to the attainment of that end.

What he has been used to, is always to consider whether the new plan is similar, in matter and form, to his previous practices. If it happens to be different, it throws him into a sort of perplexity. If the plan is a good one, and good reasons have been advanced in its favor, so that he feels unable to contest them or to bring forward preponderant disadvantages, he will be afraid to commit himself by pronouncing it bad. In order to show his candor, especially if he is on good terms with you, he may go so far as to admit that the plan is good, that is, *in theory*. But having made this concession, it being admitted and undeniable that theory is one thing and practice another, he will make a distinction, and, to repay him for his concession, he will propose that you admit that it is not the thing for practice. It is good in theory; but, alas, bad in practice.

Now it is altogether beyond dispute that there have been plans in abundance which have been found to be bad in practice, and that many others would have been found bad in practice if they had been tried. It is likewise indisputable that there have been many of each description which have appeared to be, and have been by some persons so considered, plausible in theory.

What is here meant to be denied, however, is that a plan which is essentially incapable of proving good in practice can properly be said to be good in theory. Whenever, for example, out of a number of circumstances necessary to the success of a plan, any one of them is omitted in the calculation of the expected effects, such a plan will be found defective in practice to the extent of the importance of the omitted part. If that part was important, and there were no compensating advantages, the plan might even be called *bad*. When the plan for the illumination of the streets by gas-lights was laid before the public by its alleged inventor, one item of capital expense, namely — that of the gas-pipes, was omitted. But that omission hardly proved that the whole idea was a bad one, being counterbalanced by the prodigious advantages offered.

In the field of political economy, most of the plans which have been adopted and employed by government for enriching the community by money given to individuals have been bad in practice. But if they have been bad in practice, it is because they have been bad in theory. In the account taken of probable profit and loss, some circumstance has been overlooked which has later been found necessary in order to render the plan advantageous on the whole. This circumstance has usually been the advantage which would have been reaped from the money employed, either in the form of additions to capital by other means, or by added comfort through its expenditure. In terms of wealth, we may say that the portions which were merely *transferred* from hand to hand by these operations, were erroneously considered as having been *created*.

Sec. 4. Too Good to be Practicable

There is one case in which, in a certain sense, a plan may rightly be said to be too good to be practicable, and that case a very comprehensive one. It is where, without adequate inducement in the shape of personal interest, a plan requires for its accomplishment that some individuals or class of individuals shall have sacrificed his or their personal interest to the interest of the whole. Where the success of such a plan hinges upon a sacrifice by some one individual or small group of individuals, it is not altogether beyond the sphere of moral possibility. Instances of such a disposition, though extremely rare, are not altogether lacking: by philanthropy, by secret ambition, such miracles have now and then been wrought. But when a large body of men, or a multitude of individuals taken at random, are expected to make such a sacrifice, it is then that the expectation deserves to be called *utopian*. In such a case the observation "Too good to be practicable" might not be wanting in truth.

But that is not the intimation which the phrase is commonly meant to convey. Those who employ it are generally those who, finding a plan adverse to their interests, but not open to attack on the ground of its general utility, have recourse to this fallacy as an instrument of contempt, to prevent those persons from looking into it who might otherwise have been disposed to do so. It is by the fear of seeing the plan put into practice that they are drawn to speak of it as impracticable.

Not wishing to exhibit themselves in their true character of opposers of a good plan, what they aim at is to produce, in superficial minds, the idea of a universal and natural connection between extraordinary and extensive goodness and impracticability. They hope that, as soon as the marks of extraordinary and extensive utility appear in any plan, they may act as it were as a signal inducing men to turn aside from it in neglect or active opposition. The net result will be to bestow upon the good plan the same treatment a man would be justified in bestowing upon a bad one.

" Upon the face of it, this plan carries that air of plausibility which, if you were not on your guard, might engage you to give more or less of your attention to it. But were you to take the trouble, you would find that, as it is with all these plans that promise so much, practicability would be wanting in the end. To save yourself this trouble, therefore, the wisest course that you can take is to put the plan aside, and think no more about the matter."

There is a particular kind of grin – a grin of malicious triumph with a dash of concealed foreboding and trepidation at the bottom of it – which forms the natural accompaniment of this fallacy when it is vented by any of the sworn defenders of abuse. Milton, instead of cramming all his angels of the African complexion into the divinity school disputing predestination,[1] should have employed part of them at least in practicing this grin, with the corresponding fallacy, before a looking-glass.

There is a class of predictions of which the tendency and object is to contribute to their own verification; and it includes the prediction involved in this fallacy. When objections on the ground of utility have proved ineffective or have been exhausted, objections on the ground of impracticability

[1] In the opinion of my colleague Professor D. Richard Weeks, the reference is to those fallen angels of the " Stygian Counsel " who betook themselves " to several employments as their inclinations led them, to entertain the time till Satan returned " from his mission, *Paradise Lost*, Bk. II, lines 557–61.

> *Others apart sat on a Hill retir'd*
> *In thoughts more elevate, and reason'd high*
> *Of Providence, Foreknowledge, Will and Fate,*
> *Fixt Fate, free will, foreknowledge absolute,*
> *And found no end, in wand'ring mazes lost.* – Ed.

present an additional resource by which men who are convinced of the utility of a plan and enthusiastic well-wishers to it may be turned aside from its support. Obviously the best garb to assume in making such an attempt is that of one who is a well-wisher likewise.

Until the examples are before his eyes, it will not be easy for a man who has not made the observation for himself to conceive to what a pitch of audacity political improbity is capable of being carried: how completely, when an opportunity that seems favorable presents itself, the mask will sometimes be taken off; and what thorough confidence there is in the complicity, or in the imbecility of readers or hearers.

If to say *a good thing is a good thing* is a pointless and foolish use of language; what shall we say of him who stands up boldly and says that *to aim at doing good is a bad thing?* In so many words, it may be questioned whether any such thing has ever been said. But what is absolutely the next thing to it, scarcely distinguishable from it, and in substance the same thing, has actually been said over and over. To aim at perfection has been pronounced to be utter folly and wickedness. To say that man as a species has so much as a tendency to better himself, and that the range of such tendency has no certain limits — this has been denounced as *speculation,* and observations to that effect have been set down as a mark of wickedness.

" By Priestley an observation to this effect has somewhere or other been made. Or by Godwin. Or by Condorcet, or some other Frenchman or Frenchmen of the class of those who, for the purpose of holding them up to execration, are called philosophers, an observation to this effect has somewhere or other been made. By this mark, with or without the aid of any other, these men and others of the same leaven, have proved themselves the enemies of mankind. And you too, whoever you are, if you dare to maintain the same heresy, you are also an enemy of mankind."

In vain would you reply to him, if he is an official: "Sir, Mr. Chalmers, who, like yourself, was an official, has maintained this tendency, and written a book which, from beginning to end, is a demonstration of it as clear and undeniable as Euclid's; and Mr. Chalmers is neither a madman nor an enemy of mankind." In vain would you reply to him, if he calls himself a Christian: "Sir, Jesus said to his disciples, and to you if you are one of them, 'Be ye perfect, even as our Father in heaven is perfect'; and in so doing has not only approved the tendency, but commanded it to be encouraged and carried to its utmost possible length." By such observations the sort of man in question may perhaps for a moment be silenced; but neither by this, nor by anything, nor by anybody, though one rose from the dead, would he be converted.

To various descriptions of persons, over and above those who are in the secret, a fallacy of this sort is to a singular degree acceptable and appealing.

1. To all idle men: all haters of business, a considerable class in a society where shares in the sovereignty of empire are parcelled out into portions which are private property, where votes are free in appearance only, and scarcely in appearance, and where the votes that are sold for money are in fact among the freest that are to be found.

2. To all ignorant men: all who for want of due and appropriate instruction feel themselves incapable of judging any question on its own merits, and who look out with eagerness for such commodious and reputation-saving grounds.

3. To all dull and stupid men: all whose information and reading has not yet been sufficient to enable them to decide a question on its own merits.

When a single argument or train of argument is presented which requires an operation as troublesome and laborious as that which goes by the name of *thought*, an expression of scorn is levelled at the author of this trouble as a just, though probably inadequate punishment for the disturbance he has occasioned to honorable repose.

Under the name of theory, speculation, and so on, what is it that is so odious to men of this description? What except reference to the *end* which ought to be pursued, which is — and how often must it, and ever in vain be repeated? — the greatest happiness of the greatest number. But if reference were made to this end, this inflexible standard, then almost everything that they do, almost everything that they support, would stand condemned. What then shall be the standard? Custom; custom being their own practice, blindly imitating the practice of earlier men in the same situations, motivated and governed by the same sinister interests.

CHAPTER X

Paradoxical Assertions

Ad judicium.

Exposition

WHEN THE UTILITY OF any measure, practice or principle is too far above dispute to be impeached by reasoning, a rhetorician to whose interests it has appeared adverse has sometimes, in a fit of desperation, as it were, resorted to the following attack. Taking up the word or set of words by which it is commonly designated, and without making any specific objection to the measure as such, he has assailed it with some vehement strain of invective by which its mischievousness or folly is made to appear undeniable. Exposure of such a process is hardly necessary, but for the purpose of exposition an example or two may be useful.

Utility, method, simplification, reason, sincerity – a person inexperienced in the arts of political and verbal warfare would not imagine that such concepts could be pointed out as fit objects of hatred and contempt by anyone claiming to possess the distinguishing aspects of a man. Yet so it is.

Sec. 1. Dangerousness of the Principle of Utility

" A great character in a high situation," namely Lord Loughborough,[1] then Attorney General, in 1789, has pronounced the principle of utility a *dangerous* one. That remark, reported to me soon after it was made, seemed at that time to be a gross absurdity; it was only later that I perceived its deep sincerity. For at that time I still continued to take for

[1] Alexander Wedderburn (1733–1805), first Baron Loughborough and later Earl of Rosslyn, became Attorney General in 1778 and Lord Chancellor in 1793. – Ed.

granted, such was my simplicity, that the greatest happiness of the greatest number was the end generally aimed at by government, though often widely missed. But Lord Loughborough was too well acquainted with the state of government in this and other countries not to know that the end pursued by the ruling few was the greatest happiness of the ruling few. And the interest of the ruling few is, in the greater part of the field of government, in a state of continual opposition to that of the greatest number. Hence a principle, which in case of conflict and to the extent of the conflict, called for sacrifices to be made of the interest of the class to which the noble lord belonged, and which alone was the object of his solicitude, could not but be in his eyes a dangerous one.

What must be acknowledged is, that to make right and effective use of the principle of utility requires the concurrence of those requisites which are not always found in company: invention, discernment, patience, and sincerity, each in no inconsiderable degree. While for the pronouncement of decisions without consulting it, decisions in the *ipse dixit* style, nothing is required but boldness. Not that the most decided scorner of the principle of utility fails to make use of it when it promises to suit his purpose. It is only when he feels that, if consulted, its decisions would be against him, that he ever takes it upon himself to do without it, and, in order to prove anything to be right or wrong, thinks it sufficient merely for he himself to say so.

Sec. 2. Uselessness of Classification

When the subject which a man undertakes to write about is a broad one, such as the science of morals or that of legislation, the truth and clarity of what he says will depend upon the relative goodness of the method which he employs. If, for example, snow and charcoal were both to be classed under the same name, and neither of them had any other;

and the question were asked whether the thing known by that name were white or black, great difficulty would be found in answering either yes or no. Or if, because of an identity of labels, sugar of lead was used in a pudding instead of the sort of sugar usually used for the purpose, practical inconveniences analogous to those experienced by Thornbury in eating pancakes,[2] might be expected to result from this error in the tactical branch of the art or science of living.

A system of classification and nomenclature which cannot be employed without confounding at every turn objects which have to be distinguished in order to avoid painful accidents, must be admitted, by every man who has not a decided interest in maintaining the contrary, to be very ill adapted to its purpose. This was shown to be true of the law terms used by the whole system of English penal law, in a work written in 1781 and published in 1789 entitled *Introduction to Morals and Legislation.* By demonstrating that the prevailing system of law is ill-adapted in an extreme degree to what ought to be its purpose, it extended an implied invitation to those, if any such there were, who being conversant in the subject, had any desire to improve it, to show that the system was not the radically bad one it was claimed to be, or else to take measures for making it better. But it being to the interest of everyone who is most conversant with the law to see that the whole system, instead of being as good as it can be made, should be as bad as can be endured, the invitation could not be accepted.

In any other branch of knowledge that can be named: medicine, chemistry, natural history in all its branches, the progress made in all other respects is acknowledged to be roughly commensurate to, and at once both cause and effect

[2] In the pancake in question, which, at a table at the Cape of Good Hope, was served up to a company of which Thornbury, better known by his travels in Japan, was one, white lead was employed instead of flour: some recovered, and some died.

in relation to, the progress made in the art of classification. In no one of those branches of science would it be easy to find a single individual by whom the operation of classification would be placed below the highest rank in the order of importance. Why this difference? Because in any one of those fields there is scarcely an individual who is opposed to the advancement of science; whereas in the profession of law there exists not one individual to whose interest the advancement of the art of legislation is not opposed, to whom, in other words, it would not be either immediately detrimental or ultimately dangerous.

Sec. 3. Mischievousness of Simplification

By the vice opposite to simplification, namely—*complication*, every evil opposed to the ends of justice, such as uncertainty of the law itself, unnecessary delay, expense, and vexation in respect of its execution, is either produced or aggravated. Consequently everyone who wishes to see the mass of these evils reduced entertains a fervent desire to see the virtue of simplification infused into the system of law and judicial procedure.

During a debate not long ago, however, a member of parliament was found resolute and frank enough to stand up and rank this virtue among the worst of the vices. The use of it, he said, was evidence of Jacobinism, circumstantial perhaps, but sufficiently conclusive. But if any disapproval of such a sentiment on the part of anyone present was visible, none, at least, was recorded; and if there was none, that lack alone would be good grounds for hoping for a thorough change in the character of the honorable house.

Sec. 4. Disinterestedness as a Mark of Profligacy

In his pamphlet on his Official Economy Bill, Edmund Burke declares that to give up official emolument is " a mark of the basest profligacy." On somewhat more defensible grounds, this position itself displays as pronounced a mark as ever could be exhibited, of the most shameless profligacy. One assumption among others contained in it, is that in the eyes of man there is nothing that has any value, nothing that can actuate or give direction to his conduct, but the love of wealth. This implies that the love of reputation and the love of power are both of them without effective influence over the human heart.

So contrary is this position of Burke's to the truth, that the less the quantity of money a man, not palpably unfit for the position, is content to accept for his engagement to render official service, the stronger is the presumptive evidence of his aptitude for the office. For it is proof of his relish for the business, and of the pleasure he anticipates from performing it.

Blinded by his rage, in his frantic exclamation wrung from him by an unquenched thirst for lucre, this madman, than whom none perhaps was ever more mischievous, this incendiary, who contributed so much more than any other to light up the flames of war, poured forth the reproach of " the basest profligacy " on the heads of thousands before whom, had he known who they were, he would have been ready to bow the knee. Of this verbal filth which he thus casts around him, one large mass falls upon the head of the Marquess Camden, and from his, rebounds upon those other official heads (including the whole magistracy of the empire) whose recent surrenders of official emoluments have recently drawn forth such a stream of eulogy in the documents of the day.

Sec. 5. How to Turn This Fallacy to Account

To pass off a paradox of this sort with any chance of success, you must be nothing less than the leader of a party. For if you are not, instead of gaping and staring at you, men will but laugh at you, or think of something else without so much as laughing. Moreover, a thing of this sort succeeds much better in a speech than in a book or pamphlet, and for several reasons. For the use of a speech is to carry the measure of the moment; and if the measure be but carried, the means do not matter. If, the measure having been carried, the paradox is seen to be no less absurd and mischievous than it is strange; no matter — the measure has been carried. War has been declared, or a negotiation for peace has been broken off. Peace you will have some time or other; but in the mean time the paradox has had its effect. A law has been passed, and that law an absurd and mischievous one. Some day or other the mischief may have a remedy; but that day may not arrive for two or three hundred years.[3]

In a speech, too, a paradox can be all profit, and no loss. Your point may be gained, or not gained; your reputation remains where it was. It is your speech, or not your speech, whichever is the most convenient. To A, who, under the notion of its being yours, admires it, it *is* your speech; to B, who, because it is yours, or because it is absurd and mischievous, spurns it, it is *not* your speech. If the words of your paradox are ambiguous, as they will be if they are well and happily chosen, susceptible of two interpretations, an innocuous and a noxious one; that is exactly what is wanted. A, who on your credit is ready to take it and adopt it in the noxious one which suits your purpose, is suffered silently to take it in that noxious one. But if B, taking it in the noxious one, attacks you and pushes you hard, then some adherent of yours (not you yourself, for it would be weak indeed for you to appear in the matter) brings out the innocent sense, vowing and swearing that *that* meaning was yours, and belabors poor B with a charge of calumny.

[3] Until recently the country has suffered in a variety of ways by a law made in the reign of Elizabeth to prevent good workmanship. Its effect is felt, but the cause men cannot bear to look at.

Thus it is that from spoken and unminuted speeches you may derive much the same sort of advantage that is derived by lawyers from that sort of sham law which, insofar as it is made by anybody is made by judges, and called common or unwritten law. They use it for their own purposes, meanwhile thundering charges of insincerity or folly against all who dare to ascribe to it a different word or a different meaning. To the supposed speech, as to the supposed law, they give what words they please, and then to those words what meaning they please. The common law, indeed, neither has, nor ever has had any determinate form of words belonging to it; whereas the speech could not have been spoken without a complete set of determinate words of some sort. But in a speech of which there is no producible record, the speech-maker is as safe as if he had never uttered a word of it.

The cause of the success of this fallacy, and hence of the effrontery and insolence of those who employ this species of imposition, is the intellectual weakness which shackles its victims in a state of servitude to authority. In proportion as intellect is weaker and weaker, reason has less and less hold upon it, and authority, fortified by the appearance of strong persuasion, has more and more. Strange as it may seem at first, it is thus that the more flagrant and outrageous the absurdity when addressed to minds of such a texture, the stronger its persuasive force. Why? Because without the strongest possible ground for persuasion of the truth of a proposition, it is assumed that so apparently dubious a proposition would never have been accepted by anybody in the first place. Hence that most magnanimous of all conclusions: *Credo quia impossible est.* Higher than this the force of faith, and hence the merit of it, cannot go. By this one bound the pinnacle is attained; and whatever reward Omnipotence has in store for service of this complexion is placed beyond the reach of failure. Considering how absolute a dominion is exercised over mankind by the passions of fear and hope, no matter how flagrant the absurdity, its acceptance can never afford a just cause for wonder in the light of the support which it is afforded by the most irresistible of the passions.

The understanding is not the source, reason is of itself no spring of action. The understanding is but an instrument in the hand of the will. It is by hopes and fears that the *ends* of action are determined; all that reason does, is to find and determine the *means*.

But where, at the mere suggestion of a set of men with gowns of a certain form on their backs, we see men living and acting under the persuasion that in the vice of lying there is virtue to change the crime of usurpation into justice — here it is not the will that is confounded and overwhelmed, but it is the understanding which is deluded. To form the ground for a decision, for example, a judge asserts as true, some fact which to his knowledge is not true — some fact for the assertion of which, in the station of witness, a man would be punished by this same judge with imprisonment and infamy. To screen it from the abhorrence which is its due, this lie, exceeding in wickedness the most wicked of the assertions commonly branded with that name, is decked up in the label *fiction*, which properly belongs to those innocuous and amusing pictures of ideal scenes depicted by the poetic genius. What are you doing with this lie in your mouth? Could you get along without it, your lie is a foolish one. If you have not the power, the lie is a futile one. In this mire may be seen to be laid the principal part of the foundation of English common law.

CHAPTER XI

Non Causa Pro Causa, or Cause and Obstacle Confounded

Ad judicium.

Exposition

WHEN IN A SYSTEM which has good points in it you have also a set of abuses to defend, after a general eulogy bestowed upon the system, indicating more or less explicitly the undisputed good effects, you take the abuses which you wish to defend, either separately or collectively (the latter is the safer course) and to them you ascribe the credit for having given birth to the good effects. *Cum hoc, ergo propter hoc.* (With it, therefore because of it.)

In every political system of long standing, and therefore not the product of any comprehensive design, but the piecemeal result of the casual and temporary predominance of conflicting interests at different and distant times, whatever its good or bad points at any given period, some will be seen on proper scrutiny to have been effective or promotive causes; others, obstacles or preventives; and still others, immaterial incidents or inoperative circumstances. And in any such system, whatever its prosperous results, its abuses and imperfections will not have been their efficient causes, but rather so many obstacles or preventives. But if you can order matters so that such abuses will be believed to have operated as promotive causes rather than as obstacles, nothing can contribute more powerfully to the effect which you are trying to produce.

If you cannot go as far as to cause the prosperous results in question to be attributed to the abuses by which they have actually been obstructed and retarded, then the next best thing is to arrange matters so that they will be ascribed to some inoperative circumstance having some connection or other — the nearer the better — with the abuses. At any rate, you will cause the prosperous circumstances at issue to be referred to any causes rather than the real ones. For if it should become manifest of what causes they are the results, it will also become manifest of what other circumstances they have not been the results. The outcome will be disastrous to the abuse you are defending; for someone will ask: "And this — what has been the use of this?" To which no answer will be found.

Real knowledge being among your most formidable adversaries, your endeavor must of course be to obstruct its advancement and propagation as effectually as possible. Real knowledge depends to a great degree upon being able, on each occasion, to distinguish from each other causes, obstacles, and uninfluencing circumstances. Such distinctions, therefore, it must be on every occasion your study to confuse and confound to the utmost of your ability.

Example 1. *Effect, Good Government; Obstacle represented as a cause, Station of the Bishops in the House of Lords*

Neither a bishop nor any other man can contribute to a situation any further than he takes a part in it. A man cannot bear a part in the business of the House of Lords unless he participates in the debates there; and to do this he must first attend its sessions. But of the whole body of the bishops, including since the Union those from Ireland, only a small part, perhaps on an average scarcely a tenth, are seen to attend and give their votes. As for a bishop speaking, when any instance of that takes place, it sets men a-staring and talking as if it were a phenomenon.

How comes it that the number of those who vote, and especially of those who speak, is so small? Because a general feeling exists that temporal occupations and politics are not suitable pursuits for churchmen. And why not?

1. Because in that war of personalities in which political debates to a large degree consist, a man of that class is vulnerable to a peculiar degree. Did the Apostles have a seat in, or bear any part in the Roman Senate or in the Common Council of the city of Jerusalem? Was it Peter, was it James, was it John — was it not rather Dives who used to clothe himself in purple and fine linen? Walking from place to place to preach comprised the occupation of the Apostles. If yours were only the same, would you not be rather more like them than you are?

2. Because there is a general feeling, though not often expressed in words out of a sort of decency and compassion, that a legislative assembly is not a fit place for a man who is not at liberty to speak what he thinks, and who, should he be bold enough to refer to any of the plainest dictates of political utility, might be silenced or confounded by reference to some one of the 39 Articles, or some text of Scripture out of a Testament Old or New. Those are things which, however improbable, he is bound to profess to believe, and, however indefensible by reason, to defend whenever he opens his mouth. It is a matter of duty with him to be steeled against conviction in such matters. These are so many vulnerable parts in which he is embarrassed, but in which his antagonist is not embarrassed. They are so many chains with which he is shackled, but with which his opponent is not shackled.

To a man in such circumstances, to talk reason would have something ungenerous and indecorous about it. For it would be his duty not to listen to it. It would be as if one should set about talking indecently to his daughter or his wife. In vain could it be argued that neither Jesus nor his Apostles ever meant what they said — that everything is to be explained, and explained away. By such answers only those persons are satisfied whose antecedent determination to be satisfied is immovable, and neither susceptible of being diminished by any objections, or increased by any answers.

Example 2. *Effect, useful national learning; Obstacle stated as a cause, System of education pursued in Church-of-England universities*

On the subject of learning, the treatment experienced by the Quaker Lancaster[1] is instructive in deciding whether the universities should be properly envisaged as causes or obstacles. Of this Quaker, although he did not attempt to make converts, it is certain that it could never be said that a school under his management was a school of perjury. And since, as by his means the elementary parts of knowledge made their way among the people, causing intellectual light to take the place of intellectual darkness, he might naturally have expected the hostility of those who love darkness better than light. In the age of academical and right-reverend

[1] Joseph Lancaster (1778–1838), founder of the Lancastrian "mutual" or "monitorial" system of education, dreamed of "covering England with establishments in each of which a thousand children should receive, in squads of ten, instruction from a hundred monitors, at the cost of five shillings per head per year." He hoped in this way to extend the rudiments of education to the neglected poor, using the older children to teach the younger in a semi-military fashion. Through James Mill, Bentham became interested about 1812 in extending Lancaster's idea to secondary education in a "Superior Chrestomathic day school" to be set up in Bentham's garden, a project later abandoned for lack of funds. The Royal Lancasterian Institution for the Education of the Poor, which was "directed by dissenters, liberals and freethinkers" was bitterly opposed by the established church as a threat to the latter's authority in education. Lancaster, who was extravagant and imprudent, was disowned by the Quakers, and emigrated to America in 1818. He made abortive attempts to establish schools in Baltimore, Caracas, and Montreal before his death in New York in 1838. Cf. Halévy, *The Growth of Philosophic Radicalism*, 285-96. – Ed.

orthodoxy, learning, even to the very first rudiments of it, would seem to be an object of terror and hatred to those who are striving to confine and stifle it.

In virtue and knowledge, as in every feature of felicity, the empire of Montezuma outshines, as everyone knows, all the surrounding states, even the Commonwealth of Tlascala not excepted. "Where is it," said an inquirer once to the high priest of the temple of Vitzlipultzli, "that we are to look for the true cause of so glorious a pre-eminence?" "Look for it!" answered the holy pontiff, "Where shouldst thou look for it, blind sceptic, but in the copiousness of the streams in which the sweet and precious blood of innocents flows daily down the altars of the great God?"

"Yes," answered in full convocation and full chorus the archbishops, bishops, deans, canons, and prebends of the religion of Vitzlipultzli. "Yes," answered in semi-chorus the vice-chancellor, with all the doctors, both the proctors and masters regent and non-regent of the as yet uncatholicized university of Mexico, "Yes, in the copiousness of the streams in which the sweet and precious blood flows daily down the altars of the great God."

CHAPTER XII

The End Justifies the Means

Ad judicium.

IN THIS CASE SURELY, if in any, exposition is of itself sufficient exposure. The end justifies the means. Yes; but on three conditions, any one of which failing, no such justification exists.

1. The first is, that the end be good.
2. That the means chosen be either purely good, or, if evil, having less evil in them on a balance than there is of real good in the end.
3. That the means have more of good in them, or less of evil, as the cause may be, than any others which might have been used to attain the end.

If these restrictions are disregarded, note what absurdities would follow. Acquisition of a penny loaf is the end I aim at. The goodness of it is indisputable. If by the goodness of the end, any means employed in the attainment of it are justified, instead of a penny, I may give a pound for it—hardly to be justified on the score of prudence. Or, instead of giving a penny for it, I may cut the baker's throat, and thus get it for nothing—hardly to be justified on the ground of beneficence.

In politics, what is the use of this fallacy? In the mouth of one of the INS, it will serve to confirm him in those cruelties which the INS find pleasure in committing upon those over whom their power is exercised. The INS as such have the power to commit atrocities, and that power has sinister interest for its spur. Therefore they have a continual demand for the use of this fallacy to the extent that is worth their while to employ such a cloak.

The OUTS, acting under the same spur, sharpened by continual privation and repeated disappointments, have on their part a still more urgent demand for this same fallacy, although the opportunity of using it is rarely presented to them.

CHAPTER XIII

Opposer-General's Justification: Not Measures but Men, or, Not Men but Measures

Ad invidiam.

THIS ORACULAR PARTY ADAGE was invented by the Whigs, and is said to have been a favorite one with the late Mr. Charles Fox. Not men but measures, or, not measures but men – for you may complete the sentence either way. This bold but slippery instrument of fallacy has a manifest alliance with the preceding one. For, if seating fit men in office is the end upon which everything depends, and the men in question are the only ones who can attain it; then no means can be imagined which such an end will not justify.

On one occasion we have one form of the aphorism from the pen of Charles Fox himself. "Are to be attended to" are the words he employs to complete it. "How vain, how idle, how presumptuous (says the declaimer in his attempt to assume the mantle of historian) is the opinion that laws can do everything! And how weak and pernicious the maxim founded upon it, *that measures not men are to be attended to*." Weak enough as thus expressed, it must be confessed, too weak to be worth noticing; as if anyone ever thought of denying that both measures and men should be "attended to."

Now it must be confessed that few things are more provoking to a man who wishes well to his country than to see a set of bad men in power gain credit and continuance in office by virtue of their sponsorship of a single comparatively unimportant but, as far as it goes, beneficial measure. But what seems not to have been sufficiently "attended to" is that the badness of their measures is the only real warrant one has for calling them bad men. And if they are really the bad men they are supposed to be, one need only have a little patience, and they will come out with some bad measure which can be openly attacked as such. Furthermore, if no such bad measures ever do come from them, the imputation that they are bad men is rather premature.

Distressing indeed to a man of real probity must be the alternative: to see a set of bad men fixed in their all-commanding seat and making a pernicious use of it; or, for the purpose of denying them such an advantage, to keep on straining every nerve to make the House and the public regard as pernicious, a measure of the utility of which he is himself satisfied.

In the abomination of long and regularly corrupt parliaments lies the cause of this distress. Under this system, when the whole sum of abuses has a determined patron on the throne, with a set of ministers who serve his purpose, misrule may swell to such a pitch that without any single measure being so bad that you can claim that it gives sufficient grounds for punishment or even dismissal, the State may be brought to the brink of ruin. At the same time some measure may be introduced against which, though good or at least innocuous in itself, the people may be turned by some misrepresentation of fact or erroneous opinion among them, to the disgrace and expulsion of the ministry. Then would come the distressing alternative.

But were the duration of the assembly short, and the great matter of corruption expelled from and kept out of it, no such alternative would ever present itself, because the chance of ridding the country of a bad set of ministers would be renewed continually. The question supposed to be decided at each election might then really be decided, whereas at present the only question decided is one and the same: shall or shall not the present ministry continue in office? That query is like the wager of a feigned issue, a mere farce, and not worth deciding except as it is connected with the real issue.

CHAPTER XIV

Rejection Instead of Amendment

Ad judicium.

Exposition

THIS FALLACY CONSISTS in urging as a bar or conclusive objection against the proposed measure some consideration which, if presented in the character of a mere amendment, might have more or less claim to notice. It generally consists of some real or imaginary inconvenience that may be the eventual result of the measure's adoption. But such an inconvenience constitutes a conclusive objection only if it is irremediable and accompanied by losses which outweigh its promised gains.

A frequent opportunity for the employment of this fallacy is the creation of a new office and, along with it, the mass of emolument which is habitually annexed to new offices as a matter of course. This is done by the union of habit with sinister interest, and without any inquiry into its necessity, or any concern for keeping its total quantity within the amount called for by the good of the service.

In such a case the fallacy consists in the practice of setting up two universally applicable objections: (1) the *need of economy,* and (2) the mischief or danger anticipated from an *increase in the influence of the crown,* as peremptory bars to the proposed measure.

Exposure

An objection would be classified under this fallacy if the utility of the proposed new establishment were left unimpeached, and the sole ground for the proposed rejection were one of those just mentioned. Unless accompanied by more specific objections, the case of the arguer for rejection rests only on charges which might equally be brought against almost all existing establishments, and in fact against almost the whole framework of the existing government. And even when specific objections are urged, if they are not conclusive in nature they will hardly carry much weight as long as any useless places remain unabolished or overpaid places are exempted from attack.

If a minister at present in office should see opposite to him another person who has been in office, it would be an *ad hominem* argument rather difficult to answer if the former should say: " When you were in office, such and such offices were of no manner of use. You never made any effort to abolish them, notwithstanding the gains which would have resulted from the reduction of needless expenditures and sinister influence. Yet now, when a set of offices is proposed for which you cannot deny there is *some* use, your exertions on behalf of economy are directed exclusively against these useful ones."

Arguments about economy may be carried on in terms of the actual figures of anticipated gains and losses, and a balance struck. But the mischief in terms of increased influence of the crown cannot be expressed in figures, and hence a great deal of the time spent in discussing it may be reckoned as lost time. Yet much could be done to prevent any increase in the sinister interest of the crown, not by raising objections to the creation of those new offices which promise to be useful, but by vesting appointments to them in other and more independent hands.

It is a mistake to put all places on the same footing in these respects: the necessary and the unnecessary, the properly paid and the overpaid. For it wears down and weakens the force of the effort which should be concentrated upon the task of abolishing unnecessary positions and reducing the surplus pay of the overpaid ones.

Another manifestation of this fallacy is its use in denouncing as a " job " (or graft) any public transaction from which a private individual derives some profit. The error (if sincere) or the fallacy (if insincere) consists in forgetting that individuals are the stuff of which the public is made, and that there is no way of benefitting the public without benefitting some individuals. It might even be added that unless a public measure does not sooner or later produce a profit which accrues to some individual in the shape of pleasure or exemption from pain, it is not entitled to the name of beneficial. So far from constituting an argument against the proposed measure, every single benefit that can be pointed out as accruing or likely to accrue to any determinate individual or individuals constitutes, as far as it goes, an argument in its favor.

Is the measure good? Then such a private profit adds to the mass of its advantages. Is the measure on the whole a bad one? Then such profit subtracts, by its whole amount, from the total disadvantages attached to the measure. Yet in actual practice there is no argument, perhaps, which is more frequently employed, or with greater stress, than this one, or more often regarded as a conclusive objection in its own right. To what cause is so general a perversion of the faculty of reason to be ascribed?

One explanation that is not lacking in substance is this: the private profit in question is regarded as conclusive evidence of sinister influence upon the motives of those supporters of the measure who, it is believed, will profit by its adoption. Such a possibility cannot be denied; but it has already been pointed out that considerations of motives are altogether irrelevant and fallacious (See Part II, Chapter I, Vituperative Personalities), since they tend to be unfavorable to every good cause.

Another explanation may be found in the passion of envy. To the man who is envious, the good of another man is evil to himself. The envious speaker or writer will denounce the supposed advantage to another in the character of an evil; and if his hearers or readers also are envious, the error will not be perceived, so rare is the habit of self-examination, and so gross and perpetual the errors into which, for the want of it, the human mind is capable of being led.

But to identify envy as a cause of this fallacy is by no means to denounce that passion as pernicious on the whole. So far from being pernicious, the more thoroughly it is considered, the more clearly it will be seen to be salutary on the whole, and so necessary, at least in the best state of things that has yet been realized, that society would hardly have been kept together without it.

The legislator who resolves not to accept assistance from any but social motives, from none save those which in his vocabulary can be identified as pure motives, will find his laws without vigor and without use. The judge who resolves to hear no prosecutors save those who are brought to him by pure motives might as well forego that part of his emolument which comes from fees, and might also save himself the trouble of going into court in penal cases. The judge who should determine to receive no evidence which was not inspired and guided by pure motives need scarcely trouble to hear any evidence at all.

The practical inference is that, if he would avoid drawing down disgrace upon himself instead of upon the measure he is opposing, a man ought to abstain from employing this argument in refutation of the fallacy. For if he does so, he will be refuting one fallacy by employing another which is itself easy to refute.

It is only by making use of the interests, the affections, and the passions that the legislator who labors for the service of mankind can effect his purposes. Those interests, acting in the capacity of motives, may be of the self-regarding class, or the dissocial, or the social. Social motives the legislator will, wherever he finds them already in action, not only utilize but cherish and cultivate. As for the self-regarding and dissocial, although his study will be rather to restrain than to encourage them, he will at any rate, wherever he sees them already in action or likely to come into action, use his best endeavors to direct their influence, with whatever force he can muster, to his own social purposes.

PART THE FIFTH
CAUSES OF FALLACIES

CHAPTER I

Characters Common to All these Fallacies

ON THE WHOLE the following are the characters which pertain in common to all the several arguments distinguished by the name of fallacies:

1. Whatever the measure in hand, they are irrelevant to it.

2. They are all of them such that their application affords a presumption either of weakness or of the total lack of relevant arguments on the side on which they are employed.

3. To any good purpose they are all of them unnecessary.

4. All of them are not only capable of being applied, but are actually in the habit of being applied to bad purposes, that is — to the obstruction and defeat of all such measures as have for their object the removal of abuses or other imperfections still discernible in the frame and practice of the government.

5. By means of their irrelevancy they all consume and misapply time, thereby obstructing the course and retarding the progress of all necessary and useful business.

6. By the irritative quality which, in virtue of their irrelevancy and the improbity and weakness of which it is indicative, they all possess (especially those that deal in personalities), they are productive of ill-humor, even at

times of bloodshed, and continually of waste of time and hindrance of business.

7. On the part of those who give utterance to them they are indicative either of improbity or intellectual weakness, or of a contempt for the understandings of those on whose minds they are destined to operate.

8. On the part of those on whom they operate, they are indicative of intellectual weakness; and on the part of those in and by whom they are pretended to operate, they are indicative of improbity in the shape of insincerity.

The practical conclusion is, that in proportion as the acceptance and hence the utterance of these fallacies can be prevented, the understanding of the public will be strengthened, the morals of the public will be purified, and the practice of government will be improved.

CHAPTER II

First Cause of the Utterance of these Fallacies: Self-Conscious Sinister Interest

THE CAUSES OF THE UTTERANCE of these fallacies may be named and enumerated as follows:

1. Sinister interest — self-conscious type.
2. Interest-begotten prejudice.
3. Authority-begotten prejudice.
4. Self-defense, meaning a sense of the need of self-defense against counter-fallacies.

As to the first of these causes, self-conscious sinister interest, it is apparent that the mind of every public man is subject at all times to the operation of two distinct interests: a public and a private one. His public interest is that which is constituted by the share he has in the happiness and well-being of the whole community. His private interest is made up of the share he has in the well-being of some portion of the community that is less than the major part. The smallest possible portion of public well-being which can constitute a man's private interest is that which composes his own personal or individual interest.

In the greater number of instances, these two interests, the public and the private, are not only distinct but opposite, and that to such a degree that if either is exclusively pursued, the other must be sacrificed to it. Take for example pecuniary interest: it is to the personal interest of every public man who has at his disposal public money extracted from the whole community by taxes, that as large a share as possible, and if possible the whole of it, should remain available for his own use. At the same time it is to the interest of the public, including his own portion of the public interest, that as small a share as possible, and if possible none at all, should remain in his hands for his personal or any other private use.

Taking the whole of life together, there never has existed nor can there ever exist a human being in whose instance any public interest he can have had, will not, insofar as it depends upon himself, have been sacrificed to his own personal interest. Towards the advancement of the public interest, all that the most public-spirited man, which is as much as to say the most virtuous of men, can do is to do his best to bring the public interest (meaning his own personal share in it) as often as possible into coincidence, and as seldom as possible into repugnance with his private interests.

Even if there were ever so much reason for regretting it, the sort of relation which is thus seen to exist between public and private interest would be none the less true. But the more correct and complete a man's grasp of the subject is, the more clearly will he understand that in this natural and general predominance of personal interest over every variety of more extensive interest, there is no just cause for regret. Why? Because upon this predominance depends the existence of the species and of every individual belonging to it. Suppose for a moment the opposite state of things – in which everyone should prefer the public interest to his own – and the necessary consequences would be no less ridiculous in idea than disastrous and destructive in reality.

In the ordinary course of legislation, no supposition that is inconsistent with this only true and rational one is acted upon. On this supposition is built whatever is done for the purposes of government in the way of rewards and punishments. The supposition is – that on the part of every individual whose conduct is thus to be shaped and regulated, the cause which will determine his conduct will be interest, his own private interest. And it is further supposed that in case of competition between the public interest and his private interest, it will be the latter which will predominate.

If the contrary supposition were acted upon, what would be the consequence? Rewards and punishments would no longer be effective in shaping the conduct of individuals, and the only sanctions that would remain for securing compliance to the laws would be advice and recommendation.

Hence it is that any class of men who have an interest in the rise or continuance of any system of abuse no matter how flagrant will, with few or no exceptions, support such a system of abuse with any means they deem necessary, even at the cost of probity and sincerity. A common bond of connection, Cicero says, exists among all the virtues. For the word *virtue*, substitute the word *abuse*, meaning abuse in government, and the observation will be no less true. Among abuses in government, besides the logical common bond existing among all abuses, there exists a moral common bond composed of the particular and sinister interest in which all men who are members of a government so circumstanced have a share.

As long as any man has the smallest particle of this sinister interest belonging to him, he will have a fellow-feeling for every other man who in the same situation has an interest of the same kind. Attack one of them, and you attack them all. In proportion as each of them feels his share in this common concern is dear to him, he is prepared to defend every other confederate's share with no less alacrity than as if it were his own. But it is one of the characteristics of abuse, that it can only be defended by fallacy. It is, therefore, to the interest of all the confederates of abuse to give the most extensive currency to fallacies, not only those which may be serviceable to each individual, but also to those which may be generally useful. It is of the utmost importance to such persons to keep the human mind in such a state of imbecility that shall render it incapable of distinguishing truth from error.

Abuses, or institutions beneficial only to the few at the expense of the many, cannot be defended openly, directly, and in their own character. If they are to be defended at all, it must be in company with and under the cover of other institutions which either actually or apparently do not deserve the name of abuses. For the few who are in possession of power, the principle best adapted to their interests, if it were capable of being set to work, would be that which would give an unlimited increase to the stock of abuses established at a given period. No longer than a century ago a principle of this cast was actually in force, and to an extent which threatened the whole frame of society with ruin, under the name of *passive obedience* and *non-resistance*. This principle was a *primum mobile*, by the application of which, abuses of all shapes could be manufactured for use to an absolutely unlimited extent. But this principle has now nearly if not altogether lost its force. The creation of new abuses has therefore of necessity been abandoned. The preservation of existing abuses is all that remains feasible; and it is to this work that all exertions in favor of abuse have for a considerable time past been confined.

Institutions, some good, some bad; some favorable to both the few and the many, some favorable to the few alone at the expense of the many, are the ingredients of which the existing system is composed. He who protects all together, and without discrimination, protects the bad. To this end the exertions of industry are still capable of being directed with a prospect of success, and still are directed, with a degree of success that is disgraceful to the probity of the few who practice such a breach of trust, and to the intelligence of the many who endure its consequences.

If the fundamental principle of all good government, the greatest happiness of the greatest number, were on every occasion set up as the mark and only proper end in view, then on each occasion the question would be: by what particular means can this general objective be pursued with the greatest probability of success? But by cultivating the habit of applying this one principle, the eye of the inquirer, the tongue of the speaker, and the pen of the writer would in every part of the field of legislation be driven to some conclusion condemnatory of some one or other of the abuses which depend upon the common sinister interest for their support.

In a word, as long as any one of these relatively profitable abuses continues unremedied, just so long must there be at least one person to whose interest the use of reason is prejudicial. To such a person the success of the measure which threatens to correct the abuse will be prejudicial, and so will that of every other similarly beneficial measure supported by reason.

It is under the dominion of usage, custom, precedent, that the existing abuses have sprung up and continue. Blind custom, in contradiction and opposition to reason, will be the standard which he will try to set up on every occasion as the only proper, safe, and definable standard of reference. Whatever is, is right. Everything is as it should be. These are his favorite maxims; and hc will let slip no opportunity of inculcating them to the best advantage possible. Having besides his share in the sinister interest a share in the universal and legitimate interest, there will also be good and beneficial laws and institutions of which he will be a sincere and strenuous defender. He will want to be effectually defended from the assaults of common enemies either from without or from within the community. But it is under the dominion of blind custom that such protection has always been provided.

Custom being therefore sufficient to his purpose, and reason being always adverse to it, he will try to place every institution, the good as well as the bad, upon the basis of custom. If good institutions were only shown by reason to be conformable to the principle of utility, they would be established and supported on firmer ground than they are at present. But by the application of reason that would place them on the ground of utility, the defender of abuses has nothing to gain, but everything to lose and fear from such a course. The principle of general utility he will therefore represent as a *dangerous* principle; and such, as long as blind custom continues to serve his purpose, to him it really is.

In the past, the defense of abuses and the opposition to measures of reform were conducted by fire and sword. But at present such warfare cannot be carried on completely by such engines. Fallacies, therefore, applied chiefly to directing contempt and hatred against those who apply the principle of general utility, remain the only instruments in universal use for defending the strongholds of abuse against hostile powers. These engines, accordingly, we see applied to the purpose in prodigious variety, and with more or less artifice and reserve.

CHAPTER III

Second Cause: Interest-Begotten Prejudice

IF EVERY ACT OF THE WILL and hence every act of the hand is produced by interest, that is by a motive of one sort or another, the same must be true, directly or indirectly, of every act of the intellectual faculty, although the influence of interest upon the latter is neither as direct or as perceptible as that upon the will.

But how, it may be asked, is it possible that the motive by which a man is actuated can be secret to himself? Nothing, actually, is easier; nothing is more frequent. Indeed the rare case is, not that of a man's not knowing, but that of his knowing it. It is the same with the anatomy of the human mind as with the anatomy and physiology of the human body: the rare case is, not that of a man's being unconversant with it, but that of his being conversant with it. The physiology of the body is not without its difficulties; but in comparison with those by which the knowledge of the physiology of the mind has been obstructed, they are slight indeed.

When two persons have lived together in a state of intimacy, it happens not infrequently that either or each of them may possess a more correct and complete view of the motives by which the mind of the other is governed, than of those which control his own behavior. Many a woman has had in this way a more correct and complete acquaintance with the internal causes by which the conduct of her husband has been determined, than he has had himself. The reason for this is easily pointed out. By interest, a man is continually prompted to make himself as correctly and completely acquainted as possible with the springs of action which determine the conduct of those upon whom he is more or less dependent for the comfort of his life. But by interest he is at the same time diverted from any close examination into the springs by which his own conduct is determined. From such knowledge he has not ordinarily anything to gain; he does not find in it any source of enjoyment. Indeed, in any such knowledge he would be more likely to find mortification than satisfaction.

When he looks at other men, he finds mentioned as a matter of praise the prevalence of the purely social motives, the semi-social motives, and those of the dissocial sort which have their source in an impulse supplied by the purely social or the semi-social motives. It is by the supposed prevalence of these amiable motives that he finds reputation raised, and that respect and goodwill enhanced to which every man is obliged to look for so large a proportion of the comfort of his life. In these same amiable and desirable endowments he finds the minds of other men abounding and overflowing; abounding, that is, during their lifetimes by the testimony of their friends, and after their departures by the recorded testimony set forth in some monthly magazine to the acclamation of their friends and with hardly a dissenting voice from among their enemies.

But the more closely he looks into the mechanism of his own mind, the less he is able to refer any of the mass of effects produced there to any of these amiable and delightful causes. He finds nothing, therefore, to attract him towards this self-study; he finds much to repel him from it. Praise and self-satisfaction on the score of moral worth being accordingly hopeless, it is in the sphere of the intellect that he will seek them. "All men who are actuated by a regard for anything but self, are fools; those only, whose regard is confined to self, are wise. I am of the number of the wise."

Perhaps he is a man in whom a large proportion of the self-regarding motives may be mixed with a slight tincture of the social motives operating upon the private scale. In that case, what will he do? In investigating the source of a given action, he will in the first instance set down the whole of it to the account of the amiable and conciliatory motives, in a word, the social ones. This, in any study of his own mental physiology, will always be his first step; and it will commonly be his last also. Why should he look any further? Why take in hand the painful probe? Why undeceive himself, and substitute the whole truth, which would mortify him, for a half-truth which flatters him?

The greater the share which the purely social motives have in the production of the general tenor of a man's conduct, the less irksome this sort of physiological self-dissection will be. The first view is pleasing; and the more virtuous the man, the more pleasing it will be. But the less irksome any pursuit is, the greater will be a man's progress in it, if his intellectual faculties permit.

CHAPTER IV

Third Cause: Authority-Begotten Prejudice

PREJUDICE IS THE NAME given to an opinion of any sort on any subject when considered as having been embraced without sufficient examination. It is a judgment which, being pronounced *before* evidence, is therefore pronounced *without* evidence. Now what is it that could lead a man to embrace an opinion without sufficient examination, and thus to risk being deceived into a line of conduct harmful to himself or to others?

One cause is the uneasiness attendant upon the labor of examination. A man accepts an opinion as true in order to save the labor which might be necessary to enable him to see the falsity of it. The universality of the propensity to take not only facts but opinions on trust is a matter of common observation. Pernicious as it is in some of its applications, it has its root in sheer necessity, in the weakness of the human mind.

In the instance of each individual, the quantity of opinion which it is possible for him to accept or reject on the ground of examination performed by himself bears but a small proportion to the whole of his knowledge. Most of it can have no firmer ground than the like judgments of other individuals. The cases in which it is possible for his opinions to be *home-made* constitute only a small fraction when compared to those in which, if he is to have any opinion at all, it must necessarily be an *imported* one.

But in the case of the public man this necessity furnishes no justification either for the utterance or for the acceptance of such arguments of base alloy as those which go by the name of fallacies. Such fallacies are not the less offspring of sinister interest because the force of authority is more or less involved. Where authority has a share in their production, there are two distinguishable ways in which sinister interest may also have its share.

(1) A fallacy which, in the mouth of A., had its root immediately in self-conscious sinister interest, obtains through his utterance of it and on the credit of his authority, credence among acceptors in any multitude. Having thus rooted itself in the minds of men, it becomes constitutive of a mass of authority, which in turn conduces to the planting or rooting of the erroneous notion in the minds of men in general. Thus is obtains, at the hands of other men, both utterance and acceptance.

(2) Having received the prejudice at the hands of authority motivated by the operation of sinister interest, the acceptor of the fallacy finds that his own sinister interest prompts him to bestow upon it, in the character of a rational argument, more attention than he would otherwise have bestowed. He fixes his attention, accordingly, on all considerations which have a tendency to assure its utterance and acceptance; and he keeps at a distance all the contrary considerations.

CHAPTER V

Fourth Cause: Self-Defense Against Counter-Fallacies

THE OPPOSERS OF A PERNICIOUS MEASURE may sometimes be driven to employ fallacies because of their supposed utility in answering counter-fallacies. " Such is the nature of men (they may say), that these arguments, weak and inconclusive as they are, nevertheless are those which make the strongest and most effectual impression upon the bulk of the people (upon whom ultimately everything depends). The measure is a most mischievous one; and it would be a crime on our part to leave unemployed any means not criminal which promises to contribute to its defeat. It is the weakness of the public mind, and not the weakness of our cause, which compels us to employ such engines in the defense of it."

Now such a defense might be satisfactory in instances where fallacies are employed not as *substitutes* but only as *supplements* to direct and relevant arguments. But if they are to be employed as supplements, two conditions seem necessary to prove that they are used as supplements only, and with complete sincerity.

(1) That arguments of the direct and relevant kind should be placed in the front of the battle, and declared to be the main arguments by which opposition or support of the proposed measure was decided upon.

(2) That on the occasion of employing the fallacies in question, a frank acknowledgment should be made of their true character, their intrinsic weakness, the considerations which obliged one to resort to them, and the regret which accompanies the consciousness of such obligation.

If, even when used in opposition to a really pernicious

measure, these warnings are not annexed, their omission affords a strong presumption of insincerity. For a sincere man would have nothing to fear from any avowal of their true character. Yet this person omits to make the avowal. Why? Because he foresees that, on some other occasion, arguments of this class will have to constitute his sole reliance. Thus to use fallacies without accompanying warnings is proof of either imbecility or improbity: imbecility if their weakness fails to become visible; improbity, if with full consciousness of their weakness and destructiveness they are nevertheless given currency. So close are imbecility and improbity related that it is often difficult to tell which one is chiefly to blame. On many a well-meaning man this base and spurious metal has no doubt passed for sterling; but if you see it burnished, and held up in triumph by the hands of a man of strong as well as brilliant talents — by a very master of the mint — then you may set him down without unfairness upon the list of those who deceive without being able to plead that they themselves have been deceived.

CHAPTER VI

Uses of these Fallacies to their Utterers and Acceptors

BEING ALL OF THEM replete to such a degree with absurdity, and many of them apparently composed of nothing else, the question naturally arises how they could have acquired so extensive a currency among men? Is it credible (it may be asked) that their inanity and absurdity should not be fully manifest to those persons who employ them? Is it credible that political measures should proceed upon such flimsy grounds?

No, it is not credible. To the very person by whom the fallacy is presented in the character of a reason which forms the ground of his conduct, it has probably presented itself in its genuine colors. But in all assemblies in which shares in power are exercised by votes, there are two kinds of people whose convenience has to be consulted: the speakers and the hearers. Both sorts may find such fallacies useful to an eminent degree.

(1) The speaker wishes his arguments to bring him titles to respect upon the scores of both independence and wisdom; and these fallacies promise to be of assistance in both directions. As to independence, the speaker who desires to win votes for his measure must find something in the shape of a reason to accompany and recommend it. Though in fact directed and governed by some other will behind the curtain, and by the interest which controls that other will, decency is understood to require that it is from his own understanding, and not from the will of any other person, that his own will should be understood to have received its direction. It is not by punishments or rewards, fears or hopes, threats or promises, but by something in the nature of a reason that

the understanding is to be governed and determined. To prove, then, that it is by his own judgment that his conduct is determined, it is advisable to produce something in the nature of a reason by which his judgment and hence his will has been moved. For such a purpose almost every article in the preceding catalogue of fallacies may with more or less effect be made to serve, according to the nature of the case.

To win respect for the speaker on the score of wisdom is a more complicated matter: some of the fallacies have hardly any title to such praise, while others would merely justify a reputation for prudence mixed with so much timidity as to be unacceptable to an erect and commanding mind. Such are the arguments from custom and from authority: — the hydrophobia of innovation, the argument of the ghost-seer, whose nervous system is kept in a state of constant agitation by the phantom of Jacobinism dancing before his eyes; — the idolater who, beholding in ancestry, allegorical personages, precedents, and great characters in high situations dead and living, so many tyrants to whose will, real or supposed, blind obsequiousness on the part of the vulgar of all classes may be secured by apt ceremonies and gesticulations, makes himself the first prostration in the hope of seeing it followed by still more devout prostrations on the part of inferior idolaters in whose breasts the required obsequiousness has been implanted by long practice.

But there are other arguments more calculated to place the wisdom of the orator on higher ground. His acuteness has penetrated to the very bottom of the subject. His comprehension has embraced the whole of it. His adroitness has stripped the obnoxious proposal of the delusive coloring by which it had recommended itself to the eye of ignorance. He pronounces it speculative, theoretical, romantic, visionary. It may be good in theory, but it would be bad in practice. It is too good to be practicable: the goodness which glitters on the outside is sufficient proof of the worthlessness that is within. Its apparent facility is conclusive evidence that it is really impracticable.

The confidence of the tone in which such a decision is conveyed serves as both fruit and sufficient evidence of the complete command of the subject in all its bearings which the speaker has gained by a single glance at it. His superior experience and judgment enable him at one glance to identify the features which suffice to classify the proposal as obnoxious.

The same superior tone may spring from rank and its accompanying opulence as well as allegedly superior talents. The labor of the brain, no less than that of the hand, is a species of drudgery which the man of elevated station is quick to turn over to the baseborn crowd below, to the set of plodders whom he condescends to honor upon occasion with his conversation and countenance. By his rank and opulence he is enabled in this, as in other ways, to pick and choose what is most congenial to his taste. By the royal hand of Frederick the Great, philosophers and oranges were subjected to the same treatment and put to the same use. The sweets, the elaboration of which may have been the work of years, were elicited in a few moments by the pressure of an expert hand.

(2) The praise of the receiver of wisdom is always inferior to that of the utterer; but the receiver, assuming that he derives due profit from what he receives, should not be without his praise. The advantage he may garner from these fallacies is that of being enabled to give a reason for the faith that is, or is supposed to be, in him.

For there are some circumstances in which silence will not serve a man, in which it will be construed as a confession of self-convicting consciousness that what he is doing is wrong and indefensible. It may betray the fact that what he is giving men to understand as his opinion, is not really his opinion; that the supposed facts which he has been asserting as its apparent foundation, simply are not true. Should his audience be persuaded that that was the situation, his credit and reputation would be effectually destroyed.

Something, therefore, must be said, of which it may be supposed that it operated on his mind in the character of a reason. By this means his reputation for wisdom is all that is exposed to suffer (from the actual flimsiness of the argument). His reputation for probity will be preserved intact.

Such base arguments resemble the bad money which each man passes off on his neighbor, not in complete ignorance of its worthlessness and not really expecting his neighbor to be ignorant, but in the hope and expectation that his neighbor will suppose that by him, the utterer of the base argument, its badness could not possibly have been clearly understood.

But the more generally current any such absurd notion is, the greater the probability of its being seriously entertained; for there is no notion, actual or imaginable, that a man cannot be brought to entertain, if only he is satisfied that it is being generally or extensively entertained by others.

CHAPTER VII

Particular Demand for Fallacies Under the English Constitution

THERE ARE TWO REASONS which will suffice to explain why, under the British constitution, there is bound to exist both a demand for fallacies, and a supply of them, which cannot be matched for copiousness and variety anywhere else in the world. In the first place, there can be no such demand unless discussion is to a certain extent free. Without a popular assembly taking an effective part in the government and publishing its debates, and without free discussion through the medium of the press, there is no demand for fallacies. Fallacy is fraud; and fraud is useless when everything is done by force.

The only example which can enter into comparison with the English government is that of the United Anglo-American States. There, on the side of the *Outs,* the demand for fallacies stands about as it does under the English constitution. On the side of the *Outs* the demand for fallacies is always, however, the least urgent and abundant. It is on the side of the *Ins* that the demand for fallacies thrives. Its magnitude and urgency depend upon the size of the aggregate mass of abuse, and its variety depends upon the variety of the shapes in which abuse has manifested itself.

On crossing the water, fortune gave to British America the sort of relief which the same policy gives to a fox: of the vermin by which he had been tormented, a part were left behind. In America there are no deaf auditors of the Exchequer; no blind surveyors of melting irons; no non-registering registrars of the Admiralty Court or any other tribunal; no tellers by whom no money is told but that which goes into their own pockets; no judge pocketing 7,000 pounds a year for useless work for which one must address his clerks; no judge who, in the character of judge over himself, sits in one place to protect by storms of fallacy and fury the extortions habitually committed in another; and no tithe-gatherers exacting immense recompense for minute or never-rendered service.

With respect to the whole class of fallacies built upon authority, precedent, wisdom of ancestors, dread of innovation, immutable laws, and many others occasioned by ancient ignorance and ancient abuses, it will occur to many readers that in the American Congress the use made of such fallacies is not likely to be nearly so copious as that in the august assembly which has been pleased to call itself the Imperial Parliament of Great Britain and Ireland.

CHAPTER VIII

The Demand for Political Fallacies—How Created by the State of Interests

IN ORDER TO HAVE a clear view of the object to which most political fallacies will be found to be directed, it will be necessary to point out the state in which, with a very few exceptions, the business of government ever has been and still continues to be in every country on earth. For this purpose are cited several propositions whose proof would require more space than is available here – propositions which, if not immediately assented to, will at any rate be allowed to possess the highest claims to attention and examination, even by those who are most opposed to them.

1. The end or object which every political measure, whether established or proposed, ought to have in view is the greatest happiness of the greatest number of persons interested in it, and that for the greatest length of time.

2. Unless the United States of North America be virtually an exception, in every known state the happiness of the many has been at the absolute disposal either of the one or of the comparatively few.

3. In every human breast, with the exception of rare and short-lived ebullitions resulting from some extraordinarily strong stimulus or incitement, self-regarding interest is predominant over social interest, and each person's own individual interest over the interests of all other persons taken together.

4. In a few instances, possibly, a person may, throughout the general tenor of his life, sacrifice his own individual interest to that of another person or persons with whom he is connected by some domestic or other private and narrow

tie of sympathy, but not to the whole number (or majority) of the community to which he belongs.

5. If in any political community there are any individuals who constantly place the interests of all the other members of the community ahead of their own individual interests, the number of these public-spirited individuals will be so small, and they will be so hard to distinguish from the rest, that for practical purposes they may be disregarded.

6. In this general predominance of self-regarding over social interest, when attentively considered, there will not be found any just cause either for questioning or for regretting it. Since it will be found that, without this predominance, no such species as the one to which we belong could have existence. For if it were done away with, and all persons or most persons should find respectively one or more persons whose interest throughout the whole of life was dearer to them, and more anxiously and constantly watched over than their own, the whole species would necessarily, and within a short space of time, become extinct.

7. If this be true, it follows, by the unchangeable constitution of human nature, that in every political community the holders of the supreme power will, on every occasion in which competition arises, sacrifice the interest of the many to their own particular interest.

8. But every arrangement by which the interest of the many is thus sacrificed to that of the few may properly be called (and to the extent of the sacrifice) a bad arrangement. Indeed, the only worse arrangement would be one which sacrificed the interest of *both* parties.

9. A bad arrangement, considered as already established and in existence, is known as *an abuse*.

10. The interests of the subject many being sacrificed to those of the ruling few on every occasion when the two compete, it is the constant object of study and endeavor on the

part of the ruling few to preserve and extend the existing mass of abuse. Such, at any rate, is their constant propensity.

11. In the mass of abuse which it is their interest to defend, there is a portion from which they derive a direct and assignable profit, and also another portion from which they do not derive such profit. Now the mischievousness of the portion from which they do not derive any profit cannot be exposed except by bringing to light facts and observations which would apply also to that portion from which they do derive direct and particular profit. Thus it is that in every community all men who are in power, that is, the *Ins,* are constantly engaged by self-regarding interest in the maintenance of abuse in every shape in which they find it established.

12. But whatever the *Ins* have in possession, the *Outs* have in expectancy. Thus far, therefore, there is no distinction between the sinister interests of the *Ins* and those of the *Outs,* nor, consequently, in the fallacies which they employ in the support of their respective sinister interests.

13. To this point the interests of the Outs and the Ins coincide; but there are other respects in which their interests are opposite to one another. For procuring for themselves the situations and mass of advantages possessed by the Ins, the Outs have but one mode of proceeding. This is: the raising of their own relative place in the scale of political reputation as compared with that of the Ins. This can be accomplished either by raising their own standing, or by lowering that of their successful rivals.

14. In addition to that particular and sinister interest which belongs to them in their quality as rulers, these rivals also have their shares in the universal interest which belongs to them as members of the community at large. In this latter capacity they are sometimes occupied with measures for maintenance of the universal interest, that is – for the preservation and increase of that portion of the universal

happiness which their regard for their own interests does not seem to require them to sacrifice. By every increase in such happiness they derive advantage to themselves, not only as members of the community at large, but in the shape of reputation as ruling members of it.

15. But in whatever manner the Ins may seek to derive reputation for themselves, thus raising themselves in the scale of comparative esteem, it is to the interest of the Outs to prevent them from any such rise, and, if possible, to cause their reputation to sink. Hence there exists on the part of the Outs a constant tendency to oppose all good arrangements proposed by the Ins. But, generally speaking, the better an arrangement really is, the better it will generally be thought to be. And the better it is thought to be, the higher will it raise the reputation of those who support it. The better a new arrangement proposed by the Ins is, however, the stronger is the interest by which the Outs are incited to oppose it. But the more obviously and indisputably good the measure is when considered in itself, the more incapable it is of being successfully opposed except by fallacies. This explains the general character of the fallacies which are chiefly employed by the Outs.

16. To the extent of their share in the universal interest, any arrangement which is beneficial to that interest will be beneficial to any member of the community. Therefore successful opposition to a generally beneficial measure is prejudicial to those who oppose it. Opposers of such measures must therefore calculate the probable consequences, and weigh their share in the benefits of the measure against a possible rise in the scale of reputation as compared with their political adversaries.

Under the English constitution at the present time, however, the chances are in a prodigious degree against the success of any opposition by the Outs directed against even the most flagrantly bad measure proposed by the Ins, and much more so with respect to a really good one. Hence it is, that when, the arrangement being good in itself, there is any prospect of opposing it successfully by means of fallacies without too greatly endangering their reputation, the Outs will have little to lose by making the attempt.

17. With respect to those bad arrangements which the Ins stand engaged by their sinister interest to promote, and in which the Outs, as above, have a community of interest, the part dictated by their sinister interest is a curious and delicate one. By successful opposition, the Outs would lessen that mass of sinister advantage now possessed by the Ins, but which is theirs in hope and expectancy. They must choose, therefore, between this disadvantage and the possibility of an advance in the scale of comparative reputation. But since there is almost a certainty that their opposition will fail, they are more likely to think primarily of what would happen if they should change places with the Ins. The result is that any reforms which they propose are likely to be spurious, fallacious, or at best inadequate. Their inadequacy, and the virtual confession involved in it, merely support and confirm every portion of kindred abuse which is left untouched.

CHAPTER IX

Different Roles which may be Assumed with Relation to Fallacies

AS WITH BAD MONEY, so with bad arguments, different persons assume different roles in giving them various sorts and degrees of currency. *Fabricator, utterer, acceptor* — those are the different parts enacted in giving currency to a bad shilling. And the same parts may be taken in giving currency to a bad argument.

But in the case of a bad argument, he who is its fabricator is likely to be its utterer also. Yet for one fabricator who is also an utterer, there may be any number of utterers, no one of whom was a fabricator. The law also distinguishes several different states of mind on the part of each of the actors: (1) Evil consciousness, or *mala fides*; (2) temerity, or sometimes *culpa*; and (3) blameless agency, or *actus* without intent to harm, even though mischief may result.

Whether shillings or arguments are being considered, evil consciousness consists of a man's awareness of the badness of the article which he intends to pass off as good. Generally the fabricator is least likely to be innocent of such evil intent. For be it the bad shilling or the bad argument, the making of it is bound to have cost more or less exertion. Usually such exertion will not be made unless for the purpose of utterance, and to some direct advantage. In the instance of the bad shilling, it is certain that its badness was known and understood; in the instance of the bad argument, it is more or less probable, more probable in the case of the fabricator than in that of the mere utterer. It is always possible that the badness of the argument may never have been perceived by its fabricator, or that it may have been framed without any intention of applying it to a bad purpose. But in general, the more a man is exposed to the action of sinister interest, the more reason there is for charging him with evil-consciousness, supposing him to be aware of the action of the sinister interest.

The action of the sinister interest, however, may have been either perceived or unperceived, for without a certain degree of attention a man no more perceives what is passing in his own mind than what is passing in other minds. The book lies open before him; but though it be the object nearest to him, and though he be ever so much in the habit of reading, it may even while his two eyes are fixed upon it be read or not read, according as his attention has or has not been called to its contents.

Sinister interest has two media through which it usually operates. These are *prejudice* and *authority*; and hence the immediate progeny of sinister interest are interest-begotten prejudice and authority-begotten prejudice. Whenever a bad argument owes its fabrication or its utterance to a sinister interest that is not perceived, it has for its immediate parent either in-bred prejudice or authority.

Of the three operations thus intimately connected: fabrication, utterance, and acceptance, it is obvious that the first two may be accompanied by evil-consciousness. As to acceptance, a distinction must be made before an answer can be given on that score. Acceptance may be divided into *internal* and *external*. Where the opinion, no matter how false it may be, is really believed to be true by the person to whom it has been presented, its acceptance may be termed internal. Where, on the other hand, other persons believe, whether through discourse, deportment, or other signs, that an opinion has received internal acceptance at his hands, whether or not through design on his part, we may speak of external acceptance.

In the natural state of things, both of these modes of acceptance occur together: the external mode follows the internal as a natural consequence. Either of them, however, is capable of taking place without the other. Feeling the force of an argument, I may appear as if I had not felt it; or, not having been impressed by it, I may appear as if I had received a weak or a strong impression, whichever suits my purpose best. It is sufficiently manifest that evil-consciousness cannot be the accompaniment of internal acceptance; but it may be, and actually is, the accompaniment of external acceptance as often as the latter is not accompanied by internal acceptance.

So far the distinction between evil-consciousness and temerity appears plain enough; but on closer inspection a sort of mixed or middle state between evil-consciousness and pure temerity may be observed. This is where the persuasive force of an argument admits of different degrees, as when an argument which operates with a certain degree of force on the utterer's mind is represented by him as acting with a considerably greater degree of force. Thus a man who really considers his opinion as invested only with a degree of probability, may speak of it as a matter of absolute certainty. This persuasion is not, of course, absolutely false; but it is exaggerated, and this exaggeration is a species of falsehood.

The more frequent the trumpeter of any fallacy is in its performance, the greater the progress which his mind is apt to make from the state of evil-consciousness to the state of temerity. It is said of gamblers that they begin their careers as dupes and end as thieves. In the present case, the parties begin with craft and end with delusion.

A phenomenon which seems indisputable is that of a liar by whom a lie of his own invention has been told so often that at length it has come to be accepted as true even by himself. But if such is the case with regard to a statement composed of words, every one of which finds itself in manifest contradiction to some determinate truth, it may be imagined how much more easily and frequently it may happen to a statement of such nicety and delicacy as one concerning the strength of the impression made by an instrument of persuasion. The persuasive force of the latter is susceptible of innumerable degrees, no one of which has ever yet been distinguished from any other by any external signs or tokens in the form of discourse or otherwise.

If the substitution of irrelevant for relevant arguments is evidence of a bad cause, and of consciousness of its badness, how much more so is the substitution of appeals to the will for appeals to the understanding. Arguments addressed to the understanding may, if fallacious, be answered; and any mischief they have a tendency to produce may be prevented by counter-arguments addressed to the understanding. But against punishments and rewards addressed to the will, those addressed to the understanding are altogether without effect, and the mischief produced by them is without remedy.

CHAPTER X

Uses of the Preceding Exposure

THE PRACTICAL USE of these exposures of the states of mind of those who employ these fallacies is in opposing the check of reason to the practice of fighting with such poisoned weapons. In proportion as the virtue of sincerity is an object of love and veneration, the opposite vice is held in abhorrence. The more generally and intimately the public in general are convinced of the insincerity of him by whom the arguments in question are employed, in that same proportion will be the force of the motives which will keep a man from employing them.

Suppose the deceptious and pernicious tendency of these arguments, and hence the improbity of him who employs them, could be sufficiently impressed upon the minds of men, and suppose further that virtue in the form of sincerity is an object of respect, and vice in the opposite form of aversion and contempt in the public mind in general, then the practice of this species of improbity would become as rare as those other varieties which are restrained by moral power.

If the object of this treatise were to prove the deceptious and inconclusive nature of these arguments, the exposure thus given of the mental character of the persons who employ them would not have any just title to be received in evidence. Be the improbity of those who use these arguments ever so glaring, the arguments themselves are exactly what they are, neither better nor worse. For to employ as proof of the impropriety of an argument, the improbity of him by whom it is uttered, is itself an expedient which stands in the list of fallacies brought to view in these pages.

But we may suppose the impropriety and mischievousness of these fallacies sufficiently established on other, and those unexceptionable grounds. So the object now in view is to determine by what means an end so desirable as the general disuse of these poisonous weapons may be attained in the completest and most effectual degree. Now the mere *utterance* of these base arguments is not the only, and certainly not the principal mischief in the case. What constitutes the principal and only ultimate mischief is their reception in the character of conclusive and influential arguments. To the object of making men ashamed to utter them must therefore be added the ulterior aim of making men ashamed to receive them: ashamed as often as they are observed to turn towards them any other aspect than that of aversion and contempt.

But if the practice of insincerity is something a man ought to be ashamed of, so is the practice of giving encouragement, or of forbearing to oppose discouragement to that vice. To its discouragement that man contributes most who holds the immorality of the practice up to view in the strongest and clearest colors. Nor, upon reflection, will the task be found as hopeless as at first sight it might be supposed to be. In the most numerous assembly that ever sat in either house, perhaps, not a single individual could be found who would utter an obscene word in the company of a chaste and well-bred female. And if the frown of indignation were as sure to be drawn down upon the offender against this branch of the law of probity as by such an offense against the law of delicacy, transgression would not be less effectually banished from those great public theatres than it has already been from the domestic circle.

If the tendency of the fallacies in question is really pernicious, then whoever he may be who is able by lawful and unexceptionable means to bring them into disrepute, will thereby have rendered good service to his country and to mankind. But pecuniary power in a moderate degree must also be added to this intellectual power if this good service is to be fully rendered. For example, in the printed reports of debates of legislative assemblies, their editor might well point out instances of the use of these fallacies by the usual marks of reference in the present list.[1]

The lack of sufficient time for adequate discussion, when carried on orally in a numerous assembly, has been shown by experience to be a real and serious evil to no inconsiderable extent. For this evil the table of fallacies furnishes a powerful remedy.

In the course of time, when these imperfect sketches shall have received perfection and polish from some more skilful hand, it may be that any legislator anywhere who is so far off his guard as through craft or simplicity to let drop any of these irrelevant and deceptious arguments will be greeted not with the cry of " Order! Order! " but with voices in scores crying aloud " Stale! Stale! Fallacy of Authority! Fallacy of Distrust! " and so on.

The faculty which detection has of divesting deception of her power is attested by the poet Horace: " Quaere *peregrinum,* vicinia rauca reclamat." (" Ask a foreigner, and the neighborhood shouts itself hoarse.")[2] The period of time at which this change shall have been acknowledged to have been completely effected with respect to these instruments of deception, will form an epoch in the history of civilization.

[1] This was the intention, never fully carried out, of editor Bingham in his *Parliamentary History and Review.* – Ed.

[2] Horace, *Epistles,* 1, 17, 62.

APPENDIX

The Noodle's Oration

by Sydney Smith

Editor's Note

ONE OF THE FIRST REVIEWERS of *The Book of Fallacies* in 1824 was the witty and liberal Reverend Sydney Smith (1771–1845), whose fame in America seems fated to rest forever upon his trenchant query in an earlier review.[1] Smith had been the founder and first editor of the *Edinburgh Review* in 1802; and the brilliance of his contributions was a powerful factor in its success for the next quarter of a century. So renowned did he become as a high-spirited and independent humorist that it is said to have cost him any chance he had of becoming a bishop. He was an eager and effective champion of toleration, Catholic emancipation, and Parliamentary reform. In those matters he was on the side of the radicals, even though the *Edinburgh* was, on most questions, the target of the *Westminster* group. Smith pro-

1 "In the four quarters of the globe, who reads an American book, or goes to an American play, or looks at an American picture or statue?" Review of Seybert's *Statistical Annals of the United States of America* in the *Edinburgh Review,* Vol. XXXIII (1820), 79. What is generally forgotten is that Sydney Smith was equally critical of American science and technology, for his review went on: "What does the world yet owe to American physicians or surgeons? What new substances have their chemists discovered, or what old ones have they analyzed? What new constellations have been discovered by the telescopes of Americans? — What have they done in the mathematics? Who drinks out of American glasses? or eats from American plates? or wears American coats or gowns? or sleeps in American blankets? — Finally, under which of the old tyrannical governments of Europe is every sixth man a Slave, whom his fellow-creatures may buy and sell and torture?"

fessed to have read with interest everything that Bentham had published.

His review of *The Book of Fallacies* began: "There are a vast number of absurd and mischievous fallacies, which pass readily in the world for sense and virtue, while in truth they tend only to fortify error and encourage crime. Mr. Bentham has enumerated the most conspicuous of these in the book before us." [2] Smith then tackled, as few critics have before or since, the vexing question of Bentham's later style,[3] and what should be done about it, thus: "Whether it is necessary that there should be a middleman between the cultivator and the possessor, learned economists have doubted. But neither gods, men, nor booksellers can doubt the necessity of a middleman between Mr. Bentham and the public. Mr. Bentham is long; Mr. Bentham is occasionally involved and obscure; Mr. Bentham invents new and alarming expressions; Mr. Bentham loves division and subdivision — and he loves method itself, more than its consequences. Those only therefore who know his originality, his knowledge, his vigor, and his boldness, will recur to the works themselves. The great mass of readers will not purchase improvement at so dear a rate, but will choose rather to become acquainted with Mr. Bentham through the medium of Reviews — after that eminent philosopher has been washed, trimmed, shaved, and forced into clean linen. One great use of a Review, indeed, is to make men wise in ten pages

[2] *Edinburgh Review,* No. LXXXIV (August, 1825), 367–89.

[3] Another scholar who expressed a wish that the "obscure, involuted Benthamese dialect" might be translated into English was Thomas Cooper (1779–1859), who wrote in Columbia, S. C., on March 29, 1830: "I am reviewing Bentham's late work in 5 V. on Judicial Evidence. It is really a most abstruse, but mind-exciting book. It will not be read; for I find the Hebrew lessons I have been taking these six months past, not so difficult as Bentham's pages." "Letters of Dr. Thomas Cooper, 1825–1832," *American Historical Review,* Vol. VI, 734.

who have no appetite for a hundred pages; to condense nourishment, to work with pulp and essence, and to guard the stomach from idle burden and unmeaning bulk. For half a page, sometimes for a whole page, Mr. Bentham writes with a power which few can equal; and by selecting and omitting, an admirable style may be formed from the text. Using this liberty, we shall endeavor to give an account of Mr. Bentham's doctrines, for the most part in his own words. Wherever any expression is particularly happy, let it be considered to be Mr. Bentham's: – dullness we take to ourselves."

There could hardly be a better statement of the purpose which has also inspired the present enterprise than this argument for the need of a middleman between the later Bentham and the public as stated by Sydney Smith. In his review, Smith went on to give a masterly account of the principal contents of the book, and then capped the whole by making up "a little oration" which conveys, in Leslie Stephen's words, "the pith" of "the really admirable dialectical power"[4] of *The Book of Fallacies.* He called it "The Noodle's Oration," a noodle being a simpleton, a stupid or a silly person.

The Noodle's Oration

What would our ancestors say to this, Sir? How does this measure tally with their institutions? How does it agree with their experience? Are we to put the wisdom of yesterday in competition with the wisdom of centuries? (*Hear, hear*). Is beardless youth to show no respect for the decisions of mature age? (Loud cries of *Hear*! *hear*!) If this measure is right, would it have escaped the wisdom of those Saxon progenitors to whom we are indebted for so many of our best political institutions? Would the Dane have passed it over? Would the Norman have rejected it? Would such a

[4] Leslie Stephen, *The English Utilitarians,* Vol. I, 295.

notable discovery have been reserved for these modern and degenerate times?

Besides, Sir, if the measure is good, I ask the honorable gentleman if this is the time for carrying it into execution — whether, in fact, a more unfortunate period could have been selected than that which he has chosen? If this were an ordinary measure, I should not oppose it with so much vehemence; but, Sir, it calls in question the wisdom of an irrevocable law — of a law passed at the memorable period of the Revolution. What right have we, Sir, to break down this firm column, on which the great men of that day stamped a character of eternity? Are not all authorities against this measure: Pitt, Fox, Cicero, and the Attorney- and Solicitor-General?

The proposition is new, Sir; it is the first time it was ever heard in this house. I am not prepared, Sir — this house is not prepared, to receive it. The measure implies a distrust of His Majesty's government; their disapproval is sufficient to warrant opposition. Precaution only is requisite where danger is apprehended. Here the high character of the individuals in question is a sufficient guarantee against any ground of alarm.

Give not then your sanction to this measure; for, whatever be its character, if you do give your sanction to it, the same man by whom this is proposed, will propose to you others to which it will be impossible to give your consent. I care very little, Sir, for the ostensible measure; but what is there behind it? What are the honorable gentleman's future schemes? If we pass this bill, what fresh concessions may he not require? What further degradation is he planning for his country?

Talk of evil and inconvenience, Sir! Look to other countries — study other aggregations and societies of men, and then see whether the laws of this country demand a remedy, or deserve a panegyric. Was the honorable gentleman (let me ask him) always of this way of thinking? Do I not remember when he was the advocate in this house of very opposite opinions? I not only quarrel with his present sentiments, Sir, but I declare very frankly, I do not like the party with which he acts. If his own motives were as pure as possible, they cannot but suffer contamination from those with whom he is politically associated. This measure may be a boon to the constitution, but I will accept no favor to the constitution from such hands. (Loud cries of *Hear! hear!*)

I profess myself, Sir, an honest and upright member of the British Parliament, and I am not afraid to profess myself an enemy to all change, and all innovation, I am satisfied with things as they are; and it will be my pride and pleasure to hand down this country to my children as I received it from those who preceded us.

The honorable gentleman pretends to justify the severity with which he has attacked the noble Lord who presides in the Court of Chancery. But I say such attacks are pregnant with mischief to government itself. Oppose ministers, you oppose government; disgrace ministers, you disgrace government; bring ministers into contempt, you bring government into contempt; and anarchy and civil war are the consequences.

Besides, Sir, the measure is unnecessary. Nobody complains of disorder in that shape in which it is the aim of your measure to propose a remedy to it. The business is one of the greatest importance; there is need of the greatest caution and circumspection. Do not let us be precipitate, Sir; it is impossible to foresee all the consequences. Everything should be gradual; the example of a neighboring nation should fill us with alarm!

The honorable gentleman has taxed me with illiberality, Sir. I deny the charge. I hate innovation, but I love improvement. I am an enemy to the corruption of government, but I defend its influence. I dread reform, but I dread it only when it is intemperate. I consider the liberty of the press as the great palladium of the constitution; but, at the same time, I hold the licentiousness of the press in the greatest abhorrence. Nobody is more conscious than I am of the splendid abilities of the honorable mover, but I tell him at once, his scheme is too good to be practicable. It savors of utopia. It looks well in theory, but it won't do in practice. It will not do, I repeat, Sir, in practice; and so the advocates of the measure will find, if, unfortunately, it should find its way through Parliament. (*Cheers*).

The source of that corruption to which the honorable member alludes is in the minds of the people; so rank and extensive is that corruption, Sir, that no political reform can have any effect in removing it. Instead of reforming others, instead of reforming the state, the constitution, and everything that is most excellent, let each man reform himself! Let him look at home, he will find there enough to do, without looking abroad, and aiming at what is out of his power (*Loud cheers*). And now, Sir, as it is frequently the custom in this house to end with a quotation, and since the gentleman who preceded me in the debate has anticipated me in my favorite quotation of the "Strong pull and the long pull," I shall end with the memorable words of the assembled barons — "*Nolumus leges Angliae muturi.*" ("We do not propose to change the laws of England.")

INDEX